The Sociopolitics of English Language Teaching

BILINGUAL EDUCATION AND BILINGUALISM

Series Editors: Professor Nancy H. Hornberger, *University of Pennsylvania, Philadelphia USA,* and Professor Colin Baker, *University of Wales, Bangor, Wales, UK*

Other Books in the Series
Becoming Bilingual: Language Acquisition in a Bilingual Community
    Jean Lyon
Bilingual Education and Social Change
    Rebecca Freeman
Building Bridges: Multilingual Resources for Children
    Multilingual Resources for Children Project
Child-Rearing in Ethnic Minorities
    J.S. Dosanjh and Paul A.S. Ghuman
Curriculum-Related Assessment, Cummins and Bilingual Children
    Tony Cline and Norah Frederickson (eds)
English in Europe: The Acquisition of a Third Language
    Jasone Cenoz and Ulrike Jessner (eds)
Foundations of Bilingual Education and Bilingualism
    Colin Baker
Japanese Children Abroad: Cultural, Educational and Language Issues
    Asako Yamada-Yamamoto and Brian Richards (eds)
Language Minority Students in the Mainstream Classroom
    Angela L. Carrasquillo and Vivian Rodriguez
Languages in America: A Pluralist View
    Susan J. Dicker
Learning English at School: Identity, Social Relations and Classroom Practice
    Kelleen Toohey
The Languages of Israel: Policy, Ideology and Practice
    Bernard Spolsky and Elana Shohamy
Multicultural Children in the Early Years
    P. Woods, M. Boyle and N. Hubbard
Multicultural Child Care
    P. Vedder, E. Bouwer and T. Pels
A Parents' and Teachers' Guide to Bilingualism
    Colin Baker
Policy and Practice in Bilingual Education
    O. García and C. Baker (eds)
Teaching and Learning in Multicultural Schools
    Elizabeth Coelho
Teaching Science to Language Minority Students
    Judith W. Rosenthal
Working with Bilingual Children
    M.K. Verma, K.P. Corrigan and S. Firth (eds)
Young Bilingual Children in Nursery School
    Linda Thompson

Please contact us for the latest book information:
Multilingual Matters, Frankfurt Lodge, Clevedon Hall,
Victoria Road, Clevedon, BS21 7HH, England
http://www.multilingual-matters.com

BILINGUAL EDUCATION AND BILINGUALISM 21
Series Editors: Nancy Hornberger and Colin Baker

The Sociopolitics of English Language Teaching

Edited by
Joan Kelly Hall and William G. Eggington

MULTILINGUAL MATTERS LTD
Clevedon • Buffalo • Toronto • Sydney

Library of Congress Cataloging in Publication Data

The Sociopolitics of English Language Teaching/Edited by Joan Kelly Hall and William G. Eggington
Bilingual Education and Bilingualism: 21
Includes bibliographical references and index
1. English language–Study and teaching–Foreign speakers. 2. English language–Study and teaching–Social aspects–United States. 3. English language–Study and teaching–Political aspects–United States. 4. Education, Bilingual–United States.
I. Hall, Joan Kelly. II. Eggington, William. III. Series.
PE1128.A2.S5994 2000
428'.0071–dc21   99-088694

British Library Cataloguing in Publication Data

A CIP catalogue record for this book is available from the British Library.

ISBN 1-85359-437-7 (hbk)
ISBN 1-85359-436-9 (pbk)

Multilingual Matters Ltd

UK: Frankfurt Lodge, Clevedon Hall, Victoria Road, Clevedon BS21 7HH.
USA: UTP, 2250 Military Road, Tonawanda, NY 14150, USA.
Canada: UTP, 5201 Dufferin Street, North York, Ontario M3H 5T8, Canada.
Australia: P.O. Box 586, Artarmon, NSW, Australia.

Printed and bound in Great Britain by the Cromwell Press Ltd.

Contents

Foreword   vii
Robert B. Kaplan

Introduction   1

Section 1: Language Politics, Language Practices, and English Teaching   5

1   Policy and Ideology in the Spread of English   7
James W. Tollefson

2   Linguistic Human Rights and Teachers of English   22
Tove Skutnabb-Kangas

3   Official English and Bilingual Education: The Controversy over Language Pluralism in U.S. Society   45
Susan J. Dicker

4   Non-Native Varieties and the Sociopolitics of English Proficiency Assessment   67
Peter H. Lowenberg

Additional Questions and Activities   83
Additional Reading and Resources   84

Section 2: The Social, Cultural, and Political Dimensions of Language Education   87

5   The Social Politics and the Cultural Politics of Language Classrooms   89
Alastair Pennycook

6   Educational Malpractice and the Miseducation of Language Minority Students   104
John Baugh

7   Transforming the Politics of Schooling in the U.S.: A Model for Successful Academic Achievement for Language Minority Students   117
Shelley Wong

Additional Questions and Activities   137
Additional Reading and Resources   138

Section 3: Possibilities for Action   141

8   Creating Participatory Learning Communities: Paradoxes
    and Possibilities   143
    Elsa R. Auerbach

9   Exploring the Spiritual Moral Dimensions of Teachers'
    Classroom Language Policies   165
    Ramona M. Cutri

10 Disciplinary Knowledge as a Foundation for
    Teacher Preparation   178
    William Grabe, Fredricka L. Stoller and Christine Tardy

11 Becoming Sociopolitically Active   195
        Linn E. Forhan and Mona Scheraga

        Additional Questions and Activities   219
        Additional Reading and Resources   220

Epilogue   222

References   226

Author Biographies   240

Index   246

Foreword

Robert B. Kaplan

Some twenty years ago, in a postgraduate teacher-training class, a student asked to speak with me privately, saying that she had a problem she wished to discuss. In the privacy of my office, she told me that she had been very lucky to have been hired to teach in a bilingual program, but that the program involved Spanish-speaking children; the problem, she said, was that she was bilingual in Arabic, not Spanish. What should she do? The actual resolution of her dilemma is not relevant to my argument; I make no claims to Solomonic wisdom. The argument, however, is that the educational system did the right thing (employing bilingual teachers) in a less effective way (failing to recognize that bilingualism is at best an ill-defined term and that the reality of bilingualism comes in many forms). It seems to me that such ironies are rampant in the educational system. Furthermore, it seems to me that these ironies tend to accumulate in language-teaching contexts more than in other academic contexts.

This book examines ironies of bilingualism. It shows that the act of teaching ESL/EFL is a highly politicized activity, politicized in the following relationships:

- teachers and students;
- students and students;
- students and parents;
- teachers and parents;
- schools and parents;
- teachers and teachers;
- teachers and administrators;
- administrators and the state;
- schools and communities;
- schools and society;
- languages and students, parents, teachers, administrators, schools, communities, and societies;
- teaching materials, curricula, and assessment instruments, and the individuals who create and buy and use such things;

- between any number of other pragmatic oppositions that mark the end of the twentieth century.

This volume discusses the marginalization of language teachers. To a certain extent, the marginalization of language teachers is their own fault (though I understand it is bad form to blame the victim). The absence of licensure for language teachers, the absence of evaluation of language programs, the deplorable quality of some language teacher-training curricula, the equally deplorable pay, and less than full-time employment (without benefits) of language teachers all constitute important aspects of the issue, but it is the willingness of teachers to accept (or perhaps their unwillingness to challenge) these conditions that results in the marginalization of teachers.

However, an issue not addressed in this volume is the marginalization of language teaching itself. ESL/EFL teachers are the offspring and heirs of foreign language departments and their policies (and, more recently, of English departments and their policies). Traditionally, these departments have viewed themselves as exponents of literary study; language teaching has historically been perceived as scut work, good enough to keep graduate students employed, but certainly not the concern of serious scholars. And the consequent focus on literary forms and literary language has defined what language teachers are expected to transmit. This focus is the outgrowth of assumptions about language learning—that language teaching is not a professional activity, that language learning is centered in acquiring the grammar of a language (i.e. language theory = grammar theory), and that language learning does not require much on-task time. These assumptions, further constrained by economic considerations, result in policies like that in California's "English Language Education for Children in Public Schools Initiative" (Proposition 227) enacted in 1998 (see Dicker, chapter 3).

Although this volume does not focus on the marginalization of language, what this volume does show is that virtually everything that happens with respect to curriculum, methods, teacher training, and language choices is heavily politicized and often based on conscious and subconscious bias. The following list contains 12 questions addressed in this volume about the teaching of language and myths that both educators and politicians often accept:

(1) *What language(s) will be taught in the public school system?*
Myth: language choice is driven by economic considerations; that is, languages that are thought to contribute to employability are taught. Reality: several factors influence the choice of which language to teach—convenience, student numbers, teacher expertise, and available resources.

(2) *Who will be taught these languages?*
Myth: access to language education is democratically determined.
Reality: language access is largely restricted to the best students on the assumption that language learning (i.e. literary literacy) is an intellectual exercise and therefore should be limited only to the best and the brightest.

(3) *Who will teach these languages?*
Myth: any competent speaker with appropriate training is eligible to teach.
Reality: Schools favor native speakers (however they may be defined), and some native speakers are employed without reference to appropriate training.

(4) *Who will train the teachers?*
Myth: existing schools are competent.
Reality: many schools are not competent, which may explain the less than mediocre outcomes in language curricula.

(5) *When will these languages be taught—that is, at what point in the curriculum will the languages be introduced and at what point will instruction cease?*
Myth: languages should be introduced in middle school and continued for a maximum of two school years.
Reality: significant research suggests the adolescent years may be the worst possible time to introduce language learning. Furthermore, full competence takes many years to develop. One size does not fit all.

(6) *Where will these languages be taught?*
Myth: the only appropriate place for teaching to occur is in the formal classroom.
Reality: learners need contact with authentic communities of speakers.

(7) *How will success be determined?*
Myth: "standardized" tests determine proficiency.
Reality: the very existence of "standardized" tests is in question, and, whatever such tests may measure, it is certainly not communicative competence but is, on the contrary, likely to include only grammar and vocabulary.

(8) *What is the best methodology for teaching these languages?*
Myth: a "best" methodology exists.
Reality: the language-teaching field is more beset by fads than perhaps any other area of education. The "best" methodology changes at incredibly frequent intervals, depending on which charismatic "scholar" happens to have drawn attention to him or herself lately.

(9) *What are the best materials for teaching these languages?*
Myth: a single set of materials will be equally effective for all learners.

Reality: the set of materials is often identified by the strength of the advertising campaign mounted by a publisher, or by that same charismatic scholar who happens to have a set of wonderful materials in his pocket. In any case, rarely do teachers get to choose their materials; rather, yet another bureaucracy selects materials.

(10) *What sorts of auxiliary materials best support learning these languages?*
Myth: individual schools have the resources to purchase whatever auxiliary materials they wish.
Reality: schools have budget constraints.

(11) *Who will pay for appropriate language learning?*
Myth: districts and states will pay.
Reality: districts and states are strapped for funds and are quite likely to reduce funding for language teaching (see California Proposition 227) because language learning is not "jazzy," may be perceived as "effeminate" (clear evidence suggests that far more girls than boys undertake language study; see Baldauf & Rainbow, 1996), and may also be perceived as irrelevant in the face of serious academic work like science and mathematics (or less serious but jazzier "subjects" like football).

(12) *How will it be determined that language teaching programs are doing a satisfactory job?*
Myth: if a program survives, it is successful.
Reality: survival depends on a range of variables unrelated to any known educational criteria.

The answers to all these questions are politically determined, those answers being essentially insensitive to pedagogical considerations or theoretical views. This mythology is centered in beliefs about language and language learning.

Many countries value their native language as one being worthy to be taught in schools. In the United States, for example, there is a fundamental belief that English, being a world language, is preferred for any intellectual activity. The political linkage between language and the state—between language and national identity, between language and national unity—lies at the core of this belief.

Language teaching has its historical roots in the teaching of classical languages (i.e. Latin, Greek, Hebrew, and Sanskrit). But those are dead languages, devoid of any community of speakers. The objective of study in those languages was to achieve an understanding of the thought and art of dead civilizations. Consequently, communicative competence was rarely the goal; rather the goal resided in an understanding of the grammar and vocabulary of those languages as a means to access the thought and art. For that goal, the grammar-translation approach was

ideal; translation constituted a viable teaching methodology. Although
the teaching of classical languages is (most regrettably) in decline, the
methodology is alive and well and widely practiced around the world
(where assessment often drives curriculum) for the teaching of modern
languages.

Although research suggests that something like a continuous exposure of at least 1000 hours is required to achieve any sort of competence,
and further that the 1000 hours must be administered over a duration
not so great that the rate of forgetting exceeds the rate of learning, there
are few language curricula anywhere in the world that approach the
1000-hour minimum. On the contrary, language classes tend to be large
(an average of 50 students per class), classes tend to meet for three
50-minute class hours per week for the average 35 weeks of the academic year, and the curricular limit tends to be 2 years. In a class of
50 students, then, each student gets roughly the equivalent of 1 minute
of useful instruction in every 50 minute period. If one does the arith-
metic (1 minute/period x 3 period/week x 35 weeks/academic year x 2
academic years = 210 minutes [or a total of 3.5 hours total exposure—
an average of 1.75 hours per academic year]), it will take about 541.5
years to reach the 1000-hour minimum—a duration in which the rate of
forgetting is quite likely to exceed the rate of learning.

Who is making all these bad policy decisions? Ministries of Education
(or whatever such bodies may be called in any given setting) make many
decisions. But Ministries of Education are not evil; they are not involved
in some global conspiracy to deprive students of adequate language education. Ministries of Education must operate within budgetary and social
constraints established by legislatures. The reality is that neither budgets
nor curricula are endlessly permeable. If money is spent on language
education, then some other curricular area goes begging, and if curricular
time is expended on language education, then some other curricular area
enjoys less curricular time. The relative intensity of protest depends on
whose ox is being gored. For example, a professor of history at Melbourne University, in Australia, wrote in a newspaper article (*Weekend
Australian*, 1 March 1997):

> The pressure on schools to teach drug education, physical education
> and languages has meant history has been de-emphasized to such an
> extent that it's now more important to study a foreign language than
> to learn about your own country.

Why do legislatures impose such unrealistic constraints on education,
particularly language education? Legislatures are merely ignorant and
subject to all sorts of popular misperceptions about language. Kaplan

and Baldauf (1997: 3) develop the metaphor that language education is like sex:

> Language issues have some of the characteristics of sex—everyone does it, and consequently everyone is an expert. However, it is not teachers nor even parents who teach most adolescents about sex; rather, it is a cadre of other adolescents, mostly characterized by knowing little about the matter. From there on, it is largely a matter of on-the-job training. It is not until one reaches maturity that one even discovers that there are real experts who might teach one something about the subject. So it is with language issues. Every segment of society has language and individuals competently use language for a variety of purposes. However, when users engage in talking about language—which they frequently do—that talk is largely marked by profound ignorance.

And so it is with legislatures and Ministries of Education, which are, after all, made up of fallible men and women characterized by the prevailing ignorance.

For much of human history, the relative ignorance of legislatures and Education Ministries hardly mattered. Few people went to school; the social requirements for "success" were more limited, and the influence of particular educational structures was geographically limited. But as the human population has increased, the stakes for success have escalated. As globalization has permeated educational structures (e.g. the European Community), the silliness of decision-makers has come to acquire vast significance.

In the final analysis, what this volume recommends is a dramatic re-education of all those who make decisions about language—from students, to parents and teachers, to materials and test writers, to administrators, to Education Ministries, to legislatures. Just as societies are painfully learning that the rape of natural resources has a huge cost, so they must learn that the destruction of human resources has an equally painful outcome. Just as societies have had to learn about ecological structures—how the demise of a species affects the lives of other species in a widening gyre—so they must now learn that languages too exist in an ecological structure, and that the death of a language is not a trivial event.

Although this re-education must take place in administrations and legislatures as well as in academics, Christison and Stoller (1997) have attempted to offer guidance to administrators in the field, without necessarily raising the political issues. The American Council on Education (1982) has attempted to address institutional policy. TESOL (1984, 1986) has addressed internal standards for language programs. Indeed, there is a substantial literature on the problems and solutions, though not often on the causes. Unfortunately, it is not teachers (or even Education Ministries) who are at fault. The United States Immigration and Naturalization Service (INS), for example, enforces regulations enacted by the U.S. Congress which specify who may enter the country under what conditions (including language conditions). The United States Information Agency (USIA) operates programs based in other countries and promulgates the policies that dictate answers to the dozen questions raised above. The U.S. Department of Commerce, the U.S. Agency for International Development (USAID), and dozens of other governmental agencies are involved—indeed, agencies in every cabinet department are involved to some extent. But then so are other countries in the English-speaking world—e.g. Britain's Overseas Development Administration [ODA], the British Council, the Australian Overseas Service Bureau [OSB], the Australian Agency for International Development [AusAID], the Canadian International Development Agency [CIDA], and even some agencies of nations where English is not the first language.

It would be quite impossible in this brief foreword to enumerate all the governmental agencies involved or to specify in detail all the assumptions about language and language learning that dominate their policies. And this listing essentially ignores the myriad state agencies, school district agencies, and county and city agencies that all play a role in policy determination in the U.S. Among the darkness of the "English Only" movement and the destruction resulting from the hegemony of English, there is a faint ray of hope. The Center for Applied Linguistics together with the National Foreign Language Center cosponsored the first national conference on Heritage Languages in America, 14–16 October 1999, at California State University, Long Beach, as part of the Heritage Language Initiative, intended

> to overcome [the] neglect of heritage languages … to help the U.S. education system recognize and develop the heritage language resources of this country as part of a larger effort to educate citizens who can function professionally in English and other languages. (Brecht & Ingold, 1998)

Wisely, this volume starts the re-education process with an essentially captive audience: students and language teachers. If the next generation of language teachers is better informed about what it is doing, and if it has learned to gather itself up to speak against egregious foolishness among its administrative superiors (see Forman & Scheraga, this volume), much can be accomplished. But, I fear, it will take more than talking to teachers to address the re-education of the population. The contributors and editors of this volume are to be congratulated on their courage; it is not always wise to rock the boat. But until individuals of the caliber of the contributors to this volume can speak to Education Ministries and legislatures, success is likely to be limited and may require years to penetrate the layers of bureaucracy and ignorance that interpose themselves between students and their teachers.

Introduction

The Sociopolitics of English Language Teaching

We often find that public discussions on the teaching of English as an additional language typically focus on such aspects of pedagogy as the latest teaching methods and techniques, multimedia materials and resources available for student use, and the "how to's" of managing student behavior. They may also involve discussions on the latest findings of studies whose purposes include uncovering the various psychological dimensions of learning and finding more effective ways of teaching. Less often do we find conversations on the more macro aspects of English language teaching, which include such political, cultural, and social issues as language policies and their implications for schooling practices, and the role of the teacher in (re)creating such policies and practices. On one level these issues may seem less tangible, less immediately relevant to our roles as teachers of English, than the more mundane matters of teaching techniques and classroom management may seem. However, if we look closely enough, it becomes clear that rather than being peripheral to our tasks as teachers, the political, cultural, and social dimensions of English language teaching are embedded in each and every decision we make. Language policies, both officially and unofficially sanctioned, cultural expectations about the roles of teacher and student, and our identities in terms of, for example, gender, race, ethnicity, and nationality at the same time inform and constrain what we do in the classroom. Our actions, in turn, both shape and constrain the social, academic, and linguistic consequences for our learners. Thus, as important to the development of English language teacher expertise as knowledge of effective classroom practices may be is our understanding of these more macro dimensions of pedagogy and how they shape both our roles as teachers and our students' roles as learners.

It is to these larger concerns of English language teaching that this text is addressed. Our primary purpose is to introduce these issues to aspiring teachers of English from myriad educational contexts and geographical locations for the purposes of provoking their sensibilities, stimulating discussion, and ultimately raising students' awareness of these important issues. Good pedagogy demands that teachers be well informed about the decisions they must make. The readings and subsequent classroom discussions and activities will help aspiring teachers not only to develop the knowledge they need to make such decisions but, as importantly, to assume responsibility for their own learning.

Description of the Text

The text is composed of a collection of 11 papers that were written specifically for this volume by well-known experts in the field of English language teaching. Organized around three themes, the chapters explore some of the more significant sociopolitical issues linked to the teaching of English as an additional language. Each author contributed with the understanding that he or she was to provide his or her own perspective on a topic with the aim of illuminating rather than attempting to resolve the complexities surrounding the topic. Readers will note that the chapters are written in a variety of styles and propose a variety of perspectives. Given the diversity of opinions and writing styles, readers may find themselves drawn to some chapters or to some perspectives more than they are to others. Moreover, they may find that their preferences differ from their classmates.

We should make it clear that our intent is not to prescribe any specific position on an issue or to advocate a particular perspective. Rather, as noted previously, the intent is to raise the awareness of novice teachers and others in the field of TESOL about matters that are central to their role as teachers of English but that are sometimes overlooked or ignored in teacher preparation programs. Nor do we believe that becoming knowledgeable of these issues will lead to the development of "ideal" teachers who will be able to create and teach in "ideal" educational contexts. Our educational worlds are far too dynamic and ever changing and we each approach our roles as teachers with a unique view of our world. We do believe, however, that engaging with these issues in serious, reflective ways will lead to a creative awareness of the various kinds of issues that constitute the field of English language teaching. It will also lead to an understanding of the complex and vital roles we as teachers play in the creation and re-creation of meaning in our students' lives. What we hope for readers then is their development of "practical competence" (Stanley, 1992: 214), the knowledge and skills needed to define, interpret, and reformulate goals and actions both in response to and in the creation of their locally situated educational contexts. We realize that we cannot cover all of the social, cultural, and political issues that are so important to the English language teaching field, especially to aspiring teachers in TESOL teacher preparation programs, in one volume. However, we hope that readers are motivated by the discussions on the topics that are addressed here to seek out and become involved in those issues and concerns that are of particular importance to them.

The four chapters in Section One deal with language policies and practices. Two of the chapters, those by Tollefson and Skutnabb-Kangas, address the role that language policies and, more specifically, English language policies, play in facilitating or hindering the use of other languages in international settings. Dicker's chapter focuses on similar issues as they have developed in the United States. The chapter by Lowenberg examines language policies as they are instantiated in the practice of English language testing and discusses the implications for a variety of English language speakers. Section Two contains three chapters that address the social, political, and cultural aspects of language education. Two chapters, those by Pennycook and Wong, explore some of the more salient social, cultural, and political aspects of classroom learning. Although the specific classrooms they discuss are geographically and culturally rather different, the concerns they raise are similar. Reflecting similar interest in language education, Baugh's chapter introduces the notion of "educational malpractice" and discusses its implications for language minority students. The four chapters in Section Three explore possibilities for action. The chapter by Auerbach examines pedagogical possibilities for the adult English language classroom while that by Grabe, Stoller, and Tardy discusses possibilities for the preparation of teachers of English. The final chapter, by Forhan and Scheraga, provides readers with a multitude of suggestions for "getting involved" personally and professionally.

Following each chapter is a list of questions and activities intended to facilitate class discussion of the ideas contained within the chapter. Moreover, at the end of each section is a list of additional readings on the chapters' topics and a list of additional discussion questions and activities for further exploration of the ideas and issues. In the Epilogue, the many points raised in each of the themes are brought together in song lyrics written by Lavon Smith, a graduate of the TESOL master's program at the University of Georgia who happens to be a singer/songwriter in addition to being an English language teacher. We include it here as an example of what we think is a wonderfully creative synthesis of the ideas and issues covered in the various chapters. We could not have done it better. At the end of the textbook, readers will find short biographies of the chapter authors and editors and a subject index.

Acknowledgments

We would like to recognize those people that helped in the creation of this volume, especially our families and colleagues for their patience and support. Thanks to each of the contributors for their willingness to be involved in the project and the effort spent in creating chapters written specifically to newcomers to the field. Thanks also to those who have helped in the final production of the manuscript and its preparation for publication: Nancy Hornberger, Colin Baker, and Ken Hall at Multilingual Matters for their patience, wisdom, and guidance; graduate students Paul Matthews and Julie Spilker for copyediting and proofing; and graduate student Kent Minson for proofing, production, and layout. Finally, we would like to thank all those who recognize and address the issues of English language teaching. We hope this volume will contribute and inspire others to contribute to the discussion of how we can better help those we teach.

The Editors

Section 1

Language Politics, Language Practices, and English Teaching

As English language teachers, we are the frontline deliverers of a series of formal and informal, planned and unplanned language policies which, haphazard as they may be, seem to be heading in the same general direction—a direction involving the implementation of a unique linguistic experiment on almost the entire population of the planet. This experiment addresses one overriding question: Is it possible for the vastly culturally and linguistically diverse populations of the world to develop English as a common first, second (or third ...) language, and if so, at what cost to factors such as societies and individuals as well as to cultural and linguistic diversity?

The four chapters in this first section focus on various aspects of these and related questions. The authors of these chapters ask thought-provoking questions that challenge our common understandings of what the English language teaching profession is trying to accomplish. Sometimes, the answers they provide are disturbing. We do not ask you to agree with them. Rather, we ask you to consider the underlying assumptions critically, not dogmatically. Our ultimate objective is for English language teaching professionals to realize that the enterprise we are engaged in must be handled with the utmost care.

In Chapter One, Tollefson draws our attention to a paradox. English is seen as a language of opportunity and yet it also creates significant inequalities. He touches on important issues raised frequently in this present volume, namely: Is my language better than your language? And, is my English better than your English? Tollefson also asks us to examine our language ideologies. He suggests that a series of pervasive ideologies contributes to the "hegemony" of English—the implicit acceptance that English is the language of all languages. Within this framework, Tollefson concludes by suggesting that English language teachers should be more than mere technicians of classroom practice. Citing Giroux (1988), he encourages us to be "transformative intellectuals"—professionals who are concerned about the social and political impact of what we are doing.

In Chapter Two, Skutnabb-Kangas extends Tollefson's arguments to encompass the notion of linguistic human rights. She draws our attention to two models or paradigms and suggests that most English language teaching is embedded within the "Diffusion of English Paradigm" often at the expense of the "Ecology of Languages Paradigm." This is a provocative chapter placed at the beginning of the book in order to dramatically kick-start teachers toward becoming "transformative intellectuals." Before diving into Skutnabb-Kangas's discourse, you may want to turn to the first discussion question at the end of the chapter. Here Skutnabb-Kangas asks us how we feel after reading the article. Are we furious? She then quotes Edward Said's notions of what it means to be an "intellectual." Consider them carefully. Once again, as editors, we do not ask you to agree with the notions contained within the chapter. In fact, we encourage you to challenge them. In so doing, you will eventually come to your own personal understandings of these complex intellectual and emotional issues.

Dicker, in Chapter Three, localizes some of the notions discussed in the previous two chapters by examining official English and bilingual policies currently being debated in the U.S. These debates bear striking resemblance to similar discussions currently underway not only in other nations where English is the dominant language, but in many nations where national ideological monolingualism is confronting the realities of linguistic (and cultural) pluralism brought about by large-scale immigration and recognition of the rights of indigenous and historical minorities. Dicker frames her discussion by referring to two opposing ideologies: language restrictionism and linguistic pluralism. She suggests that the language restrictionist ideology is realized in the form of the U.S. English organization—an organization that promotes official English and English-only education. She encourages English language teachers to situate ourselves within this debate.

In Chapter Four, Lowenberg connects the sociopolitics of language policy to pedagogical practice in terms of the assessment of English proficiency. He establishes the notion of a (the) standard English, but then challenges that notion by indicating "standards" in non-native varieties that differ from THE standard. He argues for the viability of "non-standard" standards, concluding that there should be a variety of standards. He then shows how these issues can have a major impact on teaching strategies and assessment procedures. For example, when an English language learner produces English structures that may not agree with a native English speaking teacher's norms, are those non-normative features "errors" or simply differences in standards? Similarly, should those responsible for the administration and teaching of standardized tests for measuring fluency in international English, such as the TOEIC, incorporate non-native standards in their assessment content?

Chapter 1
Policy and Ideology in the Spread of English

J.W. Tollefson

Edna Velasco is a graduate of Ateneo de Manila, one of the most prestigious private colleges in the Philippines. Throughout Edna's schooling, in elementary and secondary school as well as in college, English was the language of instruction. The history of U.S. colonial policy in the Philippines left a powerful legacy of English language usage, not only in education, but in government (where English is an official language), business, and the mass media. Similar to Malaysia and India, the Philippines uses English for a wide variety of purposes.

Bilingual in Filipino and English, Edna speaks the variety of English that is common among highly educated individuals in the metro Manila area. She has ten years of experience as an English teacher at the university level in the Philippines.

Edna decides to attend a doctoral program in applied linguistics at an American university, and after passing the TOEFL test, she is admitted. When she applies for a teaching assistantship in the university ESL program, however, she discovers that she must take a test of her spoken English. The test assesses not only her proficiency in English, but also her speaking style and her accent. Because she has always considered English to be one of her two native languages, she is surprised by this requirement. Although she is completely fluent in English, on the day of her examination, she is nervous, afraid of what her examiners may think about her Filipino English.

Edna Velasco's experience depicts two key features of English as an international language. First, in many nations with colonial histories linked with England and the U.S., English is used in education, government, the mass media, and business. As Peter Lowenberg shows in Chapter Four, the varieties of English in these postcolonial states are often quite different from British or American varieties. Second, these newly nativized varieties often have low status relative to varieties of English spoken in England, the U.S., Canada, Australia, and New

Zealand. Edna's experience is typical of many prospective ESL teachers in the U.S.: her English is not accorded equal status. While English speakers from the U.S., Canada, England, Australia, and New Zealand are exempt from the sort of testing that Edna must undergo, speakers of other varieties from India, Pakistan, Sri Lanka, Singapore, Malaysia, Zimbabwe, Zambia, the Philippines, and elsewhere must take tests of their English-speaking ability. In some cases, these speakers are denied employment, solely on the grounds that their English is not one of the high status varieties of English spoken internationally. (Similar issues apply to non-standard varieties of English in the United States.)

Edna Velasco's fluency in English gains her many advantages in Philippine society. She has access to jobs that require English, including the teaching profession. She has the opportunity to study abroad in countries that require a high degree of English proficiency for admission to university study. Yet her fluency in English does not lead to equal treatment as an ESL teacher in the U.S. Edna's variety of English opens doors, but it also creates difficulties, leads to uncertainty, and forces her to prove herself. Edna's experience shows that the phenomenal spread of English worldwide has not resulted in equal status or equal treatment for all speakers of English.

Thus we are confronted with a paradox: at a time when English is widely seen as a key to the economic success of nations and the economic well-being of individuals, the spread of English also contributes to significant social, political, and economic inequalities. In order to understand this paradox, we must critically examine the spread of English as an international language and the forces responsible for its rapid dissemination. Especially important is the role of language policy. What different approaches to language policies are adopted worldwide, how do they impact the spread of English, and how do those policies reinforce inequalities among speakers of different varieties of English? We will also look at the ideologies of language that play an important role in the global spread of English. Finally, we will examine resistance to the spread of English, particularly in critical pedagogy.

We begin this analysis of the sociopolitics of the spread of English with two different views of the global impact of English as an international language. In one view, the growing dominance of English worldwide is the fulfillment of a utopian dream that can be traced at least as far back as the fifteenth century. In this view, national languages play a crucial role in unifying distinct nation states, but an international language is needed for worldwide communication among governments, in business and industry, in the sciences and technology, and in education. Such a global language not only makes international communication more efficient, it also reduces the probability of political conflict resulting from competition among languages. To achieve this goal, many artificial languages, such as Esperanto, have been created, but none has ever approached widespread popularity. At various times, philosophers, linguists, and others have argued that Latin and French were appropriate choices. However, English became a serious contender for use as the primary language of international communication because of the British Empire of the nineteenth century and, after World War II, the U.S.'s rise to world economic and political dominance. With the collapse of the Soviet empire, the spread of English has accelerated as never before, now including Eastern Europe and the former Soviet Union. Braj Kachru, one of the world's best known analysts of the spread of English, concludes: "For the first time a natural language has attained the status of an international (universal) language, essentially for cross-cultural communication" (Kachru, 1983: 51). In this first view of the global spread of English, the English language fulfills the perceived need for one language of international communication. Through English, people worldwide gain access to science, technology, education, employment, and mass culture, while the chance of political conflict is also reduced.

A different view of the spread of English focuses on Australia and the U.S., where the preeminent position of English has contributed to the death of indigenous languages. Likewise, in countries such as India and Indonesia the spread of English is closely linked with the processes of economic globalization that indirectly lead to the loss of local languages. The power of English to bring about linguistic homogeneity leads Goodman and Graddol (1996) to ask whether English is a "killer" of endangered languages. More generally, critics of the spread of English point out that the benefits of English are not distributed equally. For those who already speak English, the economic value of the language translates directly into greater opportunities in education, business, and employment. For those who must learn English, however, particularly those who do not have access to high-quality English language education, the spread of English presents a formidable obstacle to education, employment, and other activities requiring English proficiency.

The Status of English

From one perspective, the spread of English reflects the high status of the language. Status can be a confusing term, in part because it refers to so much that is important in human society. For instance, it can refer to social and economic hierarchies, such as those linked with professional standing. Does a doctor have a higher status than a janitor does? Why? In this sense, status refers to what people are or what they possess. But another, perhaps more useful sense of the term is that it refers to something that people do all the time. Rich Hawkins, an actor and ESL teacher, points out that actors depict changes in status by changing their behaviors. A different way of standing, different clothing, a change in language—all can be used to depict changes in status. In this sense, status refers to beliefs that individuals hold about themselves, beliefs that others hold about them, and the intensity and direction of esteem which interlocutors give each other during interactions. Status is actively expressed in language and is subject to continuous change and negotiation. Language learning is a powerful way to develop new behaviors that express higher status. Thus the formidable task of learning English becomes a means by which individuals seek higher status. Moreover, using English in particular settings is a means for claiming higher status.

What is the source of the high status of English? One possibility is that individuals who speak English gain concrete economic advantage, or at least believe that they will gain advantage. After all, learning a language is an extraordinarily difficult, complex, and time-consuming task, not to be undertaken lightly. The fact that millions of people worldwide put such enormous effort into learning English suggests that significant economic advantages are widely assumed.

Does speaking English provide such powerful benefits that the time, effort, and expense of learning it are justified? This question is a difficult one to answer, because it is often not possible to track the particular benefits of English for particular learners over time. For one thing, learning English takes a long time, and the benefits are often delayed for many years. One way to assess the advantages of learning English is to ask people why they learn the language. When we do this, we get the answer we would expect: that English provides increased educational and employment opportunities. We also learn that English is desirable because of its connection with popular culture—U.S. film and television, popular music and other forms of mass entertainment, even McDonald's. Thus learning English is a mechanism for participating in mass consumer culture.

Another way to investigate the benefits of learning English is to search for empirical evidence showing that English provides educational and economic opportunities. When we look for empirical evidence of the benefits of English for individuals internationally, we find a highly complex and uncertain picture, in which English seems in some contexts to provide advantage for some individuals and groups, but in other contexts seems to provide little tangible benefit; and in some contexts, the need to learn English results in serious disadvantage for some groups and individuals.

Ofelia Garcia studies the tangible economic benefits of learning English for Spanish speakers in the U.S. Given the preeminent importance of English in the U.S., we would expect the U.S. to be the clearest example of a place where learning English increases one's individual income. The challenge in conducting this research, however, is to differentiate the role of language in determining income from other factors that also play a role, such as age, sex, occupation, and level of education. Garcia uses a powerful statistical tool, called multiple regression, to sort out the relative contribution of many different variables to income level.

In a particularly important study, Garcia (1995) investigated the economic value of English in three Latino communities in the United States: Mexican Americans living in selected counties of Texas, Colorado, New Mexico, Arizona, and California; Puerto Ricans in the New York area; and Cuban Americans in Dade County, Florida. If English leads to higher income levels, then Latinos who have shifted to English and are monolingual in English should have higher incomes on average than those who continue to use Spanish (i.e. those who speak only Spanish or who remain Spanish-English bilinguals). When Garcia controlled for other factors such as age and education, she discovered that Mexican Americans and Puerto Ricans who were English monolinguals did indeed have higher incomes than Spanish-English bilinguals in their respective communities; but Cuban Americans who are English monolinguals did not have higher incomes than Cuban Americans who continue to use Spanish.

In order to explain these findings, Garcia examined the different role of Spanish and English in the three regions she studied. Based upon her research, she concluded that shifting to English offers no advantage for individuals "when the minority language is not viewed as a suspicious characteristic that must be eradicated," but instead is seen as a resource for the larger community (Garcia, 1995: 156). In other words, the social and political relationship between the minority and majority communities is the key factor. Only when the minority language faces structural discrimination is it to the community's advantage to learn English. Garcia's research is of fundamental importance because it shows (1) that sociopolitical factors, including discrimination, determine the benefits of learning English; and (2) in some contexts, the link between English and economic success is a myth

Of course, in other contexts English provides substantial economic advantages. But Garcia's research suggests that we should look critically at particular learners in particular contexts to decide whether claims about the advantages of English are matched by concrete economic reality. Do the millions of English learners in Japan, China, and elsewhere really benefit from the time, effort, and expense of learning English? Which among them benefit most? Which do not?

If the benefits of learning English are not as clear as we might originally have thought, then why does English continue to spread so widely? We will look at two important aspects of the sociopolitics of the spread of English: ideologies of language that support the spread of English and language policies affecting English in different contexts internationally.

Language Policies

Researchers have long recognized that English plays different roles in different countries. Using a single term for English worldwide, such as "English as an international English," is misleading in that it suggests that the global spread of English takes place the same everywhere. In fact, the spread of English manifests itself differently in different contexts. When we take a closer look at English in different international contexts, we find that the spread of English is intimately linked with political decisions that benefit some groups at the expense of others.

In an attempt to make sense of the complexity of English as an international language, Kachru and Phillipson, two influential researchers in the field, have proposed different frameworks for analyzing English worldwide. Their work represents two competing sociopolitical perspectives regarding the spread of English. First, Kachru (1983) distinguishes between the inner, outer, and expanding circles of English-using countries. The inner circle includes countries where English is the primary, dominant language, e.g. the U.S., Canada, the UK, Ireland, Australia, and New Zealand. The outer circle includes countries where English is used in major institutions, such as government, education, and the media. Countries in the outer circle include India, Singapore, Philippines, Ghana, and many others. In most cases, a history of colonialism is the reason for the importance of English in these countries. The expanding circle includes countries where English is recognized as an important international language, but English does not have a major role in domestic institutions. In these countries, English is taught as a foreign language in school. Nations in the expanding circle include Japan, China, Russia, and Poland. Kachru is particularly interested in the spread of different varieties of English in the outer circle (e.g. Filipino English) and attitudes towards these varieties. He argues that new varieties of English deserve equal status as legitimate varieties for teachers and targets for language learners. In emphasizing attitudes, Kachru concludes that "whatever the reasons for the earlier spread of English, we should now consider it a positive development in the twentieth-century world" (1983: 51).

At first glance, Phillipson's (1992) distinction between "core" and "periphery" English-speaking countries seems to resemble Kachru's inner, outer, and expanding circles. In Phillipson's framework, the core English-speaking countries are Britain, the U.S., Canada, Australia, and New Zealand. The periphery English-speaking countries are of two types. In Japan, Scandinavia, and elsewhere, English is an "international link language," serving this important but limited communicative function. In India, Nigeria, Ghana, and elsewhere, English was imposed in colonial times and then "successfully transplanted" as an important language for intra-national communication. Thus Phillipson's categories closely resemble those of Kachru.

Yet Phillipson's framework differs markedly from Kachru's in a key way: Phillipson focuses on the unequal distribution of benefits from the spread of English. Phillipson's terms ("core" and "periphery") are borrowed from development studies, in which dominant core countries exercise major control over the economic and political fate of dominated periphery countries. Phillipson's analysis places English squarely in the center of the fundamental sociopolitical processes of imperialism, neo-colonialism, and global economic restructuring. In this view, the spread of English can never be neutral but is always implicated in global inequality. Thus Phillipson, in contrast to Kachru, argues that the spread of English is a positive development for some people (primarily in core countries) and harmful to others (primarily in the periphery). The spread of English, in this view, is a result of policies adopted by core countries to bring about the worldwide hegemony of English, for the benefit of core country institutions and individuals.

In assessing the impact of the spread of English upon social inequality, it is important to distinguish between periphery countries in which English is used for internal purposes and those in which it is used only for international communication. In the latter cases, such as Japan, the use of English is primarily associated with international government and business, as well as with access to popular culture. Although knowledge of English may provide benefits to its speakers, English is not a central basis for deciding who has access to economic resources and political power. In countries where it is used for internal purposes, such as the Philippines, English is deeply implicated in structuring social, economic, and political inequality.

How is language policy involved in the spread of English as an international language? Language policy refers to a wide range of governmental and non-governmental actions designed to influence language acquisition and language use. In many countries, government agencies play an especially important policy role in deciding issues such as the following:

- What will be the medium of instruction in schools?
- What languages will be taught?
- What language(s) must teachers know?
- What languages will be used in the courts, in government offices, in voting, and in other public arenas?

All these issues involve language policy decisions. Non-governmental agencies also may adopt language policies. For instance, how does a hospital deal with the language needs of linguistic minorities in the emergency room? What languages may employees speak on the job? All sorts of institutions, from large governmental agencies to individual workplaces, develop language policies.

A fundamental purpose of language policies is to manage language conflicts in multilingual situations. In this sense, language policy has one of the same aims as the utopian dream of a single world language—reducing language conflict. A useful framework for discussing how language policies can manage linguistic conflict is provided by Schmidt (1998) and adapted for applied linguistics by Tollefson (in press).

This framework distinguishes different approaches to language policies in multilingual situations. For our purposes, the important point is that in different contexts, each of these approaches may create possibilities for the spread of English. One approach is a monolingual policy, in which national unity and security are associated with a single dominant language and the politically dominant group holds power in part by excluding other languages from public use. The issue here is not that one language is used exclusively but rather that using a particular language is essential for economic success and political power.

The Philippines is a good example of a multilingual country where English plays a crucial role in determining access to wealth and power. Since independence in 1946, the Philippines has been dominated by a relatively small group of wealthy families who control the political system through a variety of means. One mechanism for this continuing control is the use of English as a language of government, education, business, technology, and the media. English proficiency is a major criterion for access to higher education and better jobs, yet not everyone has equal access to high-quality English education. A dual system of education operates in the country. Public schools are underfunded, overcrowded, and staffed by poorly paid teachers who can do little to overcome the structural inequalities that plague public education. In contrast, the system of private schools for elite families offers a high-quality system of education. In both public and private schools, English is a medium of instruction, but graduates of the elite schools have major advantages, including superior English proficiency. Thus the policy of favoring English in government, business, and other institutions means that the families which can afford private education are better able to benefit.

A second approach to managing language conflict is a policy of assimilation, which encourages subordinate groups to adopt the language of the dominant group as their own. In the U.S., a policy of linguistic assimilation operates in most of the school systems, as well as in special programs for immigrants and refugees. The policy of moving school children out of ESL or bilingual education to English-only instruction as quickly as possible is one of the most important examples of the overall policy of assimilation. Closely linked to such assimilationist policies are notions such as the "melting pot" and "equal opportunity," which are components of national myths designed to encourage assimilation of immigrant groups. The movement for declaring English the sole official language of the United States is an attempt to shift national policy from one of assimilation to a monolingual policy.

A third approach to managing linguistic conflict is a policy of pluralism, in which cultural and linguistic diversity is encouraged. In Australia during the 1980s, for example, government policies in education and the media encouraged the maintenance, use, and acquisition of a wide range of immigrant and indigenous languages other than English. The result was a rapid spread of language programs and a wide range of government services (e.g. libraries) for languages other than English. More recently, Australian policy has shifted toward a policy of assimilation, which requires immigrants to adopt English if they are to enjoy the full range of educational and employment opportunities. In South Africa today, an official policy of pluralism supports the use of indigenous languages, including English. The challenge for the future will be to find ways to support these languages in the educational system.

The examples of the Philippines, the U.S., and elsewhere show that language policies in individual nation states often support the use of English within those states. Equally important, however, are policies designed to further the spread of English across international boundaries. In Europe, the European Economic Community (EEC) operates as a multilingual organization, but the high cost of translation (several billion dollars per year) places increasing economic pressure on the organization to adopt English and French as dominant languages. More generally, researchers have documented in detail the role of governments, private agencies, educational institutions, and English language teaching professionals in the spread of English. Given the impact of policies favoring English, it is clear that the spread of English is not a "natural" or "accidental" process but rather the result of a billion dollar effort by governments and other agents worldwide.

Deliberate planning does not mean that a small group of individuals conspires to bring about the spread of English. Indeed, personal motives and the actions of specific individuals are not the issue. Rather, due to structural relations and historical processes, English serves the core and the periphery differently: the spread of English benefits the core, while periphery countries face the additional burden and expense of learning English, training teachers, operating language education programs, buying texts and materials, and other aspects of English education. The work of Phillipson (1992), Pennycook (1994), Skutnabb-Kangas (1995), and Tollefson (1991) shows that language policies favoring the spread of English are intimately connected with unequal social, political, and economic relationships between nations and institutions.

Ideologies of Language

We now turn from language policies to ideologies of language. A key concept in critical social theory is "hegemony," which refers to the experience of ideas, meanings, and values as absolute reality. For instance, the supremacy of English is often unquestioned, taken to be an obvious matter of common sense. In critical social theory, this acceptance of the "reality" of English is a manifestation of the "hegemony" of English—that is, the uncritical perception that it has achieved supreme global status. Central to the hegemony of English are ideologies of language, beliefs about language that shape fundamental views of reality.

Three generalizations about ideology are important for understanding the spread of English. First, individuals in social situations construct versions of reality through discourse. These realities are designed to influence the actions of others. For instance, "standard language ideology" has several powerful assumptions that influence language policy debates in the United States and elsewhere: that there is a single variety of the language (the "standard"); that everyone has more or less equal access to this standard and equal opportunity to learn it and use it; and that this standard is more appropriate than "nonstandard" varieties for government and the law, education, the media, and publishing (Lippi-Green, 1997). A wide body of research on language seriously questions all of these beliefs (see Skutnabb-Kangas, this volume), yet standard language ideology is so powerful and pervasive that these beliefs are widely accepted as self-evident "truths" or "common sense," and thus largely outside the realm of explicit debate (see Fairclough, 1989). Research on language ideology is intended to help in understanding how such beliefs become part of culture.

A second generalization about ideologies of language is that language is socially and historically situated, and always contested. This means that language ideologies are used to advance different constructions of the world; these constructions place limits on possible language policies. For instance, belief in standard language ideology was the basis for much of the uproar in the United States over the proposal to grant some legitimacy to Ebonics (African-American Vernacular English, or Black English) in the schools of Oakland, California. Similarly, standard language ideology is the basis for restricting the use of Filipino English in U.S. schools. As long as standard language ideology is pervasive, a multilingual policy in which Ebonics, Filipino English, or other "low status" varieties are granted legitimacy in education is likely to meet with fierce resistance in the U.S.

Third, in most countries, including the U.S., debates about language are conditioned by the two powerful discourses of equality and national unity. Sometimes these discourses are in conflict and sometimes they are mutually reinforcing, but in any event, they tend to force the discussion of language to focus on the degree to which particular policies achieve or sustain "national unity" and the degree to which they affect the "equality" of different linguistic groups. Thus the spread of English is justified in some settings as the key to economic equality and in other settings because it is believed to aid national unity. The ideological nature of these claims is crucial. In the U.S., for instance, learning English may be an impossible undertaking for many immigrants, and thus it is not the key to equality for them, but rather a barrier to it. In the Philippines, claims for the neutrality of English ignore the dual educational system and unequal access to effective English language education. The ideological power of "equality" and "national unity" is so great, however, that linking English with either of these discourses is an effective mechanism for its continued spread.

In order to understand English as an international language, we must critically examine the rationales that are given for its spread and its use. In what sense is it empirically accurate to claim that English in the United States is central to "equality" or to "opportunity" or to "national unity?" For which groups does the dominance of English provide the greatest opportunity? For which groups is English a barrier to education or employment? For whom does it offer "equality"? Which groups does English unify or exclude? When the use of English is justified on the grounds that it furthers national unity and offers economic opportunity, which groups benefit most? What alternative policies are available, and which groups would benefit from those policies? As we seek answers to these questions, we see that ideologies of language play an important role in the global spread of English.

Resistance to the Spread of English

Although ideological claims for the value of English are widespread, the inequalities associated with English are not completely hidden. Some critics of the spread of English recognize that its value is not the same for everyone, its spread often results in inequality rather than opportunity, and the need to learn English is often a barrier to education and employment rather an opportunity for it. For instance, Tickoo (1993) shows how the hegemony of English makes it difficult for the Kashmiri language in North India to compete as a language of education. Because the vast majority of Indians are taught English in an environment with poor teaching and little opportunity for interaction in English, the English language does not become a usable means of communication. Still, Kashmiri is blocked from use as an effective medium of instruction. The belief in the value of English-medium schools is so intense that students flock to them, despite the fact that most students are unable to learn effectively through English, with disastrous consequences for their education. In response, Pattanayak (1986) advocates resistance to English: "The cultural deprivation and sociopolitical inequality introduced by the approach of monolingual control ... make nonsense of any talk of economic benefit [from English]" (22).

In Papua New Guinea, the English-only policy in education results in two groups of students: a huge number of "school leavers," who become alienated from an ineffective and irrelevant system of English education and therefore drop out of school; and a tiny number of "elites," who graduate and obtain jobs in the market economy of the country (Ahai & Faraclas, 1993). In the Solomon Islands, the hegemony of English in the English-medium school system results in classes that are not meaningful to most children and an examination system that forces a majority of students to drop out of school, leading to work on plantations or in low-skilled jobs in town with no opportunity for advancement (Watson-Gegeo & Gegeo, 1995). Thus there is a movement for a change away from the educational policy of English monolingualism in both Papua New Guinea and the Solomon Islands. Similarly, in the Philippines, the hegemony of English means that only the small number of children from well-to-do families can afford to attend private schools and enjoy the educational and employment opportunities that English provides. As a result, groups that are excluded from the mainstream economy and political institutions resist English.

One aspect of English resistance is a call for better understanding of the social and economic costs of monolingual policies and standard language ideologies. As Pattanayak (1986) points out:

The amount of resources spent to produce the 4% of English-knowing persons in India over the past two hundred years proves the absurdity of efforts to replace many languages by one. From a predominantly monolingual point of view, many languages are a nuisance.... They are uneconomic and politically untenable.... In the case of multilingual countries, the reverse is true. For them, restrictions in the choice of a language are a nuisance, and one language is not only uneconomic, but is politically untenable and socially absurd. (22)

Another form of resistance takes place within the field of English language teaching. Many teacher preparation programs focus on learner variables such as motivation, learning style, self-esteem, age, and family background and culture. Yet the social and political context of English language education is at least equally important. If teaching methods, texts and materials, and the English language itself are largely irrelevant to the everyday lives of students in the Solomon Islands, North India, or Papua New Guinea, then it is misleading to seek explanations for the students' difficulties in factors such as motivation. Instead, English language educators must understand the direct and powerful impact of social, political, and economic forces upon their classrooms and how these forces affect students' lives.

How might English language teachers place their work within a broader sociopolitical perspective? Giroux (1988) argues that teachers should see themselves as "transformative intellectuals" rather than technicians who apply a curriculum to specified groups of learners. In Giroux's view, teachers should be fundamentally concerned with moral and ethical issues and with the impact of their classes upon the disadvantaged and oppressed. Work inspired by Paolo Freire uses problem-posing as a central classroom activity in order to ground classes in the everyday issues that affect students' lives. For example, Bonny Norton describes an effective critical pedagogy in South Africa (Peirce, 1989) and Elsa Auerbach (1992 and in this volume) offers numerous ideas for critical pedagogy. The work of these and other critical educators demonstrates that a wide range of teaching practices can place social and political issues at the center of teaching and learning.

Edna Valasco's language situation can be understood only with reference to important sociopolitical factors, especially language policy and ideology. Edna was educated in an English-language educational system that is sustained by pro-English policies and ideologies. As a graduate of elite private schools, Edna has gained enormous economic benefits from English. When she arrives in the U.S., she finds that institutional policies grant privilege to American English over her variety of Filipino English.

These policies are rationalized by a powerful and pervasive standard language ideology that justifies linguistic hierarchies. Thus Edna finds that her English, which is a source of high status in the Philippines, is now a source of suspicion and uncertainty, stigmatized as inferior to standard American English.

Yet, on balance, Edna is one of the more fortunate from her country. Her variety of English is less stigmatized than that of the majority of Filipinos, who attend public schools; indeed, Edna has advantages over most others from the "outer circle" of the "periphery." As a Filipina in the U.S., Edna is unlikely to enjoy the same access to employment as speakers of British or American English. However, her English proficiency offers her distinct advantages, a result of the complex sociopolitical forces shaping Edna's linguistic life.

Discussion Questions and Activities

1. Take a careful look at English language textbooks used to teach nonnative speakers of English. Find one that includes explicit statements about what students must know in order to be successful in employment. In contrast, find one that poses problems for discussion and expects students to find their own answers and solutions. What are the important differences between the texts? What assumptions about students are implicit in texts that provide recipes for success? What assumptions are implicit in problem-posing texts?

2. Millions of immigrants from the Philippines and other countries in the periphery have immigrated to the U.S., England, and other English-speaking countries. If there is an immigrant community in your area, interview an individual to find out about his or her language education back home. Also ask about the status of the immigrant's variety of English in the new country. You might begin by contacting an immigrant association, church, or social service agency.

3. Consider in more detail the two views of the spread of English: a utopian dream or a killer of languages. For what groups in what contexts is the spread of English a utopian dream? For what groups is it a threat to their language or identity? Be sure to consider the impact of the dominance of English on groups speaking other languages in the U.S., England, Australia, Canada, and New Zealand.

4. Choose two linguistic communities residing within the U.S. that have minimal sociopolitical or sociocultural power and list the advantages and disadvantages that the spread of Standard American English might have for each. What role does language education play in the spread of English?

5. Contrast Kachru's and Phillipson's frameworks for analyzing the spread of English. What are the advantages of each framework? Do the frameworks lead to different conclusions about the spread of English?

Chapter 2
Linguistic Human Rights and Teachers of English

T. Skutnabb-Kangas

Languages are being killed today at a much faster pace than ever before in human history. Linguistic diversity is disappearing relatively faster than biodiversity. Linguistic and cultural diversity on the one hand and biodiversity on the other hand are related to each other and possibly influence each other mutually. The fate of languages is thus vital for the future of the planet.

Legally binding linguistic human rights, especially in education, might be one of the necessary (but not sufficient) ways of counteracting language murder and therefore a prerequisite for the maintenance of linguistic diversity. Violations of linguistic human rights, especially in education, may lead to reduction of linguistic and cultural diversity on our planet.

This chapter describes what linguistic human rights (LHRs) are and what international law contains about LHRs, especially in education. It discusses to what extent present linguistic human rights are sufficient to protect and maintain linguistic diversity, to prevent ethnically articulated conflict, and to function as the necessary corrective to the "free" market. It analyzes the consequences of LHR violations, especially in education. It describes what is being done to gain basic LHRs in different parts of the world, including spelling out present problems and challenges. It discusses the consequences for education of some recent and draft human rights instruments concerning specifically language rights in education. Finally, it concentrates on The Hague Recommendations Regarding Minority Education Rights.

The existing language rights provisions will then be related to English language teaching in several parts of the world. This will first be done more generally, in terms of the organization of the teaching, comparing models which do and models which do not lead to high levels of multilingualism and which do or do not respect LHRs. Then ESL teacher competencies will be discussed in terms of the Hague Recommendations. Some of the research arguments for bilingual teachers who are NOT native speakers (NS) but second (SLS) or foreign (FLS) language speakers of English will be presented. The basic tenets that have guided ESL will be discussed as fallacies. Finally, teaching of English will be related to two paradigms, the Diffusion of English Paradigm and the Ecology of Languages Paradigm. It will be claimed that most ESL today, internally and globally, is a reflection of the Diffusion of English Paradigm. For linguistic and cultural diversity to be maintained, for the planet to have a future, an Ecology of Languages Paradigm (which also respects linguistic human rights) is a necessary (but not sufficient) prerequisite.

The State of the World's Languages

A language can be defined as a dialect promoted by the elite, a dialect with an army, or with state borders. There are probably between 6500 and 10,000 spoken (oral) languages in the world, and the number of sign languages can be equally large. Europe and the Middle East together have only around 4% of all languages, and the Americas (North, South, and Central) together around 15%. The rest of the world's oral languages, 81%, are in Africa, Asia, and the Pacific. Nine countries have more than 200 oral languages each: the two megadiversity countries Papua New Guinea and Indonesia (850 and 670 respectively) and seven others.

These countries account for more than half the world's languages. Another 13 countries have more than 100 languages each: the Philippines, Russia, U.S.A., Malaysia, China, Sudan, Tanzania, Ethiopia, Chad, Vanuatu, Central African Republic, Myanmar (Burma), and Nepal. These top 22 countries, just over 10% of the world's countries, probably account for some 75% (over 5000) of the world's oral languages. The top 11 oral languages in the world, in terms of number of mother tongue speakers, are Chinese, English, Hindi/Urdu, Spanish, Arabic, Portuguese, Russian, Bengali, Japanese, French, and German.

All have more than or very close to 100 million speakers. Although these 11 languages comprise only 0.10 to 0.15% of the world's oral languages, they account for almost 50% of the world's oral language speakers. Another 30 languages have between 35 and 100 million speakers. A very small group of the world's languages, certainly numbering less than 300, are spoken by communities of 1 million speakers and above.

Demographically these fewer than 300 languages account for a total of over 5 billion speakers or close to 95% of the world's population. On the other hand, the 95% of the world's population accounts for much less than 5% of the world's languages, probably only 3%. This means that some 95 to 97% of the world's languages have fewer than 1 million speakers each. Probably around 45% of the world's languages are spoken by between 1 million and 10,000 speakers each.

Therefore, over half of the world's (oral) languages and most of the sign languages are spoken by communities of 10,000 or fewer speakers. But half of these, in turn, meaning around a quarter of the world's languages, are spoken by communities of 1000 or fewer speakers. Demographically their speakers account for only 0.15% of the world's population. These very small and therefore endangered languages are the most vulnerable oral languages of the world (and all sign languages are threatened). Most languages in the world (84%) are spoken in one country only. The median number of speakers for oral languages is probably some 5–6000 people.

Linguists agree that many languages face extinction. Michael Krauss from Alaska divides the (oral) languages into three groups, the moribund, the endangered, and the safe languages. The moribund languages, between 20 and 50% of the world's oral languages, are the ones that are no longer being learned by children, meaning they are "beyond endangerment, they are living dead and will disappear in the next century." The endangered languages are the ones "which, though now still being learned by children, will—if the present conditions continue—cease to be learned by children during the coming century" (1992: 6). The safe languages are the ones which are neither moribund nor endangered. Krauss discusses how many speakers a language has to have to be "safe." More than one million? Then we would only have some 200 to 250 safe languages. He finally settles with a minimum of 100,000 speakers. This gives around 600 "safe" languages. This means that during the next hundred years, 90% of today's languages are going to disappear or become moribund unless something is done.

What kills languages? Some of the direct main agents for this linguistic (and cultural) genocide are parts of what we call the consciousness industry: formal education and the mass media (including television, which Krauss calls "cultural nerve gas"). Today it is formal education that makes indigenous or minority children, who come to school speaking their own language and possibly knowing a bit of the dominant language, leave school dominant or sometimes virtually monolingual in the dominant language. They may leave believing that their language is not as useful or developed as the dominant language, and that they help their future children best by speaking the dominant language to them. They may even believe in the ideology of monolingual stupidity/reductionism: that monolingualism is normal, sufficient, inevitable, and desirable, and that it is necessary to choose between the languages, to learn the dominant language subtractively (at the cost of their own) rather than additively (in addition to their own). When linguistic diversity disappears through linguistic genocide (meaning languages are killed; they do NOT disappear through any kind of natural death, but are murdered), the speakers are assimilated into the realms of other languages. The top languages in terms of number of speakers are the big killer languages, and English is the foremost among them. These are the languages whose speakers have arrogated to themselves and to their languages more structural power and (material) resources than their numbers would justify, at the cost of speakers of other languages.

If you are an ESL teacher and/or if you teach minority children through the medium of a dominant language, at the cost of their mother tongue, you are participating in linguistic genocide. You are killing the necessary diversity and the prerequisites for life on our planet. Even if you feel shocked and angry at this accusation, it is your duty to know, and to find out about alternatives. One tool in counteracting linguistic genocide might be linguistic human rights, especially in education.

Linguistic Human Rights

Transmission of languages from the parent generation to children is the most vital factor for the maintenance of languages. Children must have the opportunity to learn their parents' idiom fully and properly so that they become (at least) as proficient as the parents. Language learning in this sense has to continue at least into young adulthood, for many functions throughout life. When children have access to formal education, much of their more formal language learning that earlier happened in the community, happens in schools. If an alien language is used in schools, i.e. if children do not have the right to learn and use their language in schools as the main medium of education, the language is not going to survive because children educated through the medium of an alien language are not likely to pass their own language on to their children and grandchildren. These are being "forcibly transferred" from one group to another; this is genocide according to Article II(e) of the UN Genocide Convention (see below). "Modernization" has accelerated the death/murder of languages that had survived for centuries or millennia before the advent of formal education. One of the main agents in killing languages is thus the linguistic genocide which happens in formal education every time indigenous or minority children (or dominated group children even if they are a majority in terms of numbers) are educated in a dominant language.

Linguistic genocide sounds drastic. We need to define it. When the United Nations worked on the final draft of what was to become The

Convention on the Prevention and Punishment of the Crime of Genocide (E 794, 1948), a definition of linguistic genocide was included in Article III.1:

> Prohibiting the use of the language of the group in daily intercourse or in schools, or the printing and circulation of publications in the language of the group.[1]

In the final vote in General Assembly, Article III was voted down and is NOT part of the final Convention. Still, the definition can be used. If we accept the claim that "prohibition" can be direct or indirect, it follows that if the minority language is not used as a medium of education in the preschool/school and if there are no minority teachers in the school, the use of the language is indirectly prohibited in daily intercourse in schools, and it is a question of linguistic genocide.

For maintenance and development of languages, educational linguistic rights, including the right to mother tongue medium education, are thus absolutely vital. I would not hesitate to call educational language rights the most important linguistic human rights if we are interested in maintaining linguistic and cultural diversity on our planet.

In many of the post-WWII human rights documents, language is mentioned in the preambles and in general clauses as one of the characteristics on the basis of which individuals are not to be discriminated against in their enjoyment of human rights and fundamental freedoms. The original and basic four characteristics (in the United Nations Charter, Art. 13) are "race, sex, language, or religion." This shows that language has been seen as one of the most important characteristics of humans in terms of their human rights.

But when we move from the lofty non-duty-inducing phrases in the preambles of the human rights instruments to the real business, namely the binding clauses, and especially to the educational clauses, something very strange happens. There is a change of position. All or most of the non-linguistic human characteristics (race, sex, religion, etc.) are still there and get positive rights accorded to them: the clauses or articles about them create obligations and contain demanding formulations where the states are firm dutyholders and are obliged to ("shall") act in order to ensure the specified rights (i.e. positive rather than negative rights). Here modifications (e.g. "should" instead of "shall"), opt-out clauses ("if there is sufficient demand," "wherever possible"), and sliding-scale alternatives (the state can do XXX or X or minimally X) are rare.

In binding educational clauses, however, one of two things can often be noted. Firstly, often language disappears completely, as, for instance, in the Universal Declaration of Human Rights (1948) where the paragraph on education (26) does not refer to language at all. Similarly, the International Covenant on Economic, Social and Cultural Rights (adopted in 1966 and in force since 1976), having mentioned language on a par with race, color, sex, religion, etc. in its general Article (2.2), does explicitly refer to "racial, ethnic or religious groups" in its educational Article (13). However, it omits here reference to language or linguistic groups:

> Education shall enable all persons to participate effectively in a free society, promote understanding, tolerance and friendship among all nations and all racial, ethnic or religious groups.

The European Convention on Human Rights and Fundamental Freedoms from 1950 is equally silent on not only language rights in education but even on more general minority rights. Several new Declarations and Conventions to protect minorities and/or minority languages have been passed in the 1990s. But even in the new instruments language has been omitted in education clauses and, for instance, in racism definitions.

Generally, in human rights documents, if language-related rights are included and specified, the article dealing with these rights, in contrast to the demanding formulations and the few opt-outs and alternatives in the articles dealing with other characteristics, is typically so weak and unsatisfactory that it is virtually meaningless.

For example, in the UN Declaration on the Rights of Persons Belonging to National or Ethnic, Religious and Linguistic Minorities, adopted by the General Assembly in December 1992, most of the articles use the obligating formulation "shall"—except where linguistic rights in education are concerned. Compare, for example, the unconditional formulation in Article 1, with the education Article 4.3 (emphases added, _"obligating"_ in italics, "**opt-outs**" in bold):

> 1.1. States _shall protect_ the existence and the national or ethnic, cultural, religious and linguistic identity of minorities within their respective territories, and _shall encourage_ conditions for the _promotion_ of that identity.

> 1.2. States _shall_ adopt **appropriate** legislative _and other_ measures _to achieve those ends._

> 4.3. States **should** take **appropriate** measures so that, **wherever possible,** persons belonging to minorities have **adequate** opportunities to learn their mother tongue **or** to have instruction in their mother tongue.

Clearly the formulation in Article 4.3 raises many questions. What constitutes "appropriate measures," or "adequate opportunities," and who is to decide what is "possible"? Does "instruction in their mother tongue" mean through the medium of the mother tongue or does it only mean instruction in the mother tongue as a subject?

We can see the same phenomenon in the European Charter for Regional or Minority Languages (22 June 1992). A state can choose which paragraphs or subparagraphs it wants to apply (a minimum of 35 is required). Again, the formulations in the education Article 8 include a range of opt-outs, including "as far as possible," "relevant," "appropriate," "where necessary," "pupils who so wish in a number considered sufficient", "if the number of users of a regional or minority language justifies it," as well as a number of alternatives, as in "to allow, encourage or provide teaching in or of the regional or minority language at all the appropriate stages of education."

While the Charter demonstrates the unquestionably real problems of writing binding formulations which are sensitive to local conditions, just as in the UN Declaration above, its opt-outs and alternatives permit a reluctant state to meet the requirements in a minimalist way. It can legitimate its actions by claiming that a provision was not "possible" or "appropriate," or that numbers were not "sufficient" or did not "justify" a provision, or that it "allowed" the minority to organize teaching of their language as a subject, at their own cost.

A new Council of Europe Framework Convention for the Protection of National Minorities was adopted by the Committee of Ministers of the Council of Europe on 10 November 1994. We again find that the Article covering medium of education is so heavily qualified that minorities are completely at the mercy of the state:

> In areas inhabited by persons belonging to national minorities traditionally or in **substantial** numbers, **if there is sufficient demand,** the parties **shall endeavor** to ensure, **as far as possible** and **within the framework of their education systems,** that persons belonging to those minorities have **adequate** opportunities for being taught in the minority language or for receiving instruction in this language. (Emphases added)

The Framework Convention has been criticized by both politicians and even international lawyers who are normally very careful in their comments.

A still more recent attempt to promote language rights, a Draft Universal Declaration of Linguistic Rights, accepted in Barcelona in June 1996 and handed over to UNESCO, also suffers from similar shortcomings, even if for several beneficiaries it represents great progress in relation to the other instruments described. Still, indirectly its education section forces all others except those defined as members of language communities (which roughly correspond to national territorially based minorities) to assimilate. For all others, only education in the language of the territory is a positive right, i.e. not education in their own language. There is no mention of bilingual or multilingual territories in the Declaration. Every territory seems to have only one "language specific to the territory," i.e. territories are seen as monolingual. For those who speak a language other than the language of the territory, education in their own language is not a positive right. In addition, the Declaration grants members of language communities not only the right to "acquire a full command of their own language" but also the right to "the most extensive possible command" of any foreign language in the world. In contrast, the rights granted to "everyone" include only the right to "oral and written knowledge" (i.e. not "full command") of one's own language. This is clear in a comparison of the formulations at the end of Article 26 on language communities with Article 29 which spells out the (negative) right of "everyone":

> All language communities are entitled to an education which will enable members to acquire a full command of their own language, including the different abilities relating to all the usual spheres of use, **as well as the most extensive possible command of any other language** they may wish to know. (Art. 26 on rights of language communities, emphasis added)
>
> 1. Everyone is entitled to receive an education **in the language specific to the territory where s/he resides.**
>
> 2. This right does not exclude the right to acquire **oral and written knowledge of any language** that may be of use to him or her as an instrument of communication with **other language communities.** (Art. 29 on rights of "everyone," emphasis added)

Furthermore, Article 29.2 is formulated so as to suggest that "everyone's" own language can be learned only if it is a useful instrument when communicating with other language communities. This means that it could in principle be excluded if it is not known by any entity defined as a language community, or if it is not used as a lingua franca between people where some represent language communities. It is likely that the lack of rights in the education section will force all those not defined as members of language communities to assimilate. The

Declaration gives language communities very extensive rights but leaves "everyone" with very few rights. This makes the Declaration vulnerable in several respects. As mentioned earlier, many states claim that they do not have minority language communities or do not want to give these communities any rights. As a result, these communities are completely dependent on the acceptance of their existence by states, an acceptance that many states are not willing to grant. Thus individual rights become enormously important in the Declaration. But these individual rights are the weakest part of the Declaration. In addition, the new Declaration seems to be in many ways completely unrealistic—few if any states are willing to accept it in its present form.

The new Draft Universal Declaration, even if it were accepted, does not give any positive educational language rights to all individuals, regardless of which category they belong to—and this is exactly what individual human rights are supposed to do. If something is to be seen as an individual human right, it means, per definition, a right which every individual in the world has, simply because that individual is a human being. It means an unconditional, fundamental right that no state is allowed to take away. Thus the situation has not improved despite new instruments in which language rights are mentioned or even treated in detail.

There is a hierarchy in human rights instruments, with different rights for different groups. Dominant majority language speakers have all the rights. Traditional/territorial/national minorities have more language rights than other minority groups and most human rights instruments pertain to them. Immigrant/guest worker/refugee minorities have practically no language rights in education in relation to their own language and only few in relation to learning the official language. The UN International Convention on the Protection of the Rights of All Migrant Workers and Members of Their Families, from December 1990 but not yet in force because of lack of signatures, in its assimilation-oriented educational language Article (45) accords minimal rights to the mother tongues and is even more vague than the instruments mentioned before. Indigenous peoples have on paper some rights and more are suggested in the UN Draft Universal Declaration on Rights of Indigenous Peoples, but many of them may disappear in the revision process.

The conclusion is that we are yet to see the right to education through the medium of the mother tongue become a human right. We are still living with basic language wrongs in human rights law, especially in education policy. Denial of linguistic human rights, linguistic and cultural genocide, and forced assimilation through education are still characteristic of many states, notably in Europe and Neo-Europes (U.S.A., Australia,

Canada, New Zealand, where the first two have killed more languages during the last couple of centuries than most other countries in the world, and are continuing). Despite the small recent improvements (see below), it seems to me to be clear that the Western states do not respect what should be basic linguistic human rights, especially in education, and that they do little to prevent linguistic and cultural genocide.

Recent Positive Developments

One of the difficulties in earlier provisions has been that states can claim that they have no minorities and that there thus are no beneficiaries for provisions. This has been, for instance, the stance of France and Turkey—they claim that they have no minorities (France has changed this in May 1999). We can look at the UN International Covenant on Civil and Political Rights, ICCPR, Article 27 which still grants the best legally binding protection to languages:

> In those states in which ethnic, religious or linguistic minorities exist, persons belonging to such minorities shall not be denied the right, in community with other members of their group, to enjoy their own culture, to profess and practice their own religion, or to use their own language.

In the customary reading of Article 27, rights were granted only to individuals, not collectivities. Moreover, "persons belonging to … minorities" had these rights only in states which accepted their existence. Immigrant minorities have not been seen as minorities in the legal sense by the states in which they live. The customary reading of Article 27 interpreted it as

- excluding groups (even if they are citizens) which are not recognized as minorities by the state;

- excluding (im)migrants (who have not been seen as minorities);

- conferring only some protection from discrimination (= "negative rights") but not a positive right to maintain or even use one's language; and

- not imposing any obligations on the states.

More recently (6 April 1994), the UN Human Rights Committee adopted a General Comment on Article 27 which interprets it in a substantially broader and more positive way than earlier. The Committee sees the Article as

• stating that the existence of a minority does not depend on a decision by the State but requirements to be established by objective criteria;

• protecting all individuals in the State's territory or under its jurisdiction (i.e. also immigrants and refugees), irrespective of whether they belong to the minorities specified in the Article or not;

• recognizing the existence of a "right"; and

• imposing positive obligations on the States.

This would mean, for instance for the U.S., that those groups which fulfill the "objective criteria" for being minorities (and most immigrant minority groups do) have to be treated as minorities who have rights. This provision includes undocumented migrants. Thus the state has obligations, duties, towards them.

As a side note, using terms like "linguistically diverse students" and other nice euphemisms which are in the process of replacing the degrading, outrageous terms like LEP and NEP in the United States about minority students, actually robs these children of the only protection they have in international human rights law. Objectively they ARE minority students and you are harming them by refusing to use the term. "Linguistically diverse students" have no protection in international law; minority students do.

OSCE, Organization for Security and Cooperation in Europe, has 55 member states, including the U.S.A. and Canada. In 1992 OSCE created the position of a High Commissioner on National Minorities "as an instrument of conflict prevention in situations of ethnic tension." The High Commissioner, Max van der Stoel, is a former Foreign Minister of the Netherlands. In order to prevent ethnic conflict, the High Commissioner recently published authoritative guidelines for minority education for OSCE member states, including the U.S. These guidelines, The Hague Recommendations, were worked out by a small group of experts on human rights and education (including the author of this chapter). The guidelines are an interpretation and concretization of what international human rights law says about minority education. Even if the term "national minority" is used, the guidelines also apply to immigrated minorities, and one does NOT need to be a citizen in order to be protected by the guidelines.

In the section "The spirit of international instruments," bilingualism is seen as a right and responsibility for persons belonging to national

minorities (Art. 1), and states are reminded not to interpret their obligations in a restrictive manner (Art. 3). In the section on "Minority education at primary and secondary levels," mother tongue medium education
is recommended at all levels, including bilingual teachers in the dominant language as a second language (Articles 11–13). Teacher training is
made a duty of the state (Art. 14). Some of the central articles include the
following:

11. The first years of education are of pivotal importance in a child's
development. Educational research suggests that the medium of
teaching at pre-school and kindergarten levels should ideally be the
child's language. Wherever possible, States should create conditions
enabling parents to avail themselves of this option.

12. Research also indicates that in primary school the curriculum
should ideally be taught in the minority language. The minority
language should be taught as a subject on a regular basis. The State
language should also be taught as a subject on a regular basis
preferably by bilingual teachers who have a good understanding of
the children's cultural and linguistic background. Towards the end
of this period, a few practical or non-theoretical subjects should be
taught through the medium of the State language. Wherever possible, States should create conditions enabling parents to avail
themselves of this option.

13. In secondary school a substantial part of the curriculum should be
taught through the medium of the minority language. The minority
language should be taught as a subject on a regular basis. The State
language should also be taught as a subject on a regular basis preferably by bilingual teachers who have a good understanding of the
children's cultural and linguistic background. Throughout this period,
the number of subjects taught in the State language, should grad-
ually be increased. Research findings suggest that the more gradual
the increase, the better for the child.

14. The maintenance of the primary and secondary levels of minority
education depends a great deal on the availability of teachers
trained in all disciplines in the mother tongue. Therefore, ensuing
from the obligation to provide adequate opportunities for minority
language education, States should provide adequate facilities for the
appropriate training of teachers and should facilitate access to such
training.

Finally, the Explanatory Note states that

> submersion-type approaches whereby the curriculum is taught
> exclusively through the medium of the State language and minority
> children are entirely integrated into classes with children of the
> majority are not in line with international standards. (5)

Now compare these human rights standards to what you know of the
education of minorities in your country. Does your country or school live
up to the standards? Even California, the state that, until Proposition 227
was voted through, had more "bilingual" education than other states in
the U.S., had over 70% of linguistic minority children in submersion, even
if it was and is labeled something else.

A submersion or sink-or-swim model is a program where linguistic
minority children with a low-status mother tongue are forced to accept
instruction through the medium of a foreign majority language with high
status, in classes where some children are native speakers of the language of instruction, where the teacher does not understand the mother
tongue of the minority children, and where the majority language constitutes a threat to the minority children's mother tongue (MT), which
runs the risk of being displaced or replaced (MT is not being learned
[properly]; MT is "forgotten"; MT does not develop because the children
are forbidden to use it or are made to feel ashamed of it)—a SUBTRAC-
TIVE language learning situation. In the U.S., there is complete termino-
logical confusion. What in fact is submersion (see the definition above) is
often falsely and indiscriminately called "immersion," often with addi-
tions: "structured immersion" or "immersion with sheltered English."
The only common feature in submersion and immersion is that the language of instruction is not the students' L1, but everything else in these
two types of educational model is different. Let me remind you that
immersion programs are programs where linguistic majority children
with a high-status mother tongue voluntarily choose (among existing
alternatives) to be instructed through the medium of a foreign (minority)
language, in classes with majority children with the same mother tongue
only, where the teacher is bilingual so that the children at the beginning
can use their own language, and where their mother tongue is in no danger of not developing or of being replaced by the language of instruction—an ADDITIVE language learning situation. Neither early exit nor
even late exit bilingual programs qualify for how minority children
should be educated according the Hague Recommendations. Even late
exit transitional programs prohibit the use of minority languages in
schools later on. It would be only two-way programs which last from
K to 12 that would qualify as programs that do NOT commit linguistic

genocide. While there are some two-way bilingual programs in the U.S. in the early grades, none exist that extend across all 12 grades.

Most of Europe is no better. However, the maintenance programs we have struggled to get in a few minority schools are another positive recent development. Private but partially state-financed ethnic minority schools, with the minority language as the main medium of education, are showing excellent results in terms of high levels of multilingualism and multiculturalism and academic success. For instance, the 11 Finnish-medium schools for Finnish labor migrant minority children in Sweden show that after nine years of mostly Finnish-medium education, with good teaching of Swedish as a second language, mostly given by bilingual teachers, the children's Swedish is at the same level or better than that of Swedish middle-class children, and their Finnish is excellent. They know other, additional languages, and their school achievement is at grade level. This is what human rights-respecting maintenance programs can do, and this is what the Hague Recommendations strive to achieve.

But what about segregation? The Swedish government suspected that ethnic minority schools could contribute to increased social, cultural, and economic segregation and asked a Swedish research group to investigate the schools. The official report, published by the National Board of Education in October 1997, concludes that there is no reason to suspect that the schools lead to segregation.

The report criticized some Muslim schools—most of which do not use Arabic as the main medium of education—in terms of the very traditional content of the education and sometimes of low teacher qualifications. But the minority language medium maintenance schools (which the Swedes call "the linguistically oriented schools" in the report) get high praise for the levels of knowledge and bilingualism attained, the enthusiasm and active engagement of parents, children and teachers, and the social, linguistic, and cultural integration of the students. The Swedish team was looking for problems in these schools in order to be able to suggest solutions. But they claim, with surprise, that they found no problems—and therefore there is no reason to suggest any solutions. Instead, they

> have to agree with a student we interviewed who claimed that his
> school gave him as much as any [Swedish-medium] public school
> could give—plus some more! (my translation)

We know what we should do, pedagogically and in terms of linguistic human rights. But it is not done. Clearly, the education offered by the human-rights-loving U.S. to most of the minority children is "not in line with international standards." Likewise, some of the attempts in

California to delimit the already almost non-existing rights to bilingual education are not only against solid research evidence but they are outrageous attempts to violate central educational linguistic human rights. A question to ask U.S. educators, then, is as follows: Why is it that the U.S. can run around the world policing human rights in other countries when you are seriously violating central human rights of children in your own country? When your schools are committing linguistic genocide every day?

English Language Teaching

If we want to relate the existing language rights provisions to English language teaching, also in other parts of the world, the next question could be: Why is it that the people running around the world, posing as ESL- and EFL-experts on how to teach English as an additional language to the world, i.e. teaching them how to become high level multilingual, mostly come from the two countries, namely the U.S. and UK, which are notoriously among the most unsuccessful ones in the world in making their own majority population high level bilingual, not to speak of high level multilingual? How can they be the best experts in the world in something they have never tried out or succeeded in at home?

We need more contributions from educational situations where learning additional languages is both successful and NORMAL, and not subtractive. Additive language learners, and researchers supporting them, should unite against the pervasive spread of McDonaldized, globalized, subtractive, uncritically anglophile ESL/EFL. If we think of where good results have been achieved in EFL, many smaller European countries that do not have a big language in international use as an official language have a lot to offer. The Nordic countries, the Netherlands, and Hungary, just to mention a few, need to give everybody a good grounding in several languages other than the mother tongues. Children start to study a first foreign language as a subject in grades 3 or 4 and add another foreign language as a subject in grade 5, 6 or 7. Many go on to study even more languages in school. Given some exposure outside school later on, many people from these countries manage extremely well in several languages, while also developing their own languages and mostly using them for their university studies (even if they of course read widely in English and other languages during their studies).

When we compare their course of learning foreign languages with the five key tenets of ESL/EFL, which according to Robert Phillipson's analysis in *Linguistic Imperialism* (1992) have guided English teaching worldwide, we can see that the Nordic countries, the Netherlands, and

Hungary (NNH) have not followed any of these. The following are the five tenets, with comments on NNH English teaching in parentheses:

—English is best taught monolingually (the mother tongues are used extensively for explanations in NNH);

—the ideal teacher of English is a native speaker (English is normally taught by NNH teachers for whom it is a foreign language);

—the earlier English is introduced, the better the results (English is usually started as a subject at the earliest in 3rd grade in NNH, often later; studies show that results with early starts are not better);

—the more English is taught, the better the results (in ordinary NNH schools English is taught only as a subject; it is not used as a medium in schools except in some experiments);

—if other languages are used much, standards of English will drop (all subjects are normally taught in local languages from K to 12 in NNH).

As Robert Phillipson (along with many others) has shown, all five tenets are in fact scientifically false and can be better labeled as fallacies:

—the monolingual fallacy,

—the native speaker fallacy,

—the early start fallacy,

—the maximum exposure fallacy,

—the subtractive fallacy.

Teaching English as a second language according to the tenets would also at every point violate the Hague Recommendations. We shall discuss only one of the subpoints in terms of teacher competencies. The Hague Recommendations suggest that all teachers of minority children should be bilingual and "have a good understanding of the children's cultural and linguistic background." It is specifically suggested that this is true for teachers of the dominant language too, for example ESL teachers.

To me, monolingual ESL teachers are per definition incompetent to teach ESL; they simply lack several of the capacities or proficiencies that a learner needs and can reasonably expect from the teacher. Having a teacher who is a native speaker of English can enhance some aspects of the learner's competence, especially in EFL situations, but in an ESL situation where the learners can hear, read, and often also interact with native models every day if they desire this, nativeness is a characteristic that is peripheral when assessing teacher competence. Other aspects are much more central. We can compare native-speaker (NS) teachers with teachers who are NOT native speakers but second (SLS) or foreign (FLS) language speakers of English, in terms of some of the capacities/proficiencies that learners need in order to achieve high levels of English in an additive learning situation. These include the following:

(1) High levels of functional competence in the target language.

Both NS and SLS/FLS can have this competence. However, it is likely that NS has a higher competence in idiomatic pronunciation and some semantic nuances. But in second language situations this is not important because the teacher is not the only source of exposure to the target language.

(2) High levels of analytical competence in the target language.

Both NS and SLS/FLS can have this competence, but it is more likely found in a trained SLS/FLS teacher. Often NS have "blind spots" in relation to their own language and have not needed to analyze how their own language functions, what the rules are, etc. (When I started writing in Danish, soon after I had immigrated to Denmark, I had to give up asking Danish colleagues, even linguists, about rules for Danish; they could not answer my questions, whereas German and British linguist colleagues who had learned Danish as a foreign language could).

(3) Insight into the linguistic and cultural background and needs of their learners.

It is (much) more likely that SLS/FLS have that insight if they teach their own group.

(4) A detailed awareness of how the mother tongue and target language differ and what is difficult for learners.

It is important to know what one already knows (i.e. what is similar in both languages) and what one needs to learn. It is (MUCH) more likely that SLS/FLS have the awareness needed if they teach their own group, because they have compared the languages in their own learning process.

(5) Firsthand experience of having learned and using a second or foreign language.

SLS/FLS always have it; NS can have it but it is more unusual. A bilingual or multilingual NS is thus better able to understand what the learners experience than a monolingual one.

Clearly, then, SLS/FL ESL teachers, second or foreign language speakers of English, have more of the capacities/proficiencies which learners need than most native speakers of English, provided, of course, that their competence in the target language is high. Their pronunciation does not need to be anywhere near native pronunciation. As several studies have shown, the sometimes negative evaluations of SLS/FL teachers competence often have more to do with the prejudiced attitudes of the evaluators than the competence of the SLS/FL speaker. This is also an aspect where ESL teachers have a duty to enlighten colleagues, students, and even parents, and to work in their professional organizations to have SLS/FL competencies acknowledged. But a starting point for all ESL teachers is to eradicate monolingualism among themselves.

To Conclude

Both globally and in Europe, there is an increasing awareness about the necessity of high levels of multilingual competence in the future if one wants to have a high-level job, especially in administration or business. Big multinational companies, like the British BP Oil International, demand trilingualism from all their new career-service appointees, with English as one of the three languages.

Recent studies by François Grin (1990) and others in Switzerland show, predictably, that high level knowledge of English gives a higher salary. But Grin also shows supply and demand curves for future development. When more and more people in the world learn English—which is today's tendency—competence in English will be the self-evident norm. Very soon there will be an over-supply, which lowers the price. Knowing only English will take you nowhere, especially in business. It will be knowledge of other additional languages that gives you the career possibilities and high salary. Already today knowledge of English AND French AND German is starting to be a standard requirement for all young people in Europe who have high aspirations. A fourth and fifth language is part of tomorrow's qualifications—and these languages need increasingly to be more "unusual" languages.

Americans need to think of this, instead of killing their linguistic and cultural potential. The Chinese and the Russians are rapidly learning English, and many will soon have a high level of competence. Soon some Americans may be the only ones in the world suffering from the curable illness of monolingual stupidity, and in a hundred years' time we multilinguals may be showing some of those who are still voluntarily monolingual, in pathological museums.

In this chapter education has been presented as the big culprit. But behind education and other types of direct agents we have those structural agents which are decisive for what alternatives exist in the educational system and in other market places where languages are allocated certain values, both economic values and partially but not completely through this, market values. Languages are validated or invalidated. Their standing on the market for linguistic capital is assessed. This is where languages compete with each other, and this is where the linguicist hier-archization of languages takes place. Both when languages are killed and when monolingual English-speaking (ESL) teachers teach minority children, linguicism is involved. Linguicism is a concept which describes more sophisticated forms of racism. In biologically argued racism, groups of people were defined on the basis of what was thought to be their "race," and those who represented the "other races," i.e. who were not "white," got less than their fair share of the resources and power. Now people are defined on the basis of their culture and eth-nicity ("ethnicism") and their mother tongue ("linguicism"), and those who represent "inferior" cultures and small languages get less than their fair share. I have defined linguicism as ideologies, structures, and practices which are used to legitimate, effectuate, and reproduce an unequal division of power and resources (material and immaterial) between groups which are defined on the basis of language.

The Japanese scholar Yukio Tsuda (1994) analyzes the spread of English in terms of a "diffusion of English" paradigm where he sees sev-eral other factors related to this diffusion. As an alternative he proposes an "ecology of languages" paradigm that includes minimally bilingual-ism but hopefully multilingualism for all. Robert Phillipson and I have worked further on Tsuda's suggestions (see the discussion in Phillipson & Skutnabb-Kangas, 1996). Below I present both paradigms the way I see them today.

The diffusion of English paradigm:

(1) monolingualism and linguistic genocide,
(2) promotion of subtractive learning of dominant languages,
(3) linguistic, cultural, and media imperialism,
(4) Americanization and homogenization of world culture,
(5) ideological globalization and internationalization,
(6) capitalism, hierarchization,
(7) rationalization based on science and technology,
(8) modernization and economic efficiency,
(9) transnationalization, and
(10) growing polarization and gaps between haves and never-to-haves.

The ecology of languages paradigm:

(1) multilingualism, and linguistic diversity,
(2) promotion of additive foreign/second language learning,
(3) equality in communication,
(4) maintenance and exchange of cultures,
(5) ideological localization and exchange,
(6) economic democratization,
(7) human rights perspective, holistic integrative values,
(8) sustainability through promotion of diversity,
(9) protection of local production and national sovereignties, and
(10) redistribution of the world's material resources.

The consequences for linguistic diversity of choosing the Diffusion of English paradigm, the "free market" response, are disastrous. Most English as a Second Language teaching today, internally and globally, reflects the Diffusion of English Paradigm. Another response could be through diversity. For linguistic and cultural diversity to be maintained, for the planet to have a future, an Ecology of Languages Paradigm (which also respects linguistic human rights) is a necessary (but not sufficient) prerequisite.

The Diffusion of English Paradigm seems to mean spreading the linguistic homogenization of the world that has been sold together with the subtractive spread of English, at the cost of the development of other languages. It seems to mean the spread of the prevailing monolingualism of the "real" English-speaking Brits or Americans or Australians or the monolingualism of the "real" monolingual French or Germans. A development question to be asked is: Do we all have to become monolinguals (with a sprinkling of Japanese or other languages, good for trade, learned in school) in order to become linguistically developed? Do we all have to "suffer from monolingual stupidity" in order to be considered linguistically developed, instead of being "blessed with multilingual brains"? (Both these are modifications of slogans on T-shirts. Many Californian teachers used to give T-shirts to their high-level bilingual students, with "BLESSED WITH BILINGUAL BRAINS". I have a T-shirt [given by Portuguese-American friends] with the text "I DO NOT SUFFER FROM MONOLINGUAL STUPIDITY.")

What has been promoted especially by some of the powerful Western states so far during this century has been their own linguistic and cultural lack of awareness, their intolerance of linguistic and cultural diversity, and their conscious underdevelopment and killing off of the world's linguistic and cultural (along with biological) resources and diversity. So far, those representing the bulk of this underdeveloped diversity have been much too patient, and much too tolerant of the ignorance, of the attempts at linguistic and cultural genocide and its concomitant economic and political consequences. What we need, after the UN Year of Tolerance, is Zero Tolerance of the prevailing ideologies of monolingual reductionism, the illness that many powerful majority populations suffer from.

We also need to develop two kinds of support systems. One support system is for these patients who suffer from monolingual reductionism, so that they can be helped to diversify, to get rid of their illness. Monolingual stupidity or monolingual naivete or monolingual reductionism is one of the most dangerous illnesses on our planet, dangerous for world peace. The only reconciliatory fact about this illness is that it is curable. Education can play a major role in the cure. The second support system needed is to protect and support those who are healthy, the multilinguals, so that we are not infected by the illness virus, so that we can stay healthy and can see clearly that we are the healthy ones. Legally binding guarantees in international and national laws protecting basic linguistic human rights, especially in education, are part of this support system. ESL teachers can be part of the support system—or continue to be part of the problem.

Notes

1. I chose not to add the international documents to the bibliography as the customary practice in legal writings is to refer to them by a lot of numbers and letters. However, this does not really help an English teacher. The easiest way to access them is to consult any recent human rights web sites, e.g. the UN Human Rights Centre in Geneva or in New York. My new book (Skutnabb-Kangas, T. *Linguistic Genocide in Education—or Worldwide Diversity and Human Rights* [in press]) contains masses of web addresses of this kind.

Discussion Questions and Activities

1. How do you feel after reading the article? If you feel furious, remember what Edward Said says about the duty of an intellectual. It is

    publicly to raise embarrassing questions, to confront orthodoxy and dogma (rather than to produce them), to be someone who cannot be easily co-opted by governments or corporations.... Least of all should an intellectual be there to make his/her audience feel good: the whole point is to be embarrassing, contrary, even unpleasant.

    An intellectual is

    neither a pacifier nor a consensus-builder, but someone whose whole being is staked on a critical sense, a sense of being unwilling to accept easy formulas, or ready-made cliches, or the smooth, ever-so-accommodating confirmations of what the powerful or conventional have to say, and what they do. Not just passively unwilling, but actively willing to say so in public.

Said's "modern intellectual's role" is truly "that of disputing the prevailing norms" (Said, 1994: 27). I am not accusing you or any other individual, I am accusing a system which allows killing of diversity and eventually the planet. Reflect together on what your own role is in that. What do you want it to be? Remember, you can not say: "I did not know," when your grandchildren ask difficult questions.

2. Languages, like all biological species, get thicker on the ground as you approach the equator, and likewise, there are both fewer biological species and fewer languages when you approach the poles. There are also remarkable overlaps between global mappings of the world's areas of biological megadiversity and areas of high linguistic diversity, and likewise a correlation between low-diversity cultural systems and low biodiversity. When one takes the top 25 countries for endemic (= found in one country only) languages and endemic mammals, birds, and reptiles, 16 of the countries are on both lists, a concurrence of 64%. It is not accidental. Discuss why there are many languages where there are lots of different animals and plants.

3. If, as researchers are beginning to think, there has been a long-lasting co-evolution between humans and their environments so that biological diversity enhances cultural and linguistic diversity and vice versa, what are the likely consequences of today's sudden disruptions in that relationship?

4. Of the 4400 known mammal species, 326 (7.4%) are on UNESCO's "red list" for endangered or threatened species; of the 8600 birds, 231 (2.7%) are. Of the 6700 oral languages, over 6000 (90%) are moribund or endangered/threatened. For ALL biological species, the realistic estimates for the yearly extinction rate vary between 0.02 to 0.2%. Even with the most pessimistic figure, 20% of the species would be extinct in hundred years' time—as compared to 90% of languages. The threat in relation to languages is far more serious. Discuss why you have not heard much about it! Again, discuss your own role. If you need to find out more, use Terralingua's web page (http://cougar.ucdavis.edu/nas/terralin/home.html) and follow the links in it. Terralingua is an international organization working to support linguistic diversity and the study of the relationship between biological, linguistic, and cultural diversity.

5. Read my and Ofelia Garcia's article (see Additional Reading and Resources) about principles to follow if one wants the school to support high levels of bilingualism. Discuss to what extent you agree or

disagree with them and why. What would you suggest instead? Which of the principles does your school follow? Would you like to follow more of them? What are you going to do? How? Together with whom?

Chapter 3
Official English and Bilingual Education: The Controversy over Language Pluralism in U.S. Society

S.J. Dicker

Walk down the streets of a large U.S. city. Visit the neighborhoods called Little Korea, Chinatown, and Little Italy. Enter a public-school cafeteria at lunch time. In this process, you will run into many people who consider themselves part of the U.S. They are Americans, or soon to be. Yet, if someone were to ask you to synthesize what you have seen and heard, to describe what an American is, you would be hard-pressed to complete this task. What are the facial features of an American? What is the color of an American's skin? What language or languages does an American speak? You would have to conclude, in the end, that there is no "average" American against which to measure each individual. We are all different: we look different, we live differently, and we speak differently.

But is this pluralism a good thing? Don't we need something to bind us together, if we are to live in the same nation? And what better concept to bind us together than a common language, the one thing we need to form links with each other, to communicate with each other. If we decide on one language, which most likely will be English, what happens to all the other languages that people bring to this country, this land of immigrants? These are the questions we will deal with in this chapter.

We will begin by reviewing the history of policies towards immigrant languages in the U.S. We will then focus on the present movement to make English the official language, spearheaded by the organization U.S. English. We will examine the premises underlying official English and challenge their validity. We will then turn our attention to two particular targets of this movement. We will see that these targets are highly successful language minorities who threaten in one way or another the established power structure of American society. Finally, we will turn our attention to the official English movement's attack on bilingual education, an attack on the poorest and most vulnerable of the movement's targets. We will examine various political efforts to end bilingual education despite evidence that bilingual education is quite successful. Finally, we will discuss the implications of the controversy over official English and bilingual education for ESL professionals.

A History of Language Policies and U.S. English

As the language of the original European colonists, English has always been the preeminent language of the U.S. However, throughout the nation's history, English has coexisted with a host of other languages. Attitudes towards these other languages fluctuate with the economic, social, and political realities of the moment. These attitudes lead to policies that linguist Ofelia Garcia (1985) has categorized as *tolerance-oriented, promotion-oriented,* and *restrictive.* Under tolerance-oriented policy, minority-language speakers have the right to cultivate their mother tongues in the private sphere. Promotion-oriented policy regulates the ways in which public institutions may use or cultivate minority languages and cultures. Restrictive policy intentionally represses minority languages.

During colonial times, multilingualism was largely promoted. Along with English-speaking settlers, there were Scots, Welsh, Irish, French, Italians, Swiss, and Germans. Knowing more than one language was necessary for the purposes of trading, teaching, spreading the gospel, and diplomacy. Still, the languages of people who were considered inferior, Native Americans and Africans, were denigrated. Also, German became a suspect language in reaction to the size and power of the German-speaking population.

The 1770s to 1880s were characterized by a tolerance-oriented policy; the use of languages other than English was often considered necessary in the process of national unification. Congress formed a number of troops, for example, in which German was the language of command, and the Articles of Confederation were published in German. However, governmental use of other languages such as German was seen as a temporary measure, a means of integrating new immigrants. It was assumed that newcomers would in time abandon their native tongues and use English exclusively.

From 1880 to the 1950s, the U.S. government pursued a largely restrictive language policy. A change in the major source of immigration, from northern Europe to southern Europe, led to a rise in anti-immigrant attitudes; the new immigrants, including Italians and Jews, were considered by northern Europeans to be racially distinct and inferior. As a result, those with privilege and power sought to protect themselves by denying educational opportunities to others.

Until this point, native-language education for immigrants was common, but by 1923, 34 states allowed only English as the medium of instruction in both private and public schools. Native-American children were taken away from their reservations and placed in boarding schools, where they were expected to acculturate completely to "American" customs and language. Language restrictionism reached outside the classroom as well. In the Southwest, where parts of Mexico had been incorporated into the U.S., the use of English was enforced. The U.S.'s entry into World War I provoked hostility towards all things German; in some cities, the public use of the German language was banned.

From 1923 to 1942, there was a brief respite from language restrictive policy. The legal case of *Meyer v. Nebraska* in 1923 introduced a more tolerant attitude. In this case, the Supreme Court overturned a state law prohibiting schools from teaching any subject in a foreign language or from teaching any foreign language. In a state where the German language was well represented in the population, and was the only foreign language used in the public schools, this piece of legislation clearly reflected the anti-German attitudes instigated by World War I. The effect of the Supreme Court ruling was limited; it restored foreign-language teaching but did not encourage native-language instruction for children who were not dominant in English. However, outside of education, the federal government did make use of immigrant languages; it disseminated information on social and economic policies in various languages, and subsidized theater in German and Yiddish under the Works Program Administration. Also, Native Americans were declared citizens during this period, creating a short-lived movement to revitalize their languages and cultures. Political forces ended this period of tolerance; World War II plunged the nation again into a period of xenophobia and language repression.

From 1958 to 1980 the learning of foreign languages was promoted, leading to a degree of tolerance for ethnic languages. The Soviet launching of the Sputnik satellite in 1957 instigated concern over the ability of the U.S. to compete with other technologically advanced nations. Foreign language study, now viewed as necessary for national defense, was supported by measures such as the National Defense Act of 1958 and the Fullbright-Hays Act of 1961. The Civil Rights movement, begun in the early 1960s, paved the way for a more hospitable climate for immigrant languages. The Bilingual Education Act of 1968 recognized native-language instruction as a means of remedying educational inequities, although its goal was to lead the way into all-English education rather than to maintain native languages. Other legislation, such as the 1965 Court Interpreter's Act and the 1975 amendments to the Voting Rights Act, recognized that governmental use of non-English languages helped bring first-generation immigrants and language minorities into fuller participation in American society.

Finally, 1980 to the early 1990s was a period of tolerance toward minority languages, shadowed by the ghost of restrictionism. This period saw the birth of the official English movement and decreased governmental support for bilingual education amid renewed expectations that newcomers replace their native languages with English. As they had in the past, changes in immigration patterns opened the way for a resurgence of anti-immigrant sentiment. Beginning in 1965, immigration from Europe was overshadowed by immigration from the developing world: Asia, Africa, the Caribbean, and Latin America. Just as northern Europeans once considered southern Europeans to be inferior, many Americans of this period considered the new immigrants—people who were racially, linguistically, and culturally distinct from the American mainstream—inferior to themselves. As in the past, changes in the economy, with fading dreams of upward mobility for middle- and working-class people, cast immigrants as rivals for educational and social opportunities. All of this set the scene once again for the rise of language restrictionism.

The roots of the official English movement are embedded in the xenophobic atmosphere created out of the social and economic conditions described above. Official English activism and anti-immigrant activism have been closely connected since the inception of U.S. English, the guiding force of the movement.

The organization's founder, John Tanton, was a Michigan ophthalmologist with a long-running concern for the effects of population growth on the distribution of natural resources. In the 1960s and 70s, he was actively involved in progressive organizations such as Sierra Club and Zero Population Growth. However, his conviction that immigrants place a burdensome strain on the ability of the U.S. to sustain its population was not acceptable to the membership of these organizations. Moving away from these groups, he formed his own organization in 1979. From his new pulpit, and under the acronym FAIR (standing for Federation for American Immigration Reform), Tanton focused on Hispanic immigrants, and undocumented Mexicans in particular, as threats to the general well-being of society. With other members of his association taking a more centrist stance, avoiding attacks on the Spanish language and allegations of the failure of Hispanics to assimilate, Tanton found himself marginalized once again. This time, his response was to start U.S. English in 1983, enlisting the aid of the late Senator S. I. Hayakawa, who had proposed an official English constitutional amendment several years earlier.

Tanton's break with FAIR was not total, for he continued to serve as the head of both FAIR and U.S. English; the organizations shared office space and employees. While Tanton was now free to focus on the language issue, he still faced the taint of nativism. His constant attacks on the Spanish language convinced many of the organization's anti-Hispanic bias. In 1987, the organization chose a well-known political conservative of Mexican origin, Linda Chavez, to be its president; the subsequent resignation of many U.S. English members and survey results showing the anti-Hispanic bias of many contributors were sources of great embarrassment. Added to this was the public revelation of a memo written by Tanton to a small group of colleagues who met regularly to discuss social issues. In it, Tanton had written:

> *Gobernar es poblar* translates "to govern is to populate." In this society where the majority rules, does this hold? Will the present majority peaceably hand over its political power to a group that is simply more fertile?... As Whites see their power and control over their lives declining, will they simply go quietly into the night? (Cited in Crawford, 1992: 151)

U.S. English received additional criticism for its ties to individuals and other organizations with anti-immigrant agendas. It was revealed that contributions from U.S. English's parent organization, U.S. Inc., had gone to FAIR, Americans for Border Control, and Californians for Population Stabilization. U.S. English had also accepted financial support from Cordelia Scaife May, an heiress with a history of backing anti-immigrant causes, and the Pioneer Fund, which has funded projects involving race improvement through genetics. These revelations led to the resignation of Chavez, Tanton, and a number of well-known members of the U.S. English advisory board.

Another criticism of the organization has been its lack of commitment to English-language education. U.S. English describes its dual function as (1) promotion of official English legislation and (2) promotion of opportunities for learning English. Its lobbying arm is set up to accomplish the first goal; its charitable arm is responsible for the second. However, records show that U.S. English's expenditures for English-language education are minimal, and it failed to live up to its promises of financial backing for Project Golden Door, a program it started for this purpose. In addition, the organization has a history of battling governmental support for English-language education; in 1986, it lobbied against a measure increasing federal funds for adult instruction in English as a second language. In response to years of criticism regarding its lack of commitment to English-language education, U.S. English announced in its summer

1998 newsletter a new legislative approach in this area; it began by supporting government funding for ESL classes in Utah and Missouri. The dollar amounts of these proposals, however, are quite modest.

The organization can count a number of successes in pushing through official English legislation at the state level. Three states had passed such laws before U.S. English was created: Nebraska in 1921, Illinois in 1923, and Virginia in 1981. As of 1998, and largely as a result of intensive lobbying on the part of U.S. English, 18 additional states have official English laws: Indiana, Kentucky, Tennessee, California, Arkansas, Mississippi, North Carolina, South Carolina, North Dakota, Arizona, Colorado, Florida, Alabama, Montana, New Hampshire, South Dakota, Georgia, and Alaska. Arizona's law, the only one that prohibited state employees from using languages other than English in any way for business purposes, was challenged, and in the spring of 1998 the Arizona Supreme Court ruled that it was overly restrictive. However, the Court indicated it might uphold a law similar to those in other states; U.S. English will pursue this.

The organization has been less successful in its effort to legislate official English. Nationally, numerous bills have been introduced in Congress; only one managed to come to a vote in the House of Representatives, in 1996, and while it passed in that body, the Senate did not take it up for consideration. However, several high-profile politicians were enlisted in the cause, including Bob Dole and Newt Gingrich.

The Premises of the Official English Movement

Various arguments have been made to support the need for designating English as the official language. The major arguments are explained and then challenged in this section: (1) Language policy and national unity, (2) Linguistic pluralism and national identity, (3) Bilingualism and bilingual education, and (4) Minority language learning.

Language policy and national unity

Official English advocates argue that having one national language is necessary for the maintenance of the country's sense of unity. Mauro Mujica, current president of U.S. English, writes that "preserving our nation's unity... is one of the top priorities of the American people." He sees governmental use of many languages as destructive, stating that "the push to divide America's people along language-lines is, in fact, helping *tear our nation apart*." He characterizes official English advocates as being pitted against "those who are working to make America officially multi-lingual" (Mujica, 1994: 2).

In reality, there is no movement to make the nation officially multi-lingual. Nor is there any conflict in the present situation: English is unquestionably the major language of communication at all levels of government, while the use of other languages is minimal. A report by the General Accounting Office found that out of 400,000 documents published by the federal government, representing about half of all documents generated between 1990 and 1994, only 265 were translated into one or more foreign languages (*Hispanic Link Weekly Report,* 1995: 1). Also, when government does use other languages, it is often in the service of aiding the transition of immigrants into American life—helping them find homes, jobs, and the support that newcomers often need.

A further question is whether national unity is affected by the number of languages used by the government or the people of a nation. As noted previously in the section on the history of language policy, the use of languages other than English actually helped bring the many residents of the colonies together to fight the British and to form a new nation. A common language does not prevent civil war, as has been proven by U.S. history and the history of other nations. Looking abroad, there are examples of nations which function multilingually in effective ways; Switzerland is one of them.

Linguistic pluralism and national identity

Official English supporters contend that the government's use of languages other than English poses a threat to American national identity. Underlying their rhetoric is the idea that speaking English makes one more American, while speaking something else makes one less American. An example of this is found in the opposition to the government's current practice of allowing citizenship ceremonies to be conducted in non-English languages. The late Representative Bill Emerson, a sponsor of official English legislation, described this policy as sending a message to immigrants that "legally, you are one of us. Linguistically, you are not" (*U.S. English Update,* 1994: 4).

More broadly, critics argue that language and cultural pluralism conflict with the creation of an American essence, the end product of the so-called "melting pot" process. Alistair Cook, a British-émigré journalist on the U.S. English advisory board, enlists the aid of Theodore Roosevelt in making this point:

> Begging the country to stop talking about German-Americans and Italian-Americans and Polish-Americans, he said, "We have room for but one language here, and that is the English language, for we intend to see that the crucible turns people out as Americans.... No

more hyphenated Americans." (Cook, undated membership letter, U.S. English)

These arguments raise the question of how much language shapes an individual's personal and national identity. Emerson suggests that there are both linguistic and legal definitions of an American. Of course, nothing in the naturalization process requires applicants to replace their native tongues with English once they become citizens. However, the message Emerson sends is that the linguistic choices made by newly minted Americans will influence the way they are perceived by others. Official English advocates insist that the linguistic restrictions of government will not affect the private sphere. Mauro Mujica, born in Chile, admits, "I myself speak Spanish at home and in some of my business dealings" (Mujica, 1995: 3). However, Emerson's comment exemplifies the subtext of the official English movement: If you want to be a real American, you have to be just like us, and *we* speak only English. This subtext also comes through in more practical terms: an official English law would prohibit public funds from going to educational and cultural programs promoting minority languages, discouraging the use of such languages in American society.

Cook's remark above also exemplifies this sense of coercion. The idea that the country creates "melted" Americans has been a staple of American thought for centuries. Yet it is only an illusion. Established Americans would blanch at the idea of the melting pot if they realized their own role in it: whatever characteristics they call their own, including language, would have to be thrown into the pot along with those of newer Americans, to be melted into a new, hybrid American prototype. Instead, established Americans insist on newcomers shedding whatever makes them different, in order to blend in with existing ideas and practices. At the same time, each new group has hung onto its identity, including its language, as long as possible, until shamed and intimidated into shedding all or most evidence of its "non-Americanness." It is this contentious scenario, and not the melting pot, which most accurately describes the history of national identity in the U.S.

Bilingualism and bilingual education

Gary Imhoff, a political consultant to U.S. English, claims that Hispanics seek "a bilingual- or multilingual-nation" (Imhoff, 1990: 56). As victims of discrimination, he claims, Hispanics believe society is socially and morally responsible for their problems, and as a result, "the responsibility for learning a new language lies with the general society and not with Hispanics" (Imhoff, 1990: 58). Some academics have also voiced negative sentiments about bilingualism. Historian Arthur Schlesinger, Jr., for example, contends that bilingualism "shuts doors. It nourishes self-ghettoization, and ghettoization nourishes racial antagonism.... Using some language other than English dooms people to second-class citizenship in American society" (Schlesinger, 1992: 108). The late Aaron Wildavsky, professor of political science and public policy, referred to bilingualism as one of the "perennial problems of our time, sure to cause consternation and heartburn" and "symptomatic of a number of elemental conflicts ... that constitute running sores in American public life" (Wildavsky, 1992: 310–311).

There is a short distance between this attitude and a condemnation of any form of native-language instruction for children who are not dominant in English. Wildavsky proposed to solve the "problem" of bilingualism by substituting bilingual education with a universal second-language requirement in elementary school. Linda Chavez, former president of U.S. English, advocates English-only education. She calls Spanish-dominant children placed in bilingual programs "victims of federal, state and local policies that promote teaching Hispanic children in their native language at the expense of teaching them English"; the end result, she believes, is that the children "will end up denied the American dream their parents came seeking" (Chavez, 1991: 59–60). In its advertising, U.S. English characterizes bilingual education as a crime: "Deprive a child of an education. Handicap a young life outside the classroom. Restrict social mobility. If it came at the hand of a parent it would be called child abuse. At the hand of our schools ... it's called bilingual education" (U.S. English, 1998: 25).

The above quotes reveal rather distorted views of bilingualism. Imhoff claims that Hispanics refuse to learn English but expect others to learn Spanish; this is how he believes Hispanics define a "bilingual nation." Of course, there is no indication that Hispanics refuse to learn English while insisting that others learn Spanish. In this scenario, Hispanics would remain monolingual; instead, proponents of bilingual education seek acceptance of the idea that Hispanics can maintain their own language while they learn English.

As intellectuals, both Schlesinger and Wildavsky probably know people who benefit socially and personally from being bilingual; it would not be surprising if they themselves were bilingual. But the context in which they negatively characterize bilingualism is not their own social world. Rather they are both concerned with what Schlesinger refers to the "flood of immigration from Spanish-speaking countries" (Schlesinger, 1992: 107–108). It is interesting that, like Imhoff, they refer specifically to this socially-stigmatized language group. They see the existence of Spanish as an impediment to learning English, fearing that the use of Spanish will leave no room for English. If this were the case, it would indeed hamper the social mobility of Hispanics. In reality, however, there is no reason to substitute one language for the other; two can exist simultaneously. (Later on in this chapter we will explore further why Hispanics in particular are so often targeted).

If, as Chavez suggests, the use of Spanish-language instruction leaves no "room" for the acquisition of English and condemns children to a substandard education and a dismal future, bilingual programs would not succeed. We know, however, that this is not the case. We also know that there are many ways in which bilingual programs are set up to fail: they are often staffed with inappropriately trained teachers, filled with students who do not belong there, and are poorly funded. According to the linguist Lily Wong Fillmore, this occurs because the public views native-language instruction as "freeing [children] from the obligation of immediate and absolute assimilation.... Because bilingual education recognizes the educational validity of languages other than English and cultures other than 'American,' it is regarded with suspicion and treated accordingly" (Fillmore, 1992: 376). As long as bilingualism is not valued for those who are poor and powerless, bilingual programs for this group will be stigmatized.

Minority language learning

Just as official English advocates argue that bilingual programs hinder non-English dominant children from learning English, they also argue that governmental multilingualism hinders the acquisition of English by the parents of these children. Mujica contends that years ago, immigrants "took it as a source of pride and fundamental necessity to learn our language to become successful, contributing citizens." In contrast, today

> so-called "immigrants rights" activists insist that foreigners no longer need to learn English *and that the American taxpayer is* <u>*obligated*</u> *to pay for translations, teachers and multilingual services for immigrants who don't want to make the effort to learn our language.* (Mujica, 1995: 2)

Official English is presented as the solution to this potential burden to taxpayers. The 1997 federal legislation was titled the "Bill Emerson English Language Empowerment Act." Its stated goal was "to help immigrants better assimilate and take full advantage of economic and occupational opportunities in the U.S." Once they learn English, immigrants "will be empowered with the language skills and literacy necessary to become responsible citizens and productive workers in the U.S." The sole use of English was also described as a way to promote efficiency, by eliminating the expense of governmental use of other languages.

It is a common tactic of the official English and nativist movements to compare today's immigrants unfavorably with those of the past. However, history shows that immigrants of every era have much in common. Learning English, in particular, has been a goal of all immigrants. Some factors impede this goal, such as age, low socioeconomic status, inadequate previous schooling, lack of access to English-language instruction, social isolation, and the fact that not all immigrants learn English fluently. Yet the pressure has always been on immigrants to learn the common language of communication to the extent of their abilities. Suggesting that the government uses tax-payers' money to provide multilingual services for people who refuse to learn English is merely a means of tapping into citizens' general discontent and directing it towards those who are least able to defend themselves.

Today's immigrants are not immune to the pressure to acquire English. No evidence exists that immigrant advocates try to convince them that learning English is unnecessary. In fact, little impedes newcomers from seeking out English-language instruction. In 1986, an estimated 40,000 people waited for openings in English classes in Los Angeles County alone (Ingram, 1986: 3). In 1990, New York State's Division of Adult and Continuing Education Programs enrolled 69,200 adults in free English classes, up from 45,000 the previous year (Howe, 1990: 26L). Ironically, these were the years that official English advocates were insisting on the need for legislation to convince immigrants to learn English.

The statements in official English legislation about the advantages of knowing English cannot be denied. Yet, there is little evidence that such legislation will actually facilitate English-language acquisition. For example, the legislation does not guarantee governmental support for English-language classes. The 1997 bill states that monetary savings from the act will be used to provide such classes. However, it is unclear where these savings will come from; as noted previously, the government's translation of printed documents is minimal, and there is no evidence that multilingual services consume large amounts of money. Eliminating such services will do nothing to help people learn English; instead, it may simply discourage immigrants from seeking the assistance they need. Furthermore, as we have seen, the record of U.S. English with regard to supporting English-language instruction, either through its own or governmental resources, has been dismal.

Targets of Language Restrictionism: Threats to Territory and Power

The goal of official English activists is to preserve the governmental and societal status of English over all other languages. However, the hundreds of languages spoken in the U.S. do not receive equal attention by language restrictionists. In certain places and at certain times, particular languages spoken by specific national-origin groups are singled out for this attention. In this section we will examine two such instances. In both of these examples, the groups in question came to wield considerable social and economic power in the cities where they settled, posing a threat to the waning power of the people they were displacing—people who were, among other characteristics, monolingual speakers of English.

Monterey Park, California

In the 1950s and 60s Monterey Park, California, considered itself, and was considered by others, an average town. Its population was predominantly European-American and its culture decidedly mainstream; in 1985, the newspaper *U.S.A Today* named it an "all-American city." By that time, however, its character had begun to change. Real estate prices had plunged and the city was experiencing what is known as "white flight." In the 1970s, investors from Taiwan and Hong Kong, recognizing the potential in Monterey Park, began buying up property and establishing businesses there. By the mid-1980s, 50% of the city's residents were Chinese. Commercial signs in the Chinese language appeared everywhere.

It is not difficult to imagine the reaction of Monterey Park's remaining European-American residents, those who did not have the financial means to join their neighbors in exodus. They were losing control of the economic and cultural domains of the city. They felt as if Monterey Park was no longer "theirs." In 1985, the city council, in which European-American residents predominated, adopted a proposal making English the official language. One council member was ultimately convinced to change his vote, and the resolution was voided.

However, the battle over language did not end. Several years later, the city council voted down the allocation of funds for the purchase of Chinese-language books for the public library. Explaining the vote, councilman Barry Hatch said, "People from other parts of the country should not be faced with volumes of foreign books they cannot read when they come to our city library." Another council member, Judy Chu, arranged for the donation of 1,000 Chinese-language books from the Lions Club International of Taiwan. However, this caused another problem: where to put the new books. Hatch proposed adding an annex to the library, saying, "I think our library should house mainly English books. There is definite educational values [*sic*] to these donated books, but the contributors will probably not stop here" (Siao, 1988).

Older residents felt uncomfortable about the changes in their city and found a convenient target in the Chinese language. To attack the Chinese residents themselves would be too blatant and might lead to charges of racism. To attack the language of these residents was safer. But the symbolism was obvious. The Chinese language was viewed as foreign just as the Chinese residents were viewed as foreigners, not authentic members of the community. The predominance of Chinese business signs, and the growing use of Chinese as the language of business proprietors and customers, signaled that the town itself was becoming foreign to those who spoke only English. Monterey Park was no longer an "All-American city," at least in the eyes of the city's remaining English-dominant citizens.

Since that time, the Chinese influence in Monterey Park has remained strong. The city's "New Chinatown" is a major center of Chinese commerce and culture in Southern California, rivaling, in the eyes of some, the older Chinatown of Los Angeles (Kang, 1997). The 1986 passage of California's official-English law has had little actual effect; it calls for the state to preserve, protect and strengthen the English language but does not give the state the power to restrict other languages. Efforts like the ones in Monterey Park to stifle non-English languages have never received legitimacy under state law.

Miami, Dade County, Florida

Miami, Florida, also underwent a huge change as a result of immigration. This famous city is culturally and historically connected to the exodus of the middle class from communist Cuba beginning in 1959. These Cuban émigrés, together with smaller numbers of immigrants from Latin American countries, helped create what sociologist Max Castro calls "a lightening Latinization," transforming "the social and cultural climate of the city from one monopolized by dominant North American norms and styles to one in which other traditions and forms competed powerfully for cultural and linguistic space" (Castro, 1992: 181). This change affected all areas of life: business, architecture, fashion, popular culture and, of course, language.

The Hispanics of Miami shared an important characteristic with the Chinese of Monterey Park: economic power, the key to affecting change. So overwhelming was this power that an important qualification for many jobs in the city was bilingualism in English and Spanish. For long-time residents, who had existed quite comfortably in a state of English monolingualism, this was a source of humiliation and a particularly irritating reminder that Miami was no longer "theirs."

This state of affairs led, unsurprisingly, to the passage of an "antibilingual" ordinance by the citizens of Dade County in 1980. The law prohibited funds for projects utilizing any language other than English or promoting any culture other than that of the U.S. It also insured that all county governmental meetings, hearings, and publications would be in English; an amendment was added excluding emergency medical and other essential services. Exit polls showed that ethnicity was a strong determinant in the vote, with non-Hispanics voting overwhelmingly for the measure and Hispanics voting overwhelmingly against it. The non-Hispanics who supported the ordinance hoped that it would make Miami a less attractive place for Spanish-speakers and expressed a desire to move away from Dade County if they could.

A number of challenges to the ordinance were mounted, but it was only 13 years later that one was successful. In March 1993, for the first round of a special county election, voter information was distributed solely in English. The Justice Department ruled that the county had violated a provision of the Federal Voting Rights Act, which requires that non-English language voting material be available when more than 5% of the voting-age population of a district are native speakers of a language other than English. The county responded by distributing Spanish-language voting information for the second round of the election. In May of that year, the county commissioners repealed the ordinance.

Like California, Florida is an official English state; its legislation was passed in 1988. However, as in California, the law is largely symbolic and does not restrict the use of other languages. Little has changed in Miami since the time of the "antibilingual" ordinance. Over half the population is Hispanic, and Cuban Americans hold many of the top positions in government and education (Clary, 1997a). Spanish and English mix freely in newspaper want ads, in notices posted on grocery store bulletin boards, on local talk shows, and in popular music (Clary, 1997b). Like Monterey Park, the history of Miami has proven that cities, and the nation as well, do not "belong" to any one group of people; those who make the choice of living in a particular place, who bring an entrepreneurial spirit and the resources to affect the life of that place, are free to do so. As a result, the language of the people who live and work there is one aspect of city life that is liable to change.

Targeting Bilingual Education and the Spanish-Speaking Community

In the section above, I described two instances in which official English advocates targeted groups wielding considerable economic power. The most virulent attacks of the movement, however, focus on bilingual education and a group that is large in number but relatively low on the socioeconomic scale, Hispanic-Americans.

Hispanics, bilingual education, and politics

Between 1981 and 1990, 57% of all legal immigration to the U.S. came from Latin American countries (Fix & Passel, 1994). In the fall of 1991, of the 2,314,079 students with limited English proficiency enrolled in American public grade schools, 72.9% were Hispanic (Fleischman & Hopstock, 1993). While limited-English proficient children are in general more likely to be poorer than English-dominant children, Hispanic children are likely to be the poorest. For example, 57% of Spanish-speaking families have incomes below $20,000, compared to 35% for families speaking Asian/Pacific Island languages (McArthur, 1993).

Hispanic children thus represent a large proportion of the government's charges in the public schools, and they are likely to be among those most in need of special attention. Such special attention may include the use of their native language in instruction. Because of the large number of Hispanic children, Spanish-English bilingual programs predominate over bilingual programs in other languages.

The large number of Hispanics needing bilingual programs makes these programs the target of official English advocates. Because of its strong presence in American culture, Spanish is seen by many Americans as encroaching on the English language and threatening its predominance. English-dominant parents fear that the attention given to Hispanic children's special needs detracts from attention given to their own children; just as English-speaking residents of Miami and Monterey Park felt squeezed out of their cities, English-speaking children are viewed as being squeezed out of their schools. U.S. English argues for the efficiency of using only one language in government; eliminating native-language instruction is viewed as saving financial resources. Finally, official English advocates contend that the use of Spanish detracts from children's acquisition of English, just as governmental use of Spanish allegedly detracts from their parents' ability to learn the language.

It is important to see that the official English movement and its attack on bilingual education reflect conservative trends in the broader political scene. In the 1980s, conservative forces began to yield a growing degree of power in Washington. The elections of Ronald Reagan and George Bush were part of this trend. The American public in general showed up less often at the polls, but conservative-to-right-wing voters came in disproportionately large numbers. Politicians seeking reelection played to these voters in particular. As a result, many of the nation's social programs have been attacked and scaled down. "Welfare reform" became the code word for the dismantling of many support programs for the poor. Financial support for public education began to decline. Innovations in educating children outside of the established system have further weakened public education: voucher programs allow children to move from public to private schools, bringing public money with them; charter schools cede the running of publicly funded schools to private groups. The politicians who spearhead this downsizing of government call for the disadvantaged to pick themselves up and support themselves, to become more independent. The private sector is supposed to fill in for the allegedly bloated governmental bureaucracy.

Official English fits neatly into this scenario, calling for immigrants to stop relying on government for multilingual services and learn English on their own. The depiction of immigrants as unwilling to learn the common language parallels the depiction of single mothers unwilling to find jobs. Both arguments rely on the belief that people with needs just have to straighten out their value systems and acquire a new morality. Public education is also too much of a burden; these schools, it is held, just have to learn to compete with allegedly better private and parochial schools. Bilingual instruction is a particular encumbrance; children should buckle down, sit in all-English classes, and learn the language as quickly as possible. This argument hits a particular chord for English-dominant parents of the working and middle classes, who are also being affected by the decline in support for public education. It cleverly deflects attention away from the government's cost-cutting activities by pitting English-speaking parents against poorer, minority-language parents in the debate over bilingual education. Also, because Hispanics are a large and growing part of the population, official English advocates fear that if Hispanic children do succeed in school, they may compete for ever-scarcer jobs and economic opportunities with English-dominant children in the near future.

Official English advocates thus have two modes of attack with regard to bilingual education: it is both fiscally irresponsible and educationally unsupportable. The former argument, we have just seen, is part of the wider justification for scaling down government services to people in need. The latter argument, that bilingual education impedes the learning of English, faces strong scholarly evidence to the contrary.

The case for bilingual education

Decades of research in countries around the world have been devoted to native-language instruction for children whose mother tongues differ from that of the larger society in which they live, and the evidence points to its positive effects. One of the foremost investigators, the linguist Jim Cummins (1998), summarizes three main principles that have come out of this research: (1) While immigrant students quickly acquire conversational fluency in the second language, it takes a minimum of about five years, and often longer, for them to catch up to native-speakers in academic aspects of the language. (2) There is a positive association between additive bilingualism—the acquisition of a second language while the first language continues to develop—and students' linguistic, cognitive, and academic growth. (3) Instruction in the native language is effective in promoting proficiency in the second language when students are exposed to and motivated to learn the second language.

Cummins warns that bilingual education is not a panacea: "The reasons why some groups of culturally diverse students experience long-term persistent underachievement have much more to do with issues of status and power than with linguistic factors in isolation." In judging the effectiveness of bilingual programs, Cummins believes the criterion should be the extent to which they generate "a sense of empowerment among culturally diverse students and communities by challenging the devaluation of students' identities in the wider society" (Cummins, 1998: 1). Programs that acknowledge the native language of students and support its development, rather than viewing the native language as a temporary bridge to monolingualism in the second language, support this empowerment. In addition, adequate funding, well-trained teachers, appropriately sized classes, and proven teaching methodology are essential. However, many programs for immigrant children, whether bilingual or monolingual, lack these qualities specifically because they serve a population that is without power and status.

An example of a recent U.S. study that gives credence to Cummins's principles is the Ramirez Report (Ramirez *et al.*, 1991). Sponsored by the U.S. Department of Education, it ran from 1982 to 1989 and involved approximately 2,000 Spanish-dominant students living in five states: New York, New Jersey, Florida, California, and Texas. The students were enrolled in one of three programs: (1) English immersion programs, beginning in kindergarten, were taught by instructors trained in bilingual education or ESL. All instruction was in English, and students were expected to be mainstreamed by the second grade. (2) Early-exit bilingual programs were also taught by specially trained instructors. Spanish was used initially for the instruction of reading skills and for the purpose of clarification   but was quickly phased out over two years. Mainstreaming was also expected by the second grade. (3) Late-exit bilingual programs used Spanish for a minimum of 40% of instructional time. Students were expected to stay in the program until the sixth grade even if they were determined to be fluent in English before that time.

Little difference in academic achievement was found in the students in the first two programs by the end of the third grade, as measured by tests in math, English language arts, and English reading. Students in these

programs progressed at the same rate as students in the general population but remained significantly behind the control group in achievement.
Also, many students were not considered ready for mainstreaming by
the end of the second grade and were held in the program longer than
anticipated.

In contrast, students in the late-exit program were able to decrease the
achievement gap between themselves and the general population. In particular, students who were in the program with the greatest use of
Spanish, and who had begun with the lowest academic skills, progressed
in all three skills faster than the general population. Compared to students in the two other programs, these children were less likely to have
been in all-English preschool programs and came from families with
lower incomes. In one late-exit program, students who were transferred
into mainstream classes before the sixth grade eventually fared worse
than those who remained in the program.

These results show that when children are instructed in their native
language it does not impede their acquisition of English or their general
academic development. On the contrary, more instruction in the native
language appears to give students an academic edge. Also, expecting
programs that use little or none of the students' native language to prepare them for mainstreaming into all-English classes in one or two years
is unrealistic. These results support Cummins's call for long-term programs that nurture the development of the native language. They show
bilingual instruction to be an effective approach to the education of children whose native language is not English.

The political battle to end bilingual education

Considering the positive results of bilingual education and its support
in the academic community, one might expect societal support to follow.
However, this has not been the case. As previously noted, there are strong
political motives to end bilingual education, motives which turn a blind
eye to the realities of its success.

California is one state in which these motives are particularly strong.
California has a large proportion of foreign-born residents, and in periods
of general discontent, anti-immigrant sentiments are easily tapped for
political effect. The state's laws also allow popular initiatives to be added
to regular election ballots when enough citizens' signatures are gathered.
These initiatives are backed by organizations or individuals with the
financial resources to wage a wide-ranging campaign to win over voters.
Such was the case in 1986, when California passed an official English
proposal sponsored by U.S. English. Its main target was bilingual education, but the law proved to be ineffective; bilingual education remained

protected by federal statute. Then in 1994 California passed Proposition 187, another popular initiative, which would deny undocumented immigrants access to virtually all public services, including education. The constitutionality of this law was quickly challenged in the courts, where it remains today.

The bilingual education issue resurfaced in 1998 with a third popular initiative. The English Language Education for Children in Public Schools Initiative, or Proposition 227, owed much of its rhetoric to the official English movement. It referred to English as "the national public language of the U.S. of America and of the state of California"; it reminded the government of its duty "to provide all of California's children ... with the skills necessary to become productive members of our society, and of these skills, literacy in the English language is among the most important." Characterizing California's record of educating immigrant children a failure, the initiative required that all children who are not native speakers of English be placed in sheltered English immersion programs (in which all instruction is in English geared to the learning stage of the students, sometimes called "structured immersion") for no more than one year, after which they would be transferred to mainstream classes. Waivers could be requested by parents to allow their children to receive native-language instruction. Finally, 50 million dollars was to be allocated for English-language classes for adults who are non-native speakers of the language; these adults would then pledge to provide English-language tutoring to the children in their communities.

The terms of this initiative show little familiarity with the research. English immersion programs are generally less effective than bilingual programs; one year in such a program would undoubtedly prove insufficient for most students. The research shows that children need to acquire academic English, which takes a long time; it is unlikely that the adults in a minority-language community, many of whom are poorly educated themselves, would be able to acquire the kind of sophisticated, literate English they would need to be able to tutor their children adequately.

It is no surprise that the author of the initiative, Ron Unz, is not schooled in this research. Unz is a wealthy software entrepreneur with no professional background in education; he had never visited a bilingual class. Yet he became convinced that immigrant children were not learning English fast enough, and he had the political and financial means to mount his attack. He was also rather successful in winning over public opinion. The measure passed with the support of 67% of white voters, 57% of Asian voters, 48% of black voters, and 37% of Hispanic voters (Bronner, 1998). A legal challenge was issued at once by a coalition of educators, civil rights groups, and immigrant advocates; like California's Proposition 187, it may end up in the courts for some time.

Interestingly, few political figures in California supported the initiative; the growing number of newly naturalized voters, English-learners themselves, may be one reason. Criticism from Washington came in the form of a statement by Secretary of Education Richard W. Riley, who maintained that "the one year time limit and one-size-fits-all approach to learning English flies in the face of years of research" and that the initiative "is an educational straitjacket for teachers and parents" (Riley, 1998: 2). He also mentioned President Clinton's intention to increase funding for child and adult learners of English.

Even so, the anti-bilingual education movement had the backing of many members of the 105th Congress in 1998. In the House of Representatives, efforts were made to amend the Elementary and Secondary Education Act of 1965, replacing any mention of "bilingual education programs" with "English language education programs" and changing the name of the Office of Bilingual Education and Minority Language Affairs (OBEMBLA) to the "Office of English Language Acquisition." The English for the Children Act, also introduced in the House of Representatives, called for the repeal of the Bilingual Education Act, the termination of OBEMLA, and the one-year transition of all students in bilingual programs into "special alternative instructional programs ... that do not make use of the native language of the student." The wording of this bill came directly from several official-English bills introduced into Congress several years earlier.

Official English, Bilingual Education, and the ESL Profession

ESL teachers and administrators may wonder why they should be concerned with the official English and anti-bilingual education movement; it seems that people of all political ideologies support the teaching of English to immigrants. Nonetheless, this movement should be fought by ESL professionals for both practical and moral reasons.

On a practical level, we need to support good bilingual education because it helps our students' acquisition of English and general academic development. It is also important to be aware that specific instruction in ESL by trained teachers is endangered by those trying to change the current system. Good bilingual programs include ESL instruction; official English and anti-bilingual education legislation does not guarantee it. On a moral level, everyone who is professionally involved in the teaching of English needs to be aware of the context of this teaching. If it is assumed that the English learned will replace the learners' native languages, then the professionals involved are condoning what is called "linguicism," or linguistic genocide. Official English creates an atmosphere making linguicism possible; it contributes to the denigration of minority languages with the refusal of government to make use of them in its daily business and to publicly support the dissemination of the languages through cultural and educational projects. Minority-language children already learn to reject their native languages in the face of the overwhelming influence of English in the general culture; official English policy would only reinforce this. A national policy diametrically opposed to official English, one encouraging government and social support for language pluralism and including educationally sound bilingual education for all children, is the antidote to the prospect of linguistic and cultural impoverishment that an official-English future threatens.

Conclusion

In this chapter, we reviewed the history of policies toward immigrant languages in the nation. We examined the present movement to make English the official language of the U.S. and the organization most closely connected to this movement, U.S. English. The premises underlying official English were described and then rebutted. We focused on two minority-language groups that became the focus of early official-English efforts because of their socioeconomic influence in the communities where they settled: the Chinese of Monterey Park, California, and the Cubans of Miami, Florida. We then turned to the virulent attack of official-English advocates against Hispanics and bilingual education, examining the political context of this attack, the academic evidence supporting native-language instruction, and some of the legislative efforts to end such programs.

As ESL professionals, we stand at a symbolic gateway for newcomers to this country; we try to ease their way into their new home. Most of us have a vision of this home as an open, democratic society, one that will accept our students as they are. Official English and anti-bilingual education advocates have a different vision: their concept of who and what is American is a restricted one, and their view of how children should be educated is equally constrained. We have an obligation to see that this narrow vision does not become the most widely accepted one and that linguistic and cultural diversity continues to enrich our present and future identity as a nation.

Discussion Questions and Activities

1. Find an article or editorial on the issue of language pluralism in a current local or national periodical. Do the ideas in this piece of writing

describe or support a policy that is *tolerance-oriented, promotion-oriented,* or *restrictive*? In comparing what you found with what your class-mates discovered, do you see a local or national trend in terms of these categories?

2. Investigate whether and to what extent your county, city, or state government uses languages other than English. Is there a historical basis for this policy? Has this policy changed over time? Is there now or has there been in the past resistance to this policy?

3. Write a language history of your own family. If possible, interview family members of different generations. Trace the changes in native-language use and language attitudes over the generations, and spec-ulate about the factors involved in these changes.

4. Ask a neighbor, relative, or friend about his or her interpretation of the expressions "bilingualism" and "bilingual education." Does his or her interpretation mirror the views of linguists or those of lan-guage restrictionists? What are the consequences of these views to your community, if any?

5. Ask a neighbor, relative, or friend what the consequences of an "offi-cial English" law might be. Do you agree with this person's views? What factors do you think influence his or her views? What are the consequences of these views to your community, if any?

Chapter 4

Non-Native Varieties and the Sociopolitics of English Proficiency Assessment

P.H. Lowenberg

Over the past few years, considerable attention has been paid to many social and cultural issues relevant to the assessment of non-native English proficiency. Among their many advances, researchers and practitioners have successfully begun to incorporate a large number of learning, teaching, and contextual variables in the design and evaluation of assessment instruments.

However, far less consideration has been given to a variable that is much more central to the sociopolitical impact of proficiency assessment—the linguistic norms for English against which proficiency in English is generally assessed, that is, the *norms* of Standard English. Rather, an implicit, and frequently explicit, assumption has been that the universal target for proficiency in Standard English around the world is the set of norms which are accepted and used by highly educated *native speakers* of English.

This assumption is no longer valid in light of the current demographics of the world's English-using population. Many specialists in language and language teaching, such as the British linguist David Crystal (1997), have observed that English is currently used by many more non-native than native speakers. In fact, the late Peter Strevens, a renowned British specialist in TESOL, estimated that native speakers now comprise only "a fifth or less" of the world's English users (Strevens, 1992: 27). A corollary of this development is that by far the majority of English-language interactions in the world today are solely between non-native speakers, without even the presence of native speakers.

In many countries where non-native speakers use English mainly as a "foreign language," that is, for international communication, with few in-country uses—as in Japan, Thailand, and Korea—ESOL instruction is based primarily on native-speaker norms. However, this chapter will demonstrate that native-speaker norms do not necessarily apply in a large number of settings where "non-native varieties" of English are used. These are varieties which have developed in countries formerly colonized by Britain or the United States where English continues to be widely used as a "second," often official, language by substantial numbers of non-native speakers for a broad range of *intra*national purposes. A partial list of countries where English as a second language has some official functions (for example, as a language of government, the judicial system, and instruction in the school system) includes the following: Bangladesh, Botswana, Brunei, Cameroon, Ethiopia, Fiji, Gambia, Ghana, India, Israel, Kenya, Lesotho, Liberia, Malawi, Malaysia, Malta, Mauritius, Myanmar, Namibia, Nigeria, Pakistan, the Philippines, Sierra Leone, Singapore, South Africa, Sri Lanka, Sudan, Swaziland, Tanzania, Tonga, Uganda, Western Samoa, Zambia, and Zimbabwe (McCallen, 1989: 7–9; Crystal, 1997: 55–60).

In certain of these countries, the total population (much less the number of English speakers) is quite small. However, other nations in this list have extremely large populations of non-native English speakers. For example, Braj Kachru, a pioneer in the study of non-native varieties, estimates conservatively that 60 million people in India use English on a regular basis, giving India the third largest population of English speakers in the world, after the United States and Britain (Kachru, 1998).

During these countries' colonial eras, English was introduced as the dominant language of government, finance, commerce, and transportation. As colonial administrations and economies expanded, employment opportunities opened up for non-Westerners who could speak English. Therefore, the local elites began to receive English-medium educations and came to use English increasingly in their daily affairs, both as a language of power and prestige and as a language of interethnic communication (Kachru, 1986).

Since their independence, these countries have continued using English to varying degrees. In many of them, English is still used for some of the legislative, administrative, and judicial functions of government and is the principal medium of instruction in the educational system, especially in secondary and postsecondary institutions. In most of these countries, English is also important in securing higher status employment and in obtaining promotions, and English is widely used in literature and in the mass media. In addition, English is often an important code for interpersonal communication, especially as an interethnic link language in multilingual countries (Platt *et al.*, 1984; Kachru, 1992b).

In these countries, English is used daily by non-native speakers in the absence of native speakers, in non-Western sociocultural contexts, and in constant contact with other languages in multilingual speech communities. As a result, it often undergoes systematic changes at all linguistic levels, from phonology and morphology, to syntax and semantics, to discourse and style. Many of these changes would be considered deviant if used in countries where the more established "native-speaker" varieties of English are used, such as Australia, Britain, or the United States. However, in their non-native contexts, these linguistic innovations and modifications are so widespread that many have become *de facto* local norms for English usage. In fact, attitudinal research reported in Shaw (1981), Sahgal (1991), and Kachru (1992b) indicates that in at least two of these countries, India and Singapore, 50% or more of college-educated English users believe that at least some local innovations should be the local norms for English teaching and use.

The remainder of this chapter examines a number of such non-native innovations that have developed in contexts where Standard English is used. In some cases, differences between non-native and native-speaker norms result from variation in a limited number of linguistic processes which are also highly variable in and often produce differences between native-speaker varieties. Other stylistic differences between the norms of non-native and native-speaker varieties arise from differences in sociocultural values expressed by specific language usage. This discussion is followed by an analysis of actual items from existing tests of proficiency in English as a world language which, by not reflecting the sociopolitical reality of non-native varieties, may unfairly discriminate against speakers of these varieties.

Characteristics of Standard English

Standard English, like other "standard" languages, has always been extremely difficult to delimit. In this chapter, based on sociolinguistic research by Peter Trudgill (1983), Mary Tay and Anthea Gupta (1983), and Makhan Tickoo (1991), the standard model of a variety of English—native or non-native—is operationally defined as the linguistic forms of that variety that are normally used in formal speaking and writing by speakers who have received the highest level of education available in that variety. Standard English is the accepted language usage for official, journalistic, and academic writing; for public speaking before an audience or on radio or television; and for use as a medium and/or subject of instruction in the schools. A crucial tenet of this perspective is that the norms of Standard English in any variety—native-speaker or non-native—are not what any outsider—native speaker or non-native speaker—thinks they should be. Rather, based on Dell Hymes's (1972) notion of communicative competence, they are the linguistic forms that are *actually used* by institutions and individuals that have power and/or influence in the above contexts of Standard English use.

In the absence of language planning academies for any of the world's English-using speech communities, such as exist for French, Spanish, and Swedish, the identification of particular normative features of Standard English in any variety—native-speaker or non-native—can at times be extremely problematic, especially regarding innovations. Fortunately, previous research by established scholars has identified many Standard English norms for specific varieties; a comprehensive survey of much of the early research on non-native norms appears in *The New Englishes*, by Platt, Weber, and Ho (1984). In other cases, non-native norms have been institutionally codified by the same types of authorities who make such decisions in the native-speaker varieties, such as occurs in newspaper style sheets, grammar and ESOL textbooks (government-authorized or from major publishers), and examinations which have been standardized for each variety. Still other possible variety-specific norms occur in the usage of English speakers with high sociolinguistic status in the relevant speech community and in texts likely to have been prepared and edited by speakers who are highly proficient in English (in journalism, for example, in the front-page news rather than in "Letters to the Editor"), especially when these features are used repeatedly. Data in the following analysis and discussion are taken from these kinds of sources in both the non-native and native-speaker varieties.

Actually, the many contexts and situations in which English is used with mutual comprehensibility in international communication among both native and non-native speakers around the world indicates that Standard English differs only minimally across varieties, generally sharing a large set of common norms. Examples of such universal norms are rules concerning the marking of plurals on count nouns, subject-verb agreement, and the use of the past participle in the perfect tenses. Violations of these norms in contexts of Standard English occur in examples (1) through (3) from major English-language newspapers in the United States, Singapore, and Fiji, respectively.

(1) * *Hundreds of student* gathered this morning to watch a television set in the lobby of the Parliament building.
     (*The New York Times*, May 21, 1998: A10)

(2) * *They* [World Wide Web mirror sites] speed up readers' access to information and *reduces* the overall load on the network.
     (*The Straits Times*, September 17, 1996: 2)

(3) * Maciu on the other hand just couldn't fulfill his fans' expectations but *had succumb* to Atu's deadly punches.
(*The Daily Post,* May 10, 1994: 26, cited in Lotherington-Woloszyn, 1994)

The italicized phrases in these examples would be considered deviations from Standard English in all native-speaker and non-native varieties that have been identified to date.

Extension of Productive Linguistic Processes

Nevertheless, there are a number of ways in which Standard English frequently *does* diverge across varieties, and these differences, as will be discussed below, can be very significant for the construction of ESL tests. A major source of innovation in Standard English of non-native varieties is the extension of certain innovative processes of morphology and syntax that are also very productive in, and frequently cause differences between, the native-speaker varieties of English. One of the most frequently occurring of these processes is the conversion to countability of noncount nouns which semantically comprise a collection of countable units. Examples of variations in the application of this process which result in differences between native-speaker varieties occur in items (4) and (5).

(4) Some small initial fall-off in *attendances* is unavoidable.
(*Times of London,* October 27, 1986: 17, cited in Algeo, 1988: 7)

(5) ... iceberg *lettuces* are down in price and should be selling for between 35p and 55p, depending on size.
(*Daily Telegraph,* August 9, 1985:6, cited in Algeo, 1988: 7)

Attendance and *lettuce,* as seen in these examples, can be countable in British English, but are always noncount nouns in American Standard English.

This process, which is restricted to specific vocabulary items in each variety of English, likewise results in innovations in non-native varieties, as in (6) from Nigeria, (7) and (8) from the Philippines, and (9) from Malaysia.

(6) I lost all my *furnitures* and many valuable *properties.*
(Bokamba, 1992: 82)

(7) He has many *luggages.*
(Gonzalez, 1983: 167)

(8) No. of *Luggages*
("Daily Service Report" form, Century Park Sheraton, Manila)

(9) Thank you for upkeeping the *equipments* and facilities provided
     on this train.
     (Permanent metal sign riveted to the interior of railway passen-
     ger carriages, Malaysian National Railway, December 1997)

The innovative productivity of this process is demonstrated in (10),
from the United States, in which *equipment,* as in Malaysia, appears as a
count noun in a context of Standard American English.

(10) West said they used *a digital equipment* that was capable of trans-
     mitting both video and still images.
     (*San Jose Mercury News,* July 17, 1997: 16A)

This example also illustrates how innovations usually begin in particu-
ar contexts, such as electronics, from which they may or may not spread
to other contexts.

Other differences across varieties of Standard English frequently occur
in fixed combinations of verbs and prepositions. An example of such
variation between native-speaker varieties arises in British English with
approximate to and *agree in* (11) and (12), taken from texts written by
respected British scholars in the TESOL profession.

(11) The learner will only be able to show that his `knowledge' of the
     text is *approximating to* that of the teacher through tests, repro-
     duction, and answers to `higher inference' questions.
     (Porter & Roberts, 1987: 182)

(12) Examples at task level would include such things as *agreeing a
     definition* of the problem.
     (Breen, 1984: 56)

Equivalent sentences in American English would require only *approxi-
mating* in (11), but would require *agreeing on* in (12).

Once again, the same type of variation occurs between native-speaker
and non-native varieties in the construction *discuss about,* which is frequently used by ESL students in the United States but is considered to be
a redundant use of the preposition in American English. Yet, as shown
below, *discuss about* has been attested as a feature of Standard English in
several non-native varieties, including Nigeria (13), Zambia (14), and
Singapore and Malaysia (15).

(13) We shall *discuss about* that later.
     (Bamgbose, 1992: 106)

(14) They were *discussing about* the proposed opening of a gym at the
     school when the head arrived.
     (Chisanga, 1987: 65)

(15) They *discussed about* the mistakes and *emphasized on* the need for
      greater care.
      (Platt *et al.*, 1984: 84)

Additional types of morphological and syntactic divergence from
native-speaker norms in the non-native varieties are described in Platt,
Weber, and Ho (1984); in Lowenberg (1986, 1990); in Kachru (1992); and
in numerous issues of the journals *World Englishes* (Blackwell Publishers),
English World-Wide (John Benjamins Publishers), and *English Today*
(Cambridge University Press). However, even the few examples given
above suffice to demonstrate that innovations in the non-native varieties
of English often arise from the same linguistic processes that often produce differences across the native-speaker varieties.

Types of Stylistic Difference

Standard English in the non-native varieties diverges more noticeably
from the native-speaker varieties in several markers of a formal spoken
and written style. For example, in (16), from the Prime Minister of
Malaysia, and in (17), from the president of a leading political party in
India, *would* appears in conditional constructions where *will* is required
in the native-speaker varieties.

(16) We accept the verdict of the Kelantan people and we *hope they*
      would accept the verdict of the rest of the country.
      (Dr. Mahathir Mohamad, Prime Minister of Malaysia, quoted in
      the *Washington Post*, October 22, 1990: A15)

(17) ... *if they persist* with their exposures about the scandals relating
      to submarines, Swedish guns and Swiss bank accounts, they too
      would be in for trouble.
      (L.K. Advani, president of India's Bharatiya Janata Party, quoted
      in the *Washington Post*, September 2, 1987: A24)

In this use of *would*, the native-speaker use of *will* and *would* to distinguish between open and hypothetical conditions (Quirk *et al.*, 1985)
appears to have been replaced by a stylistic function. The late Raymond
Tongue, long a respected researcher of English in Singapore and
Malaysia, reported in the 1970s that Malaysian and Singaporean English
speakers whom he interviewed considered *would* to be more polite and
formal than *will*. He further posited that this stylistic distinction is
applied identically in the use of *can* and *could* (Tongue, 1979).
  This apparently systematic difference in modal usage between non-
native and native-speaker varieties of English is further illustrated in
(18) and (19), from ESOL textbooks written and published in Malaysia.

In these examples, *should* is used as a marker of politeness or formality in situations where American English calls for the use of *would*.

(18) Dear Sir,
I *should* like to be considered as an applicant for appointment as sales representative.
(Nandy, 1995: 93)

(19) With reference to your advertisement in the 'New Straits Times' of December 11th, 19—, I *should* be grateful if you would send me an application form.
(Howe, 1974: 163)

Such marking of formality also frequently creates divergences between non-native and native-speaker norms in larger chunks of discourse. Braj Kachru observes (1992c: 313) that the norms for much writing in the native-speaker varieties include "directness in presenting the point, very little stylistic ornamentation and emphasis on the information content." In the non-native varieties, Kachru continues, a more deferential, indirect, and ornamental style is often transferred from the speakers' other languages. In India, for example, the Indian linguist Subrahmanian reports (1977) the common occurrence in South Asian languages of similes, metaphors, and alliterations. "We are fascinated by embellished expressions: we equate objectivity and matter-of-factness with dullness." As a result, when Indians write in English, "most write and like 'poetic' prose because of such a tradition in our literature" (Subrahmanian, 1977: 24).

Examples of such "poetic prose" appear in the simile and metaphor reported from India by Yamuna Kachru in (20) and (21), and in the description of an art exhibit from Malaysia in (22).

(20) Noam Chomsky, *a young rebel with a brain like a burning blue flame,* appeared on the linguistic scene with a book called *Syntactic Structures* (1957), which promised a new direction in linguistics.
(Cited in Kachru, 1988: 46)

(21) Akhtar had already published some excellent short stories when he received the call *to turn the sods in the field of the novel.*
(Cited in Kachru, 1988: 48)

(22) Ibrahim Hussein enmeshes the pictorial surface with sensuous entanglements of lyrical linearity.
("Forward" to brochure, National Art Gallery, Malaysia, 1988)

All of these passages are written in Standard English, but they are considerably more embellished than would be similar texts from Standard

American English. These passages may even be difficult for many native speakers of English to comprehend, but they certainly cannot be considered the output of writers whose proficiency in English is in any way deficient.

Implications for Testing Non-native English Proficiency

Awareness of these types of grammatical and stylistic divergence between normative features in non-native varieties and corresponding norms in the native-speaker varieties is essential for evaluating non-native speakers' proficiency in English in the world context. To assess this proficiency accurately, examiners must be able to distinguish _deficiencies_ in the second language acquisition of English by these speakers (errors) from varietal _differences_ in the speakers' usage resulting from their having learned such non-native norms as those previously discussed.

Examples of the importance of this distinction appear in items (23) and (24), which are modeled on an ESL placement test regularly administered to international students at a major American university.

(23) Mr. Smith has modern _____ in his office.
    (a) a piece of furniture   (c) pieces of furnitures
    (b) furnitures   (d) furniture

(24) If I had not missed the bus, I _____ them before they left.
    (a) should see   (c) should have seen
    (b) could see   (d) could have seen

Many educated speakers of Standard English in non-native varieties would have considerable difficulty in answering these questions since they might find quite acceptable (23b) _furnitures,_ as in (6) above, and (24c) _should have seen,_ as in (18) and (19) above. On the basis of "incorrect" answers on items such as these, international students who speak non-native varieties might receive scores underestimating their actual English proficiency and be erroneously forced to enroll in remedial ESL classes, at great expense to their time and financial resources.

Speakers of Standard American English would encounter similar difficulties in attempting to supply the correct prepositions in items (25) through (27), which are taken from preparation materials for the standardized Primary School Leaving Examination (PSLE) in Singapore.

(25) The highest mark _____ the Mathematics test was 76 out of 100.
    (a) on   (c) in
    (b) at   (d) for
    (Practice Test #5 for the Primary School Leaving Examination, Singapore; distributed by Bookland, n.d.)

(26) I got the job which *payed* ten dollars per hour. I was still short *for* ten dollars.
(Chen, 1993: 51)

(27) Is your sister still angry _____ me?
(a) with   (c) at
(b) to   (d) by
(Sharma, 1987: 13)

The correct answer to (25) is (c) *in*, but the norms for prepositions in Standard American English would dictate (a) *on*. Similarly, in (26), a speaker of Standard American English would realize that *paid* has been misspelled, but probably wouldn't know that the correct preposition to replace *for* in Standard Singapore English would be *of*, rather than *by* or no preposition at all, which would be acceptable possibilities in the United States. In (27), the correct answer is (a) *with*. However, Standard American English would allow either *with* or (c) *at* in this sentence; thus, a speaker of Standard American English encountering item (27) on a test would have to choose from two acceptable answers.

Clearly, the use of items like (25) through (27) in testing speakers of Standard American English would not provide a valid measure of their English proficiency. Likewise, items such as (23) and (24) are no more valid in assessing the over-all English proficiency of international students in the United States who speak non-native varieties. Of course, these students' success at American universities will be enhanced if they follow the norms of Standard American English, since the average American instructor will have no familiarity with the concept of non-native norms. But the students' task in this case would be similar to that of American students studying in Britain; they would need to learn a few alternative norms for use while studying within a different variety of English. However, the non-native students' initial unfamiliarity with American norms would reflect no more on their general English proficiency than would the Americans' unfamiliarity with British norms.

The sociopolitical ramifications of non-native norms for Standard English become much greater in the high-stakes standardized tests that are used to assess English proficiency internationally. One such test is the Test of English for International Communication (TOEIC), which the Educational Testing Service (ETS) and, more recently, an ETS subsidiary have been administering worldwide since 1979. In its informational brochures, the TOEIC describes itself as "designed to test the English language as it is used internationally in business, commerce, and industry" (Educational Testing Service, 1990: 2). Over 1.5 million candidates sit for the TOEIC annually (Educational Testing Service, 1998: 6), a volume exceeding the annual number of candidates who take ETS' Test of English as a Foreign Language (TOEFL) (Educational Testing Service, 1996a: 2).

A former director of the TOEIC, Stephen Stupak, explains that the TOEIC "is for people working internationally who need to be able to communicate in English with both native and non-native speakers" (Stupak, nd: 1). Concerning the Standard English norms for international communication, the former director claims that "International English, for purposes of the TOEIC, is the English that one non-native speaker uses to communicate in English with another non-native speaker, in the context of business, commerce, and industry." This definition certainly sounds reasonable. However, he then reports that, with a few exceptions, "the language of the TOEIC is natural, native-speaker English" (Stupak, nd: 3).

This assumption that communication between non-native speakers is necessarily based on native-speaker norms raises serious problems of validity for the TOEIC. As the following examples demonstrate, certain items in past tests have not reflected the above findings that normative features in non-native varieties frequently diverge from native-speaker norms. Example (28) is an item that appeared in a now retired form of the TOEIC. The candidate's task here is to identify the italicized word or phrase that is ungrammatical.

(28) The new *equipments shipped* from Hong Kong will be *the only* items *on sale* this week.
(Educational Testing Service, 1993: 9)

TOEIC considers ungrammatical the countability of *equipments*. However, the use of *equipments* instead of *equipment* results from the same process that has produced examples (4) through (10) above. As reflected in (9), *equipments* may well be acceptable to educated speakers of the Malaysian non-native variety of Standard English. Moreover, example (10) suggests the possibly developing acceptability of *equipments* in at least one context of Standard American English.

A similar problem occurs in item (29), taken from another now retired form of the TOEIC, in which the candidate's task once more is to identify the underlined portion of the sentence that is ungrammatical.

(29) *To obtain a full* refund on your purchase, you must *return back* the merchandise *within* ten days.
(Educational Testing Service, 1980: 28)

In this case, the incorrect segment is *return back*, reflecting the fact that in Standard American English, the combination of *back* with *return* would be considered redundant. But as illustrated in examples (11) through (15)

above, allowable combinations of verbs with prepositions can differ substantially across both native-speaker and non-native varieties.

Items (28) and (29) are most likely not valid indicators of proficiency in
Standard English as it is used around the world. Of course, only a small
number of the items included in any test administration of the TOEIC are
affected by such cross-varietal differences in norms; most of the items
assess features that are normative in Standard English in all native-speaker
and non-native varieties, as illustrated in (1) through (3) above. However,
given the importance attributed to numerical scores in such large-scale,
often high-stakes, tests as the TOEIC, only two or three items of question-
able validity could jeopardize the ranking of candidates in a competitive
test administration.

A partial solution to this dilemma would be to screen out items which
test the types of norms which are known to differ considerably across
varieties, such as specific verb+preposition combinations (e.g. *approximate to* and *discuss about*) and the conversion to countability of noncount
nouns which semantically comprise collections of countable units (e.g.
lettuces and *equipments*).

A second solution would be to supplement the current multiple-choice
format of the TOEIC with a holistically scored essay question in order to
compensate for any remaining multiple-choice items that might not accurately reflect Standard English as it is used internationally. The following
essay excerpt (30) is from an ETS-published set of model essays for the Test
of Written English (TWE), which is often administered with the TOEFL.

> (30) Contrary to the belief that it is safe, nuclear power has a way of
> destroying whole cities. It is not like a fire that can be put out
> with water or CO_2, but special *equipments* have to be used.
> (Educational Testing Service, 1996b: 41)

This paper received the highest possible score from ETS readers, a "6,"
despite its use of *equipments*, for which the same candidate could have
been penalized on item (28) above.

However, this second solution will require accommodation of the
types of differences in discourse style that occur across native-speaker
and non-native varieties, as exemplified in (20) through (22) above. The
writers of the TOEIC seem to be unaware of the appropriateness of stylistic elaboration to mark formality and deference in many non-native varieties. Rather, Stephen Stupak, the former TOEIC director mentioned
above, assumes (Stupak, nd: 3) that

> International English ... does not contain idiomatic expressions, low
> frequency vocabulary, or complicated structures. In the business
> world people try to speak as simple a language as possible.

Such a claim exhibits lack of recognition of the marked embellishment—at least, in comparison to American norms—that often occurs in business and professional correspondence in non-native varieties. An example of this embellishment is (31), an excerpt from a letter written to an American professor in 1985 by the Educational Attaché of the Embassy of Pakistan in Washington, D.C.

(31) It is regretted to inform you that the material you have requested is not available with us.

Similarly embellished is (32), from a letter of invitation to an American professor to attend a linguistics conference in India in 1991.

(32) Please treat this as an invitation. The next circular will intimate you about the modalities of participation, accommodation and other aspects in detail.

A clearer contrast between norms for business correspondence in native-speaker and non-native varieties of English arises in (33), from the United States, and (34), from India. Each of these examples contains the greeting and introductory sentence of a letter written to an American professional inviting the addressee's listing in a biographical reference volume.

(33) Dear Professional:
Our editors have identified you as a biographical candidate for the forthcoming 23rd edition of WHO'S WHO IN THE SOUTH AND SOUTHWEST.
(*Marquis Who's Who*, Wilmette, IL, 1991)

(34) Dear Sir/Madam:
We come back upon the correspondence resting with the inclusion of your biographical-note in the forthcoming volume of our 'Biography International' and thank you much indeed for your esteemed cooperation in sending to us the same.
(*Biography International*, Delhi, 1986)

That examples (31) through (34) actually reflect norms for business and professional writing in their respective varieties is indicated by similar differences in the models for business writing that appear in ESOL textbooks and test materials. Item (35), a letter of recommendation used as the text for a reading comprehension task on a now retired form of the TOEIC, demonstrates the characteristics of business communication noted above by Stupak.

(35) Dear Mr. Simpson:
Mr. John P. Logan has informed me that you are considering him for the position of management trainee in your credit division.

For the past three summers Mr. Logan worked with our firm while earning his degree in economics at Riverdale College. Although his duties were basically clerical, we were very much impressed by the accuracy and thoroughness of his work, as well as his pleasant personality and cooperative nature.

He appears to have the ability, initiative, and personal integrity to succeed in a management position. I recommend him highly, without reservation.

Sincerely yours,
Carl J. Striker
(Educational Testing Service, 1980: 36)

In contrast, example (36), from a letter of application for employment found in a Malaysian textbook for students of business communication in English, exhibits characteristics of the more embellished style common to many non-native varieties.

(36) Dear Sir:

I should like to be considered as an applicant for appointment as Sales Representative.

I am 31 years of age and am married. My health is perfect and, as the records I send herewith will show, my power of work is great. Since leaving school at 18, I have been in the employ of Mobil Malaysia Berhad. After several promotions, I was in 1989 appointed Sales Representative of this company throughout the southeast region of Malaysia.

The rapid and continuous increase in sales in this region, particulars of which, abstracted from my accounts you will find below, indicates my success in that capacity.

I am presently seeking opportunities that my present employers cannot provide. Their note of appreciation on my last year's returns will show how well I stand with them. A copy of this note I enclose.

I shall be happy to wait upon you at your convenience. Please do not, however, refer to my people before you have seen me.

Yours faithfully,
Alex Lee
(Nandy, 1995: 93–94)

The development of test items that accommodate for such stylistic differences as those illustrated in examples (31) through (36) will not be easy for test designers. However, any test of Standard English as it is actually used internationally will require such accommodation in order to provide valid assessments of proficiency in English as a world language.

Conclusion

Though still only in its early stages, research on non-native varieties of English has already provided considerable evidence that many grammatical and discourse features of Standard English in these varieties differ from corresponding norms in the native-speaker varieties. Some of these grammatical differences result from the same linguistic processes which also produce differences between native-speaker varieties. Other non-native innovations are more stylistic and reflect sociocultural imperatives to mark formality and deference in several contexts of communication.

These observations challenge at least two faulty assumptions that are widely held by many of the qualified professionals who construct and administer tests of English proficiency, particularly tests of English as an international language, such as the TOEIC. The first of these assumptions is that native-speaker varieties of English still provide the norms which all of the world's non-native speakers—who now comprise by far the majority of the world's English users—attempt to follow, even when no native speakers are involved. This assumption may still be accurate in settings where English is used primarily as a foreign language with few intranational functions, such as Japan, Egypt, and Spain. However, the data presented here offer strong counter-evidence that this assumption is not true of the millions of English users who speak non-native varieties.

The second, almost neo-colonial, assumption held by many who design English proficiency tests is that the native speakers still _should_ determine the norms for Standard English around the world. As one such native-speaking expert has said of the TOEIC (Educational Testing Service, 1991: 2), "The desire of those who first urged the _creation_ of an international standard for English in business and industry has been realized" (emphasis mine). What such experts fail to realize is that the authority to "create" Standard English no longer resides solely with its native speakers. Braj Kachru poses and then answers the crucial question (1992a: 8): "What is standard English and what are its models and norms? This is essentially a question of attitude and _power_" (emphasis in original). Regarding this power, the late Charles Ferguson, an internationally renowned sociolinguist, observed about language change in general that "there are ... cases where the control of the future passes to non-native speakers" (Ferguson, 1992: xvi). This is indeed the case in many areas of the English-using world today, and to provide valid assessments of proficiency in English as a global language, tests of English must become sensitive to this change.

Discussion Questions and Activities

1. How would you respond to the following assertion?

   The teaching model for learners of English should be Standard English, not a non-native variety of English.

2. How would you respond to this claim?

   Non-native varieties of English will always remain but "inter-languages" that approximate native speaker norms. They represent only partial rather than "successful" learning of the original target.

3. One frequently stated objection to the development of non-native varieties of English is that as divergent norms arise around the world, English will transform into distinct languages that will not be mutually comprehensible, and the value of English for international communication will be lost. Why do you agree or disagree?

4. Consider the underlined segments in the following examples, taken from essay examinations written by graduate students from Malaysia when they were studying at American colleges and universities.

   a. For example, <u>when the first time I came here</u>, I did not have enough <u>vocabularies</u>.

   b. In the past, <u>several</u> interesting <u>research</u> had been conducted.

   On what basis is it possible to distinguish clear errors in Standard English from possible differences across varieties of Standard English?

Additional Questions and Activities

1. Find out which 7 countries, in addition to Papua and New Guinea, have more than 100 languages each. Start with the *Ethnologue*, 13th edition. Teach your students how to use it! (The address is http://www.sil.org/ethnologue). Discuss what might explain the number of languages.

2. How much do you know about your state's language policies? Other states' policies? National language policies? About the history of language policies in the United States? Explore the language policy web site created by James Crawford, a journalist and freelance writer who has written quite a bit on language policies, and be prepared to share with others your findings to these questions. His web site can be found at the following address:

    http://ourworld.compuserve.com/homepages/JWCRAWFORD/new.htm

3. What is your definition of a "native speaker"? What kinds of linguistic standards should someone who wants to teach English as an additional language be expected to meet? How do your criteria for a native speaker compare to the standards needed to be an English teacher? How well do you measure up? What issues and concerns about language standards and linguistic rights are most important to you as an aspiring teacher of English?

4. Choose two educational issues that are in some way related to linguistic diversity and that are currently being publicly discussed and follow their development in newspapers and/or other written public sources (e.g. weekly magazines, electronic listserves, etc.). Make a scrapbook documenting their development and write an evaluative response to the issues from your perspective as a teacher.

5. What are some linguistic features that you share with others (accent, grammatical structures, vocabulary etc.)? What are some common social attitudes about those features? About those who regularly use those features? What are some linguistic features shared by members of a linguistic group that differs from yours? What are some common social attitudes about those features? About those who regularly use those features? What kinds of consequences (social, political, academic, etc.) can arise from the attitudes held by others about your features? From those you hold of others about their features?

6. Gather information on the Office for Civil Rights and its role in ensuring equal educational opportunities for all students by visiting them on the U.S. Department of Education's web site at:

    http://www.ed.gov/offices/OCR/

Be prepared to share the findings of your exploration with your class-mates.

7. For information, documentation, and research into regional or minor-ity languages in education, explore two of the following web sites. Prepare a written summary of your findings.

    European Bureau for Lesser Used Languages
        http://www.eblul.org
    European Language Council Homepage
        http//www.fu-berlin.de/elc/
    Mercator-Education
        http://www.fa.knaw.nl/mercator/
    World Bank
        http://www.worldbank.org/html/extdr/educ/edu_econ/
        biling_g.htm

Additional Reading and Resources

Bautista, M.L.S. (ed.) (1997) *English Is an Asian Language: The Philippine Context.* Australia: The Macquarie Library Pty.

Benson, P., Grundy, P. and Skutnabb-Kangas, T. (eds) (1998) Special volume: Language rights. *Language Sciences* 20, 1.

Crawford, J. (1992) *Language Loyalties: A Source Book on the Official English Controversy.* Chicago: Chicago University Press.

Cummins, J. (1996) *Negotiating Identities: Education for Empowerment in a Diverse Society.* Ontario: California Association for Bilingual Education.

Daniels, R. (1990) *Coming to America: A History of Immigration and Ethnicity in American Life.* New York: HarperCollins Publishers.

Dicker, S.J. (1996) *Languages in America: A Pluralist View.* Clevedon: Multilingual Matters.

Fishman, J. (1991) *Reversing Language Shift: Theoretical and Empirical Foundations of Assistance to Threatened Languages.* Philadelphia: Multilingual Matters.

Fishman, J. (1997) *In Praise of the Beloved Language. A Comparative View of Positive Ethnolinguistic Consciousness.* Berlin & New York: Mouton de Gruyter.

Garcia, O. (ed.). *Bilingual Education. Focusschrift in Honor of Joshua A. Fishman.* Amsterdam/Philadelphia: John Benjamins.

Herriman, M. and Burnaby, B. (eds) (1996) *Language Policy in English Dominant Countries: Six Case Studies.* Clevedon: Multilingual Matters.

Joseph, J.E. (1987) *Eloquence and Power: The Rise of Language Standards and Standard Languages.* New York: Basil Blackwell.

Kachru, B. (ed.) (1992) *The Other Tongue: English across Cultures* (2nd edn) Urbana: University of Illinois Press.

Kontra, M., Phillipson, R., Skutnabb-Kangas, T. and Vrady, T. (eds) (1998) *Approaching Linguistic Human Rights.* Budapest: Central European University Press.

Lang, P. (1995) *The English Language Debate: One Nation, One Language?* Springfield, NJ: Enslow Publishers.

Lippi-Green, R. (1997) *English with an Accent.* London and New York: Routledge.

Machan, T.W. and Scott, C.T. (eds) (1992) *English in Its Social Contexts: Essays in Historical Sociolinguistics.* Oxford University Press.

Maffi, L., Skutnabb-Kangas, T. and Andrianarivo, J. (in press) Language diversity. In D. Posey and G. Dutfield (eds) *Cultural and Spiritual Values of Biodiversity.* New York: United Nations Environmental Program & Cambridge: University Press.

McArthur, T. (1998) *The English Languages.* Cambridge: University Press.

McArthur, T. (ed.) (1992) *The Oxford Companion to the English Language.* Oxford: Oxford University Press.

McKay, S.L. and Wong, S.L.C. (eds) (1988) *Language Diversity: Problem or Resource?* New York: Newbury House Publishers.

Nieto, S. (1992) *Affirming Diversity. The Sociopolitical Context of Multicultural Education.* New York & London: Longman.

Pennycook, A. (1994) *The Cultural Politics of English as an International Language.* New York: Longman.

Pennycook, A. (1998) *English and the Discourses of Colonialism.* New York: Routledge.

Phillipson, R. (1992) *Linguistic Imperialism.* Oxford: Oxford University Press.

Ricento, T. and Burnaby (1998) *Language and Politics in the United States and Canada: Myths and Realities.* Mahwah, NJ: Lawrence Erlbaum Associates.

Ricento, T. and Hornberger, N. (eds) (1996) Special topic issue: Language planning and policy. *TESOL Quarterly* 30 (3).

Skutnabb-Kangas, T. (1996) Educational language choice—multilingual diversity or monolingual reductionism? In M. Hellinger and U. Ammon (eds) *Contrastive Sociolinguistics* (pp. 175–204). Berlin & New York: Mouton de Gruyter.

Skutnabb-Kangas, T. (1998) Education of ethnic minorities—language, ethnic identity and human rights. In J. Fishman (ed.) *Language and Ethnic Identity: Before and After the "Ethnic Revival." Comparative Disciplinary and Regional Perspectives.* Oxford: Oxford University Press.

Skutnabb-Kangas, T. (in press) *Linguistic Genocide in Education—or Worldwide Diversity and Human Rights?* Mahwah, NJ: Lawrence Erlbaum Associates.

Skutnabb-Kangas, T. and Cummins, J. (eds) (1988) *Minority Education: From Shame to Struggle.* Clevedon, UK: Multilingual Matters.

Skutnabb-Kangas, T. and Garcia, O. (1995) Multilingualism for all—general principles? In T. Skutnabb-Kangas (ed.) *Multilingualism for All* (pp. 221–256). Lisse: Swets & Zeitlinger, Amsterdam, Series European Studies on Multilingualism.

Skutnabb-Kangas, T. and Phillipson, R. (eds) in collaboration with Mart Rannut (1994) Linguistic human rights. Overcoming linguistic discrimination. Contributions to the *Sociology of Language* 67. Berlin & New York: Mouton de Gruyter.

Tatalovich, R. (1995) *Nativism Reborn? The Official English language Movement and the American States.* Lexington: University of Kentucky Press.

Thomas, L. (1996) Language as power: A linguistic critique of U.S. English. *Modern Language Journal* 80 (2), 129–140.

Tollefson, J. (1991) *Planning Language, Planning Inequality.* New York: Longman.

Section 2

The Social, Cultural, and Political Dimensions of Language Education

As pointed out in various ways in the chapters of Section One, language policies and practices are key components of the formation and maintenance of all social institutions, informing the ways in which languages are defined, used, and evaluated. Consequential to our development both as language teachers and language learners then are the policies and practices that constitute the institution of schooling. The three chapters of this section, concerned specifically with schooling, examine the social, cultural, and political dimensions of the policies and practices constituting language education and the consequences for both teachers and students of English. Although each looks through a different lens, together they attempt to tease apart the complexities and consequences of language policies and language practices and in doing so raise some interesting questions about our role as teachers of English.

In Chapter Five, Pennycook explores the idea of classrooms as permeable spaces where local conditions intersect with the social and cultural politics of the communities, broadly defined, within which classrooms are situated. In making his argument, he uses case studies of two classes of adults learning English. One group is located in Sri Lanka, the other in Toronto, Canada. In his discussion, Pennycook considers how such seemingly mundane aspects of the learning environment as classroom texts, pedagogical tasks, and the physical location of the room are themselves "culturally motivated." He explains the intricate relationships between these aspects, the sociocultural identities of the teacher and students, and the goals and aspirations for teaching and learning English held by the individual members of the classroom communities. Finally, he makes apparent how these circumstances are at the same time in dynamic interaction with the more macro dimensions of social and cultural life outside the classrooms. Pennycook concludes the chapter by highlighting the challenges that await aspiring English language teachers.

Acknowledging the complexities of education, Baugh, in Chapter Six, considers the social and academic implications of particular schooling practices for language minority students in a provocative discussion of the notion of "educational malpractice." Comparing it to medical malpractice, Baugh asserts that the potential for injury resulting from the miseducation of language minority students should be considered as significant as that resulting from professional negligence in the medical field. In his definition of language minority students, Baugh includes both those who speak a dialect other than standard English and those for whom English is not a native language. After presenting several examples of what he means by "educational malpractice," Baugh suggests several possibilities for the collaboration of policy makers and educators in the move toward educational reform.

In many ways, Wong, in Chapter Seven, takes up where Baugh leaves off. The chapter opens with a chronicle of schooling practices made available to historically marginalized groups in the United States. In her narrative, Wong makes the point that for many, these practices were, and continue to be, limited in scope and potential, thereby creating fairly intractable—but not irreversible—patterns of inequality. To transform these patterns, Wong argues that we must first understand how such patterns are formed and second work in systematic ways toward creating more effectual schooling practices. Teachers, she argues, play a crucial role in such work. In the last part of the chapter Wong proposes a three-dimensional model for creating educational programs that can lead to academic success for all language minority students.

Chapter 5

The Social Politics and the Cultural Politics of Language Classrooms

A. Pennycook

When we think of language classrooms, of language teaching and learning, it is often in terms of methods, competencies, strategies, grammar, tasks, exercises, drills, activities, and so on. Although it might already seem that such a list implies a wide diversity of ideas and approaches, I want to suggest by contrast that such a list in fact is part of a very particular view of classrooms. This perspective tends to view the classroom as something of a closed box, an educational context separated from society. Inside this box, teachers try to help their students learn a language. The language is a set of structures, pronunciations, or communicative acts that students need to master. The main concern, therefore, is how teachers can encourage the students to learn, to remember, internalize, and use the necessary pieces of language. And the main research questions have to do with how learners learn to communicate: In what order do students acquire certain structures? What kinds of communicative strategies may help learning? Does task-based learning help students more than grammar-focused learning? Is it helpful to teach generic text structures to students?

I do not want to suggest that these questions do not matter. Rather I want to argue that they form only a small part of what we need to understand in terms of what matters in language education. The problem is that so much of what we read about in TESOL and Applied Linguistics, or hear in teacher education classes, tends to view classes as closed boxes. I would like to consider an alternative view—that classrooms, both in themselves and in their relationship to the world beyond their walls, are complex social and cultural spaces. In order to do this, I shall introduce briefly two English classrooms in different parts of the world, one in Canada, another in South Asia. Although these classrooms may seem different from one's own context of work, I would suggest that there are many connections here that we need to understand.

The first classroom I discuss is Suresh Canagarajah's (1993) classroom, consisting of 22 first-year students doing a mandatory English class at the University of Jaffna in Sri Lanka. They are using *American Kernel Lessons: Intermediate* as a core text. The 13 female and 9 male Tamil students are mainly from rural communities and the poorest economic groups. Few of their parents have much education. English has "limited currency" in their lives outside the class and the university. The university's academic year began late because of "renewed hostilities between the Sinhala government and Tamil nationalists" (1993: 612). These tensions provide a backdrop to the classes, with government planes bombing the vicinity of the university during placement tests.

In his critical ethnography of this class, Canagarajah shows how anything from student annotations in textbooks to preferred learning styles and resistance to his own preferred teaching approaches are connected in complex ways to the social and cultural worlds both inside and outside the classroom. Despite the dramatic urgency of the real dangers outside this classroom, Canagarajah goes on to argue for an understanding of the relative autonomy of classrooms, suggesting both that they are social and cultural domains unto themselves and that they are interlinked with the world outside.

Before discussing this point further, however, I will describe briefly another classroom, an ESL class in a Chinese community center on a leafy street in Toronto, Canada (Morgan, 1997). The program has continuous intake, mixed-streaming, and no compulsory testing: "Some students have been in my class for several years, others for only a few months" (1997: 437). In the particular lesson he describes, all 15 students "claim Chinese ethnicity," 13 being from Hong Kong, with 2 from Malaysia and Taiwan; 11 were women, and 12 were over fifty. Morgan goes on to describe a "high-intermediate" lesson to practice oral and written English. The important questions for this chapter are concerned with how we relate these classrooms and the students in terms of social class (mixed in one, more homogeneous in the other), age (two rather different populations), ethnicity (in both classes a fairly homogeneous ethnic group), gender (one class fairly equally split, the other with predominantly women), and location (Toronto and Jaffna) to broader social, cultural, and political contexts.

Classrooms and the "Real World"

As I suggested above, there is often a tendency to view classrooms as isolated spaces; classrooms are "just classrooms." I want to suggest, by contrast, that classrooms are sociopolitical spaces that exist in a complex relationship to the world outside. I use the term "sociopolitical" here to address a further important dimension of how I want to approach these questions. The term political in both "sociopolitical" and "cultural political" is used not to address a formal domain of politics or policy but rather to suggest that I view questions of social and cultural relations from a critical perspective. Earlier chapters of this book have already shown the importance of understanding language teaching in relation to language policy: how, for example, choices we make in the classroom between using "English only" or several languages must also be seen in the context of broader language policies. But the notion of politics I am working with here is a different one. In his discussion of approaches to learner autonomy, Phil Benson (1997) has made this distinction nicely:

> We are inclined to think of the politics of language teaching in terms of language planning and educational policy while neglecting the political content of everyday language and language learning practices. In proposing a political orientation for learner autonomy, therefore, we need a considerably expanded notion of the political which would embrace issues such as the societal context in which learning takes place, roles and relationships in the classroom and outside, kinds of learning tasks, and the content of the language that is learned. (32)

It is this political understanding of the language classroom that will be the primary focus of this chapter. By this I mean that I view social and cultural relations not as casual contexts of consensus but rather as sites of struggle over preferred social and cultural worlds, as domains imbued with relations of power. From this perspective, an understanding of the social politics and cultural politics of classrooms is not just about describing what is going on; it is about making critical interpretations and suggesting possible alternatives.

Initially, two main dimensions in understanding classes as sociopolitical spaces may be suggested: on the one hand, classrooms themselves are social spaces; on the other hand, the larger social context of the classroom determines social relations in the classroom. This first view suggests concerns about "democracy" in the classroom and power relations between students and teachers. Although some arguments for student autonomy or independence are based purely on a view of the psychological benefits of "independent learning," others are based on this more social understanding of classrooms and therefore are based more on a concern for social equality in learning and teaching relationships (see Benson and Voller, 1997). This approach to sociopolitical classroom relationships, however, remains rather limited if it operates simply in terms of teachers having power and students not having power, and with a belief that "democratic" classrooms involve "handing over" power to students. Such a view, I suggest, is a simplistic understanding of social relations and "power sharing," ending up with little more than an argument for group work or student input to the curriculum. This view fails to relate social relations in the classroom to the larger social context.

The second approach, which suggests that the social world outside classrooms determines what happens inside them, offers a broader scope. From this perspective it matters fundamentally what is going on outside Canagarajah's classroom. Students do not leave their social relations, their rural upbringings, or their relationships to their parents at the classroom door; instead, they bring them in with them. And the screaming of the government jets over the classroom reminds us, if admittedly in an extreme way, that the outside world is never far away. Similarly, in Brian Morgan's classroom, it matters that this is a Chinese community center, that it is close to Toronto's China Town, that each segment of that Chinese community has a different socioeconomic status, and that older members of this community who attend ESL classes will not likely be part of the wealthier sections of that community. It matters that one of his students describes herself as an "astronaut's widow," referring to the Hong Kong term (*astronaut*) for those who have gained citizenship outside Hong Kong and then returned there to work.

But it is important to note also that Canagarajah argues that classrooms are "relatively autonomous" spaces. This is an important argument because it suggests that the view sketched above—that the social world outside classrooms determines what happens in them—is too deterministic. That is to say, it maps too dependent a relationship between social relations outside classrooms and social relations in classes. What we need to understand is that there is a complex interplay between classrooms and the outside world, or rather that classrooms are not so much a reflection of the outside world, but rather part of the outside world, and in fact play a role in how that outside world operates. From this perspective, the walls of classrooms become permeable, with social relations outside classrooms affecting what goes on inside, and social relations inside affecting what goes on outside. Indeed, we need to reject the common but unhelpful terminology that contrasts the "real world" with our classrooms: our classrooms are part of the real world. This last perspective has significance for understanding the implications of pedagogy.

Social Relations: The Micro and the Macro

Elsa Auerbach (1995) has explained that she sees language classrooms as socially located: "Pedagogical choices about curriculum development, content, materials, classroom processes, and language use, although appearing to be informed by apolitical professional considerations, are, in fact, inherently ideological in nature, with significant implications for learners' socioeconomic roles" (1995: 9). From this point of view, "the classroom functions as a kind of microcosm of the broader social order" (*ibid.*), that is to say the political relationships in the world outside the classroom are reproduced within the classroom. From this perspective, then, everything we do in the classroom can be understood socially and politically. And, furthermore, we need to have some notion of ideology (or discourse) that suggests not only that social relations are reproduced inside classrooms but that social relations are linked to ideologies and thus to the way we think.

A key issue in a critical social view of education concerns the tension between, on the one hand, large-scale analyses of how inequitable social relations are reproduced and, on the other hand, an understanding of how people confront such social and ideological forces. If we see small-scale action, the micro-politics of the classroom, as reflecting large-scale social structure, we can start to see how social relations are reproduced in daily classroom interactions. I have also been suggesting that we need to understand ways that people can act against and resist such forces. In this section, therefore, I shall look in more detail at social reproduction in the context of education, before discussing the concepts of cultural reproduction, cultural politics, and resistance.

An optimistic liberal view of education is that it provides opportunity for all: anyone can go to school, receive equal treatment, and come out at the end as whatever they want. Yet it does not take a very sophisticated critical analysis to suggest that this is far from what actually happens. Crudely put, rich kids tend to go to private schools and get good jobs, while working-class kids tend to go to poorer state schools and work in the same social and economic positions as their parents. One might simply account for this in terms of good and bad schools: wealthy families can afford good schools, while poorer families have to send their children to schools that provide an education of lower quality. Such a solution, however, fails to look at the broader functioning of society. What we need, instead, is an understanding of how schools operate within the larger field of social relations, and a realization that schools, as a key institution within society, ultimately serve to maintain the social, economic, cultural, and political status quo rather than upset it. Indeed, Bowles and Gintis (1976) have shown that schools in the U.S. operate to reproduce the labor relations necessary for the functioning of capitalism, suggesting that social relationships outside the classroom are mirrored and reproduced in the classroom.

From this perspective, two principal dimensions explain language classrooms and their relationship to the social and political context. First, language classrooms are part of a much larger social world. As Tollefson (1991) and Auerbach (1995) argue, for example, education for Indochinese refugees, either in resettlement camps in Southeast Asia or in ESL classrooms in the U.S., needs to be understood as part of a larger social and economic policy. As Tollefson (1991) explains, "Refugees are educated for work as janitors, waiters in restaurants, assemblers in electronic plants, and other low-paying jobs offering little opportunity for advancement, regardless of whether the refugees have skills ... suitable for higher paying jobs. Thus refugee ESL classes emphasize language competencies considered appropriate for minimum-wage work: following orders, asking questions, confirming understanding, and apologizing for mistakes" (108). Similarly, Auerbach points out that

> work-oriented content often is geared, on the one hand, toward specific job-related vocabulary and literacy tasks (reading time cards or pay stubs) and, on the other, toward 'appropriate' attitudes and behaviors and their concomitant language functions or competencies (learning how to call in sick, request clarification of job instructions, make small talk, follow safety regulations). (1995: 17)

From this perspective, then, we can see ESL in the U.S. as part of a social system that positions people of non–English speaking background into a particular socioeconomic niche.

Second, we need to understand the classroom itself as a social domain, not merely a reflection of the larger society beyond the classroom walls but also as a place where social relations are played out. As Auerbach points out, such relations between the society and the classroom can be seen at many levels, including curriculum, instructional content, materials, and language choice. For Auerbach (1995) these concerns point in two directions: on the one hand, classrooms need to "include explicit analysis of the social context" outside the classroom, and, on the other hand, "students must be involved in making pedagogical choices inside the classroom" (28). Thus we can see how classrooms need to turn outwards to the broader social worlds as well as inwards to their own social world. But we should be wary of viewing this as only a two-dimensional relationship: we also need to consider the relationships between classrooms and schools or community centers, between these and local communities, between communities and larger social institutions, and between classrooms and global relations.

What emerges most clearly from this perspective is that it is impossible to believe any longer in the myth that teaching English can be reduced to helping people gain access to social and economic power. Rather, we are part of complex social, economic, and political relations that flow back and forth through our classroom walls. Thus, the social relations inside Canagarajah's class must be seen in relation to class and ethnic relations in Jaffna and Sri Lanka. Likewise, we need to understand that the gender, age, ethnicity, and social class of Brian Morgan's "Chinese" students are inextricably linked to English and their communities and, more generally, to immigration and other policies of Canada, Hong Kong, Taiwan, and Malaysia.

Cultural Reproduction, Resistance, and Cultural Politics

Giroux (1983) argues that theories of cultural reproduction take up where theories of social reproduction leave off: they focus much more closely on the means by which schooling reproduces social relations. One important figure whose work has become well known in this area is Pierre Bourdieu, a sociologist perhaps best known for his introduction of the now widely used term, "cultural capital." The development of the notion of cultural capital was an attempt to theorize the systems by which certain children brought certain valued attributes to school that could be exchanged for other forms of capital (e.g. social connections or school certificates), while other students' capital was not valued or exchangeable. Cultural capital, Bourdieu explains, was first developed

> as a theoretical hypothesis which made it possible to explain the unequal scholastic achievement of children originating from the different social classes by relating academic success, i.e. the specific profits which children from the different classes and class fractions can obtain in the academic market, the distribution of cultural capital between the classes and class fractions. (1986: 243)

Shirley Brice Heath's (1983) ethnography of how different communities in the Carolinas in the U.S. socialize their children into different ways of "taking from books," and how the language and literacy skills of these children were valued differently in school, fleshes out how such cultural capital is developed, valued, or devalued. In comparison to Heath's more subtle analysis of different community cultures—the Black community of Trackton and the White community of Roadville were both working-class communities—Bourdieu's more critical social analysis tends to equate forms of cultural capital with a rather overgeneralized and static notion of class. Thus, although Bourdieu provides some useful tools for thinking about how schools reproduce social inequality, his view tends to be rather closed and deterministic. As Jenkins (1992) explains, Bourdieu's view of cultural reproduction does not allow for change and does not explain how people take up and resist cultural capital.

These critical understandings of social reproduction in education locate schooling in the context of social class and inequality, showing how schools are precisely part of society, both reflecting and reproducing social relations. Yet, as Giroux (1983) and Canagarajah (1993) argue, there is a danger that this view of reproduction allows no understanding of opposition and resistance, of the complex ways students and teachers act within the context of schooling. Canagarajah (1993) describes how his students resisted many aspects of the English course: "On the one hand, they oppose the alien discourses behind the language and textbook. On the other hand, they oppose a process-oriented pedagogy and desire a product-oriented one" (617). Thus, we also need to account for ways students and teachers act with a degree of autonomy within these broader social and cultural relations.

What is needed, then, is a way of understanding resistance and change, a better understanding of what actually goes on in classrooms, and a sense that we, as educators, can do something. We need to escape over-deterministic, over-totalizing critical analyses to show how education may make a difference. For these reasons Giroux (1988) talks of the need to develop a language of both critique and hope in critical educational theory, and Roger Simon (1992) talks of a "pedagogy of possibility."

Nevertheless, it has been useful to look at culture as the means by which social inequality is reproduced, because this view insists that we understand culture in political terms. One of the difficulties in talking about culture in a TESOL context is the tendency for culture to be reduced to different behaviors of our students. This is a deterministic view of culture, whereby students "belong" to certain cultures (Chinese, Japanese, or Spanish) that determine the way they behave (see Kubota, 1999; Pennycook, 1998). On the one hand culture is a determining factor in one's behavior; on the other hand, culture tends to deal only with the "exotic" and superficial of cultural behavior: food, dress, and religious festivals. But if we start from the premise that cultures are not static frameworks but competing ways of framing the world, we can start to understand the cultural politics of classrooms. Thus, in both Canagarajah's and Morgan's classrooms, the Tamil and Chinese backgrounds of their students are not reduced to learning styles or food preferences but instead are part of a complex world that students bring to the classroom, a world in which culture and ethnicity is bound up with other political domains such as social class, gender, and age.

Cultural politics, then, gives us a more open way of addressing questions of struggles over difference, such as whose versions of reality gain legitimacy and whose representations of the world gain sway over others (see Jordan & Weedon, 1995). It is clear that representations of the world that are given credence tend to be the views of powerful and influential groups. And the official sanctioning of such knowledge and culture, particularly in institutions such as schools through set curricula, reinforce the position and the worldview of those groups. From this perspective we can see the ideologies that operate in our classrooms and the social relations that they produce. This view of cultural politics allows us to see classrooms as sites where different worldviews or discourses come into dynamic contact.

The Cultural Politics of ELT

Once we open up this perspective of the cultural politics of classrooms, we can start to see that everything we do in the classroom is related to broader concerns. This relationship of classrooms to the outside world is a reciprocal one: the classroom is not determined by the outside world, but the classroom is part of the world, both affected by what happens outside its walls and affecting what happens there. As I suggested earlier, the very fact that we are teaching English needs to be understood in terms beyond those of national language policy. As Robert Phillipson (1992) and I (Pennycook, 1994) have argued, this global spread of English is bound up with many cultural, economic, and political forces: the dominance of U.S. media, the role of international corporations, the spread of particular forms of culture and knowledge, and the development of a very particular "world order."

As English teachers, whether we are working in a so-called English-speaking country or not, we cannot escape the implications of these global connections. As Benson (1997) observes, teachers of English "are more often than not engaged in political processes of a distinctive kind." On the one hand, the "acceptance of English as a second language very often implies the acceptance of the global economic and political order for which English serves as the 'international language.'" To understand English teaching in an international context, then, we need to be able to understand how English is connected to other global forces. On the other hand, "learning foreign languages (and again English in particular) is more often than not premised upon inequalities between learner and target communities" (Benson, 1997: 27). This is part of the social and cultural context of our teaching. It matters that Canagarajah is teaching English to his students in Sri Lanka, because of its colonial and current history in Sri Lanka and India, and because of its current role in the world. It matters that Brian Morgan is teaching English to students of Chinese background, students who live in complex relations to families in Hong Kong or Taiwan, and to the Toronto community in which they now live.

What we do in classrooms also needs to be seen in similar terms. Not only are there social relations in the classroom in terms of who speaks and who sets the agenda, but the very ways we run classes need to be seen in terms of cultural politics. Assumptions about "active" and "passive" students, about the use of group work and pair work, about self-interest as a key to motivation ("tell us about yourself"), about memorization being an outmoded learning strategy, about oral communication as the goal and means of instruction, about an informal atmosphere in the class being most conducive to language learning, about learning activities being fun, about games being an appropriate way of teaching and learning—all these, despite the claims by some researchers that they are empirically preferable, are cultural preferences. And this means that the classroom becomes a site of cultural struggle over preferred modes of learning and teaching.

As Canagarajah observes, his students started to resist his more Westernized teaching approach and opted instead for an approach to learning with which they were more familiar. Such cultural preferences cannot be mapped simply onto cultural bodies: Canagrajah is, like his students, a Tamil Lankan; but he is also a "young (in my early 30s), male, 'progressive,' Christian, culturally Westernized, middle class, native Tamil, bilingual, director of English language teaching at the university" (620). Similarly, Morgan argues that what might look a fairly homogenous label of "Chinese in Toronto" covers a vast range of diversity. We bring mixed cultural identities to teaching moments. But to say that students may have different preferences does not mean that we should just do what students want; Canagarajah feels that the students did themselves little good by pursuing this route. What it does mean, however, is that we need to understand the cultural politics of these moments.

One of Canagarajah's interests is in the ways that students react to and reinterpret the textbooks, *Kernel Lessons*, used for the class. Since these valuable foreign texts were handed out and taken in again at the beginning and end of each class, he was able to see the annotations and comments the students made in their textbooks. These comments varied from the Tamilization of the characters, the addition of phrases (in English) such as "I love you darling," and dialogues, to the inclusion of references to the struggle for Tamil independence. Students also had difficulties interpreting some pictures, being confused, for example, by a picture of a character in prison, when he was pictured alone in his cell with a uniform and shoes (all unlikely in a Lankan context). The important point to take from this, however, is that all textbooks, all teaching materials carry cultural and ideological messages. The pictures, the lifestyles, the stories, and the dialogues are full of cultural content; all may potentially be in disaccord with the cultural worlds of the students. Everything we use in class is laden with meanings from outside and interpretations from inside.

Once we start to look at classrooms as an intersection of different ideologies and cultures, we can start to see that language learning is not an abstract cognitive process where bits of language become lodged in the brain. Rather, it is a highly complex social and cultural process. Once we start to understand that cultural politics happen not only in the classroom and the world but also, inevitably, in the heads of our students, then we have to see classrooms as sites where identities are produced and changed. We need to understand that these identities are multiple and shifting and tied to language and language learning.

Brian Morgan illustrates this well by showing how a simple class on intonation, in fact, has a great deal to do with social and cultural relations, history, community, and identity. As we are taken through various stages of this class, Morgan shows how questions of social identity are constantly being reworked in classrooms: "Each ESL classroom is a unique, complex, and dynamic social environment . . . : Each classroom . . . becomes a resource for community development, where students re-evaluate the past (i.e. the rules of identity) in the context of the present and, through classroom reflection and interaction, forge new cultural traditions, histories, and solidarities that potentially improve their life chances for the future" (432–433). Morgan discusses how the students' exploration of different possibilities of intonation in dialogues—some more acquiescent, some more aggressive—raised questions of social and gender relations in the Chinese community. Such possibilities have major significance for the relationship between the classroom and the broader social context, as well as for our understandings of ESL methodology and research:

> ESL teachers should pay close if not equal attention to the historical and local conditions that influence identity formation when contextualizing language activities in the classroom. A far more difficult challenge for teachers, however, will be to address their own sociopolitical assumptions inscribed within TESOL's theories and technologies of language acquisition, methodology, and research. (1997: 447)

Towards Resistance, Change, and Engagement

A number of teachers and researchers have met the demands of this sociopolitical and cultural political understanding of language classrooms and have developed relevant pedagogical or research strategies.

I chose to discuss Morgan's and Canagarajah's classrooms not only because they show these relations but also because their articles are written as teacher/researchers. They write both as teachers teaching English and researchers trying to relate their classrooms to a broader social world. This raises further pedagogical and research-oriented questions. In order to be pedagogically more effective, we need not only better theoretical understandings of classrooms but better researched classrooms as well. As Canagarajah (1993) argues, what we are lacking at present is critical ethnographies of language classrooms, which he defines as

> an ideologically sensitive orientation to the study of culture that can penetrate the noncommittal objectivity and scientism encouraged by the positivistic empirical attitude behind descriptive ethnography and can demystify the interests served by particular cultures to unravel their relation to issues of power. (605)

That is to say, the perspective on the classroom outlined here demands a response in terms of research that keeps one eye on the workings of the classroom and another eye on the broader social and political context.

We can approach such study in a number of ways, from inclusivity, to issues, to engagement. An inclusivity focus points to the importance of making sure that people of different backgrounds are represented in our texts and our classroom possibilities. Many ESL textbooks still work with a 1970s Kellogg's® Cornflakes vision of the family: a blond, white, heterosexual family, with one daughter and one son (all of whom clearly visit the dentist regularly). An argument for greater inclusivity acknowledges that both inside and outside the classroom we live in a world different from Kellogg's®. Arguments for the inclusion, for example, of women in occupations other than at the kitchen sink, have more recently included arguments for alternative lifestyles, of gay and lesbian couples, gay and lesbian parents, single parents, people of color, people with disabilities, and so on.

A different focus (though by no means incompatible) looks to include issues of identity and difference in the language teaching curriculum. This I shall call the issues focus. It is an attempt not just to have difference as a background possibility in the textbooks but also to raise more overtly such issues as a content focus in class. Thus, we may find textbooks or curricula include sections on "gay marriages" or "women in the workforce." While this does seem to put issues of difference on the agenda, there are often also problems here, since at least from within the textbook world, we tend to get a very sanitized version of difference. Much of what is presented occurs within an overarching liberal agenda that works with a bland notion of alternatives and social issues. Fundamental questions of identity get slotted into a framework of issues, so that one week we may be dealing with the environment or animal rights and another with issues of gender or sexuality. There is also a tendency to deal with a fixed set of dichotomous possibilities (e.g. nature or nurture; is homosexuality normal? etc.) (see Pennycook, 1997).

A third possibility is what I term an engagement focus. This is an approach to language education that sees such issues as gender, race, class, sexuality, postcolonialism, and so on as so fundamental to identity and language that they need to form the basis of curricular organization and pedagogy. Arleen Schenke (1996) has strongly criticized what she calls "the tired treatment of gender and 'women's lib' in many of our ESL textbooks" (156). In place of these tired liberal, issues-based approaches, she proposes what she calls a "practice in historical engagement," a focus on "the struggle over histories (and forgetting) in relation to the cultures of English and to the cultures students bring with them to the classroom already-knowing" (156). From this point of view, then, questions of difference, identity, and culture are not merely issues to be discussed but are about understanding fully how discourses structure our lives. Questions of gender or race are not themes to be discussed but make up the underlying rationale for the course. "Feminism," Schenke argues, "like antiracism, is thus not simply one more social issue in ESL but a way of thinking, a way of teaching, and, most importantly, a way of learning" (158). Such a view also informs the thinking of Canagarajah and Morgan. Understanding the social and cultural politics of classrooms ultimately has to do with a way of thinking, teaching, and learning.

Auerbach deals with the social politics and cultural politics of classrooms through what she terms "participatory action research." This research aims to do two things: (1) to give students control of the curriculum so that they start to research questions regarding language and the community that are important to them; and (2) to bring the outside community into the classroom to make it a focus of classroom work and discussion. An extensive explanation of this is given elsewhere in this volume. Similarly, Norton Peirce (1995), following Heath's (1983) suggestions for involving students and teachers in researching the literacy practices of their communities, argues for "classroom based social research" in order to "engage the social identities of students in ways that will improve their language learning outside the classroom and help them claim the right to speak" (1995: 26). Once we view classrooms as both social sites in themselves and as part of the larger social world, the types of materials we use and the activities we engage in become open to a range of questions of difference and identity with which it becomes impossible not to engage. Thus, it is not enough to acknowledge the social and cultural dimensions of our classrooms: we also need to engage students with the implications.

Conclusion: The Heart of the Crucial Issues of Our Time

A typical applied linguistic view of the classroom has tended to see it as some sort of quasi-laboratory in which languages are learned and teaching methods performed (with possibly some connection between the two). This chapter, by contrast, has argued for the importance of seeing the classroom as a social and cultural space. This sense of the social and cultural, furthermore, is not the liberal dream of equitable social relations and celebratory multiculturalism, but a view always concerned with questions of power. From this sociopolitical and cultural political viewpoint, the language classroom becomes a site of contestation, where different codes, different visions of the world, and different pedagogies are in competition and conflict. Auerbach suggests:

> Once we begin looking at classrooms through an ideological lens, dynamics of power and inequality show up in every aspect of classroom life.... We are forced to ask questions about the most natural seeming practices: Where is the class located? Where does the teacher stand or sit? Who asks questions? What kinds of questions are asked? Who chooses the learning materials? How is progress evaluated? Who evaluates it? (Auerbach, 1995: 12)

The classroom is a microcosm of the larger social and cultural world, reflecting, reproducing and changing that world. This should not be seen, however, as a pessimistic view of language teaching but as a necessary understanding of the competing demands we face as teachers. Everything outside the classroom, from language policies to cultural contexts of schooling, may have an impact on what happens in the classroom. And everything in the classroom, from how we teach, what we teach, and how we respond to students, to the materials we use, and the ways we assess the students, needs to be seen as social and cultural practices with broad implications. The challenge is to understand these relationships and to find ways of always focusing on the local while at the same time keeping an eye on the broader horizons. The view of our classroom walls as permeable means that what we do in our classrooms is about changing the worlds we live in. As James Gee notes:

> English teachers can cooperate in their own marginalization by seeing themselves as "language teachers" with no connection to such social and political issues. Or they ... accept their role as persons who socialize students into a world view that, given its power here and abroad, must be looked at critically, comparatively, and with a

constant sense of the possibilities for change. Like it or not, English teachers stand at the very heart of the most crucial educational, cultural, and political issues of our time. (Gee, 1994: 190)

Along with the difficulties and dangers such a view brings, it also presents us with exciting challenges, and it can help us see that once we take the social politics and cultural politics of our classrooms seriously, what we do as English teachers matters, for we indeed stand at the very heart of the most crucial educational, cultural, and political issues of our time.

Discussion Questions and Activities

1. Reconsider a classroom with which you are familiar. Discuss how on the one hand you might have seen it only in terms of language learning and teaching methods, and how on the other you might now start to see it in its broader social, cultural, and political contexts.
2. What pedagogical and research responses would you suggest to a view of the classroom as a social political and cultural political space?
3. Look at some of the different contributions to Benson and Voller's book on learner autonomy. How do the different writers understand autonomy? What is your view of learner autonomy?
4. Some people will argue that as English teachers "we already have enough on our plates" without dealing with social and cultural politics. What are some arguments for and against such a claim? What is your personal position?
5. What is a "good teacher"? A standard TESOL answer might have focused on knowledge of language, classroom manner, use of activities, and so on. The perspective here would suggest we need to add a number of dimensions to this. How might you now characterize a good teacher?

Chapter 6

Educational Malpractice and the Miseducation of Language Minority Students[1]

J. Baugh

Educational malpractice has rarely been discussed in the quest for higher educational standards or other educational reforms. However, the relevance of educational malpractice—along with its eventual elimination—is especially salient when it comes to teaching language minority students.[2]

Such students have tended to perform poorly on high-stakes standardized tests, and they often attend overcrowded schools with inexperienced teachers in classes that are seldom equipped to handle their special needs. Even the most skilled teachers eventually burn out from the sheer weight of attempting to serve large numbers of students. Teachers who teach in classrooms with substantial linguistic heterogeneity typically face a more difficult challenge due to multiple discrepancies in linguistic competence, along with other potential sources of cultural incompatibility.

Recent results from state-wide standardized tests in California have confirmed the obvious: scores for low-income and language minority students remain far behind those of students from affluent homes whose first language is not only English, but mainstream U.S. English (i.e. MUSE: see Lippi-Green, 1997). The consequences of socially stratified linguistic diversity and the miseducation of language minority students are the primary focus of this discussion. More specifically, I consider language minority miseducation resulting from professional negligence, incompetence, and malfeasance, and other forms of malpractice in educational contexts.

For the purpose of these remarks, I make a distinction between students with linguistic disabilities and students who do not speak MUSE and thus are at an educational disadvantage. While racially motivated affirmative action has been strongly criticized, several federal categorical educational programs confirm legal bases for affirmative intervention: Title I, Title VII, and the Individuals with Disabilities Educational Act (IDEA).

Title I serves students in poverty, and a host of Title I programs strive to combat some of the detrimental consequences of poverty among poor children who attend school. Such tasks remain daunting and they rarely receive adequate funding. The Individuals with Disabilities Educational Act serves students who suffer from pathological educational impediments. And Title VII funds, although quite limited in comparison to Title I, are provided to support students for whom English is not native (ENN).

The classification of students by these different programs has caused controversies. For example, the Oakland Ebonics controversy surfaced largely because of differing linguistic classifications for African-American students, who have never been designated as ENN. Rather, educational policies have always classified African Americans as native speakers of English. The legal consequences of a binary language classification, between ENN and native English speakers, is problematic and discussed in more detail elsewhere (Baugh, 1998, 1999). For the purpose of this discussion all students for whom MUSE is not native may suffer from "a linguistic handicap" in schools and particularly so in schools that are insensitive as to how students from other than MUSE backgrounds should be taught.

I suspect that any discussion regarding educational malpractice and the miseducation of language minority students could easily descend to the lowest depths of pedagogical muckraking, but such an exercise is unlikely to advance the education of students who now suffer the consequences of intentional-to-benign malpractice in private or public schools. Since few poor students attend private schools, the bulk of this conversation focuses on public education. Ultimately, we seek means of reducing, relieving, and eliminating malpractice in educational contexts, including programs and classes that are intended to benefit nonMUSE students.

My remarks begin with an operational definition of educational malpractice, along with some examples that are salient to the miseducation of low income and language minority students. Next, I discuss important legal distinctions between various forms of malpractice, along with legal implications pertaining to alternative sources and forms of professional incompetence, negligence, and malfeasance that may afflict students who have been or may be educationally harmed as a result of malpractice that is beyond their control. Since the educational welfare of students is our primary concern, these remarks strive to be positive and consistent with efforts to enhance teacher professionalism. The discussion considers differences in allocations of time and funding and provides further analogies to malpractice issues in other professions.

I conclude with an appeal to avoid replicating the divisive mistakes that have befallen physicians and attorneys who pay exorbitant insurance premiums to defray potential expenses incurred from malpractice litigation. Educators and other interested parties are strongly encouraged to seek nonlitigious, low-cost means of malpractice relief. At a time when educational funding is restricted, we can ill-afford to squander those precious resources on activities that do not directly advance the educational well-being of students. Were any additional funding available it would be far better spent on competent professional education, particularly whenever tax expenditures maintain that education.

Educational Malpractice

For the purposes of this chapter, I define educational malpractice as professional negligence. Although the following was written about doctors, it applies to teachers as well.

> The general rule the courts apply to determine if malpractice has been committed is to ask: Has this doctor performed in a manner consistent with his educational level and training, and in a manner consistent with the work of doctors of similar education and training in the community? (Flaster, 1983: 3)

He also notes that

> two additional elements that are necessary to make a clear case on the basis of this doctrine are:
> (1) The "agent" (object) that was the cause of the injury was under the exclusive control of the alleged wrongdoer, i.e. the doctor being sued.
> (2) The injury was not caused by or contributed to by the patient. (Flaster, 1983: 29–30)

By substituting "teacher" for "doctor" and "student" for "patient" in the preceding quotes, we direct the locus of educational malpractice toward individual students, which is comparable to medical malpractice where injury to patients is the most common basis of malpractice suits.

Although educational and medical malpractice definitions are similar, one distinction between them is important to make. Whereas the typical physician attends to one patient at a time, a teacher typically teaches several students simultaneously, with glaring differences in class sizes across the private-to-public educational spectrum. Those who purchase private education often do so to avoid placing their children in large classes.

Also, because private education is unregulated, many detractors of school vouchers fear the prospect that public taxes could support private educational institutions that need not comply with national, state, or local educational policies.

Returning, then, to public education, the following illustration considers malpractice against an entire class of students, many of whom attended an inner-city school. Educational officials eventually intervened in the following case. It has been selected for two main reasons: (1) it is factual, and (2) it appears to meet all of the criteria described previously pertaining to malpractice for physicians, that is, recognizing that teachers teach to groups of students in various sizes. The Associated Press reported the incident in question. The text has been modified slightly to eliminate specific references to individuals associated with the episode.

Use of Parody Test Costs Teacher His Job

Chicago (AP) 1994. A teacher who gave sixth-graders a math test with questions about pimps, drug dealers, and illicit sex agreed to resign from the Chicago public school system.

The Board of Education attorney said Wednesday that the teacher in question, who was transferred to a desk job away from students last month, will leave Chicago's schools.

"His use of a document—I hate to call it a test—was inappropriate as an instructional tool," stated the attorney.

The so-called exam was a racist parody that had been copied and faxed to schools and offices around the country this spring. It included questions such as these:

* "Hector knocked up six of the girls in his gang. There are 27 girls in the gang. What percentage of the girls in the gang has Hector knocked up?"

* "Martin wants to cut his half-pound of heroin to make 20% more profit. How many ounces of cut will he need?"

The teacher, who administered the test, could not be reached for comment.

The test created a furor among parents at an elementary school in a low-income neighborhood, marred by drug activity and crime.

Parents said they felt betrayed because the school is supposed to be the one place where their children are shielded from the storm of the streets. (Associated Press, March 9, 1994)

As far as educational malpractice is concerned, the teacher in question did not perform in a manner consistent with his educational level and training, nor was this test consistent with the work of other teachers of similar education and training in the community. Additional considerations confirm malpractice and imply potential malfeasance: The teacher in this case was the "agent" who caused psychological and/or emotional injuries, and the relevant instruction was under the exclusive control of the alleged wrongdoer. Also, any resulting injuries or mental anguish were not caused by or contributed to by the students.

Consistent with the orientation of teacher-focused case studies, potential injury in this instance corresponds to a class of students, not merely a single student. But this brings us to another matter regarding the locus of educational malpractice. In medical cases it is the individual patient who may sue as the victim of professional negligence or incompetence. Individual students who are enrolled in public schools are not afforded this same legal recourse; again, one obvious reason for this paradox lies in the fact that teachers serve "a class" of students simultaneously, whereas the attending physician normally attends to one patient at a time. It is this fundamental difference in the professional-to-client ratio of teachers in contrast to physicians that challenges the essential proof of causality that is required in any successful malpractice litigation. The preceding case differs in the sense that the entire class of students who received the document (i.e. test?) in question were all potential victims of harm, especially in the form of mental anguish.

Elsewhere (Baugh, 1999) I describe some of the relevant resource allocation issues that are pertinent to a complete discussion of educational malpractice, but the present remarks draw more pointed attention to students for whom standard English is non-native (SENN and ENN, see below for definitions). Students who learn Standard English natively are at considerable educational advantage when compared to students who are SENN or ENN.

Three linguistic divisions are central to this discussion, and they encompass all students:

   X = Students for whom standard English is native (SEN)[3]
   Y = Students who speak English but for whom Standard English is not native (SENN)
   Z = Student for whom English is not native (ENN)

This chapter considers African-American and bilingual populations from different linguistic perspectives. The Ebonics controversy indirectly called attention to the creole history of African-American language, while exposing that most educators remain perplexed as to how best to teach Standard English to SENN students. Speakers of Hawaiian Pidgin English are also considered SENN students; they too are classified as native English speakers in need of linguistic enrichment to enhance their educational prospects. Although the pidginization and creolization processes are most pronounced among African Americans and Hawaiians,

ENN immigrants also lack Standard English proficiency, and these linguistic distinctions are vital to a more complete understanding of effective pedagogy.

I contend that classes composed of students primarily from Y and Z are often the inadvertent recipients of educational malpractice, and they frequently attend schools where allocations of time and money are stretched thin in a regulatory void where thresholds for a minimum educational standard have yet to be established.

Whereas most of the effort to reform education has responded to calls for higher standards, malpractice requires that we confirm "minimum standards." Stated in other terms, at what point does education, or parts of the educational system, operate beneath thresholds of acceptable educational norms? While much of the educational literature discusses high standards, including important "opportunity to learn" standards, discussion of minimum standards is less frequent but no less important, especially to the children who may fall prey to incompetent miseducation.

Until minimum standards for educating SENN and ENN students are established, prospects for educational malpractice will remain high. In the wake of the Ebonics controversy and efforts to dismantle bilingual education throughout the country, educators and the American public seek positive solutions to these problems, and educators and educational policy makers would benefit from deliberations that address America's growing linguistic diversity.

Two cases illustrate the S/ENN distinctions that are central to this thesis: the 1979 Black English trial, and the 1974 *Lau v. Nichols* ruling. Both cases point toward the need to take students' language backgrounds into account prior to imparting instruction, but such linguistic assessments tend to be impressionistic at best and ill conceived at worst. For example, plaintiffs in the Black English trial were evaluated with pathological diagnostics that triggered the following case.

The Black English trial revisited

The Black English trial occurred in 1979 and centered around 11 African-American students who were diagnosed as being "linguistically handicapped." In this case a certified speech pathologist conducted a series of diagnoses that resulted in the plaintiffs' being placed in special education classes that delayed their academic development. Judge Charles Joiner, whose opinion appears in full in Smitherman (1981), ruled in favor of the plaintiffs. He observed that students were being asked to perform using standard English, but the teachers failed to acknowledge their native vernacular dialect (i.e. African-American English), which does not coincide with the prevailing linguistic norms necessary for academic development in typical public schools throughout the nation.

The judge's ruling failed to address a concern that I have previously discussed at considerable length (Baugh 1988, 1995). Differences between Standard English and dialects that are not standard should not be attributed to pathological causes. The linguistic consequences of slavery in the U.S. are well known to linguists (see, for example, Baugh, 1983; Green, 1995; Labov, 1972, 1982; Rickford, 1986; Smitherman, 1977; Wolfram, 1969). Educators who are mindful of these linguistic differences have devoted themselves to finding suitable educational solutions in support of African-American students (see Ball, 1991, 1992, 1995; Banks, 1994; Baugh, 1994; Foster, 1997; Ladson-Billings, 1994; Lee, 1995; Rickford & Rickford, 1995). Speech pathologists have also recognized that linguistic diagnostics for African-American students require special attention, and much of that recognition grew directly from issues raised during the Black English trial (Pollock & Berni, 1996; Stockman & Vaughn-Cooke, 1992; Washington & Craig, 1994; Wyatt, 1995).

Much relevant research in linguistics, education, and speech pathology has demonstrated the history of dialect differences and presented solutions for working with SENN students. However, I contend (Baugh, 1998) that many African-American students continue to be ill-served by linguistic misclassification, owing in large measure to a combination of inadequate linguistic diagnostics and educational policies that otherwise dismiss nonstandard English as a barrier to academic success. Some of these policies, and their lack of adequate linguistic dexterity, help to explain racial discrepancies in academic performance on standardized tests (Williams, 1975; Steele *et al.*, 1993).

Besides misclassification, other problems are associated with the linguistic circumstances surrounding African-American students who do not speak standard English. Most likely, teachers who place students based on pathological speech diagnostics will not be "guilty" of educational malpractice according to my criteria: (a) they perform in a manner consistent with their training and peers (as did the teachers in the Black English case); (b) they do not cause ensuing educational harm under their exclusive control, and (c) they are not the "cause" of educational injuries resulting from the dual legacy of slavery and a prior history of racialized educational apartheid. Therefore, any suggestion that classroom teachers of SENN African-American students are causal agents of willful educational malpractice is extremely unlikely to prove true, but while this may be welcome news to educators in inner-city (and rural) schools that serve large populations of students from low income and minority backgrounds, it does little to truly improve educational prospects for African-American students.

Lau v. Nichols and California's Proposition 227

Lau v. Nichols (1974) may be well known to readers of this chapter; it is the Supreme Court case that affirmed that school districts must attend to languages other than English for ENN students. In June, 1998, however, California voters passed Proposition 227 (_a.k.a._, "English for the children"), which has expanded to other states where advocates seek to dismantle bilingual education programs in favor of a single year of English immersion for all ENN students, thereby restricting educational options available to traditional language minority students.

Lau v. Nichols confirmed that educators must acknowledge languages other than English for students who are ENN, but in so doing the Supreme Court did not specify how this should be accomplished. These matters were left to professional educators. Revisions in the 1994 "Equal Educational Opportunity Act" provided greater flexibility to educators of low-income and language minority students who receive federal funding, particularly through Title I programs intended to bolster educational prospects for students in poverty—many of whom are SENN and ENN students.

Focusing for the moment on ENN students, it is clear that changing social demographics will increase linguistic diversity in many schools throughout the nation, and it will be incumbent upon educators who serve these students to identify and employ the most effective educational strategies in support of ENN students. California's Proposition 227, however, defies the public trend toward greater educational choice in favor of a singular educational approach, and it is likely that the courts will continue to play a role in approaches California schools (and perhaps schools elsewhere) must take to be legally compliant.

Seeking Solutions

What, then, do Proposition 227 and _Lau v. Nichols_ have to do with miseducation or malpractice? Those of us who seek to advance the teaching of English to ENN students must help to confirm the array of programs and procedures that are most effective. For the moment I leave any interpretation of "most effective" to your personal judgment. From a legal perspective, however, courts will not be able to determine educational malpractice that harms ENN students until we can legally distinguish between competent bilingual education programs and those that are ineffective-to-harmful for ENN students. Even though the public appears to have a growing appetite for increasing as many school choices as possible, California voters have placed highly restrictive constraints on educators who are responsible for the education of ENN students. This tumultuous state of affairs regarding bilingual education places considerable demands on professionals who educate ENN students.

In order to satisfy educational claims put forward by proponents of Proposition 227, students will need to demonstrate advanced English proficiency on standardized tests. Educators would be well advised to emulate and replicate programs that demonstrate success, based on the best available evidence, and programs that are ill conceived should be transformed or disbanded. As with studies of medical malpractice, I think local educators who are intimately familiar with the needs of specific schools, in close consultation with parents, are best suited to determine if ENN programs meet minimum professional educational standards. In anticipation of this need, educational researchers and policy makers continue to collaborate in the hope of finding common ground upon which to advance the education of ENN students.

Resource allocations have not been adequately addressed here, but they can offer valuable evidence regarding how best to educate ENN students. Are resources available to successful ENN programs different from resource allocations to ENN programs that lack success? Service capacity, including the establishment of minimum technological capabilities for various schools, are also relevant to the educational welfare of all students. Affluent schools tend to have much more technology than do less affluent schools; this is obvious to anyone who is familiar with American schools and their impact on local real estate markets.

Malpractice also requires clear and concise criteria regarding assessments of "harm" or "injury" resulting from professional negligence in educational contexts, and such criteria are closely aligned with efforts to establish high educational standards. I believe that knowledge of "minimum standards" must be implemented on the road to confirming potential cases of educational malpractice that have inflicted harm or injury to individuals or classes of students.

By comparing medical and educational malpractice we can see other areas to improve in education. One significant difference between educational and medical malpractice is that doctors do not treat their patients without diagnoses. Educators rarely employ anything comparable to an individualized medical diagnosis, with the significant exception of "Individualized Education Programs" (IEP), which are often provided as part of special education but are not routinely provided to every student. The role of confidentiality also differs considerably in education as compared to medicine. For example, medical confidentiality far exceeds educational confidentiality, and courts may eventually decide if breaches in educational confidentiality may have harmed or injured students, similar to the physician who wrongly divulges information about a patient that consequently results in harm or injury to that patient.

Educators of ENN students must fully understand that we stand at an important juncture in American education. Efforts to reform education for all students continue to raise the bar in search of ever higher standards to ensure that American students are second to none. Those efforts, combined with an awareness of the potential for educational malpractice, place education, especially minority education, in a position to advance malpractice reforms in innovative ways and thus begin to ensure that schools are places where students are unlikely to be physically or academically harmed.

The example of the math teacher who used inappropriate problems is perhaps the most apparent instance of educational malpractice; it is an example of unprofessional conduct by a teacher that ultimately required external intervention to protect students from potentially harmful effects. Educators must therefore be cautious in trying novel or experimental approaches to improve educational prospects for language minority students. Any such efforts must adhere to an analogous medical dictum: "First, do no harm."

In order to be most helpful to educators and S/ENN students, time and money should not be spent on litigation that is unlikely to advance effective educational practices. Those in positions of legal authority or policy implementation should add "minimum acceptable standards" to other systemic educational reform efforts to establish the thresholds for educational practices beneath which public education should not fall. Again, this paradox grows from the fact that all children residing in the U.S. must attend school (or show good cause for not attending school), but there is no equally compelling law or social ethos which demands that all children residing in the U.S. must attend a good school.

Minimum standards, in contrast to high standards, confirm "the floor" rather than the ceiling of educational reform. At present, educational practices pertaining to language minority students are in an advanced state of flux and disarray as educators, legislators, scholars, voters, and the courts attempt to sort out their various ideas regarding the best ways to enhance English proficiency among all students. Minimum educational standards should also be reassessed periodically as educators seek to improve them. Evaluations of time and funding allocations may help all parties better understand the distribution of educational resources and how that evidence corresponds to effective schools in contrast to their ineffective counterparts.

In conclusion, the worst possible prospect for drawing attention to educational malpractice would be the escalation of expenses that are extraneous to the welfare of students. The best future prospects lie in the potential for educators to become national leaders in malpractice reform. A combination of legal and fiscal considerations have, thankfully, kept educational malpractice litigation to a minimum, as compared to medical malpractice or malpractice in other professional venues.

The available evidence suggests that "official intervention" may take too long to eliminate sources of educational misconduct, and the courts have been extremely reluctant to offer specific guidance in cases won by plaintiffs who have been victims of educational malpractice. Most judges ask cognizant educational authorities to submit formal plans to their courts that indicate how the educational wrong-doing will be eliminated, thereby forcing plaintiffs and educational defendants to negotiate and agree upon suitable forms of future educational relief.

As a child of dedicated African-American educators, I know all too well that teachers are often blamed for educational problems that are beyond their capacity to control or repair, and it is with the utmost respect for conscientious educators that I would hope that teachers be given leading roles in finding solutions to eliminating potential or real sources of malpractice in their midst. More top-down mandates from the federal government, or state government, or local governments, are unlikely to be as successful as grass-roots efforts by teachers who are enlisted in support of this cause. Physicians who are accused of malpractice usually answer to local review boards composed of their peers, who then determine appropriate "next steps" regarding allegations of professional neglect, incompetence, or misconduct. Educators could benefit from similar models, in contrast to the current external intervention that is often contentious. Greater teacher involvement is essential to the eradication of educational malpractice.

Although teacher review boards may be well suited to evaluate the conduct of fellow teachers, alternative procedures will need to be developed to monitor educational progress, and the delivery of education at taxpayer expense. Low income and language minority students represent an even more challenging population to protect from the possible ill effects of educational practices that fall beneath minimum thresholds of acceptable educational norms.

Because of the resourceful manner in which excellent educators continue to accomplish their Herculean tasks, I believe that educators also have the skill and potential to implement educational reforms, be they reforms to advance educational prospects for low-income and language minority students, or larger reforms that are applicable to every student. The potential exists for educators to play a leading role in professional malpractice reform that could be the envy of other professions that tend to resolve such conflicts through costly litigious expenditures of time and money, neither of which are in adequate supply to serve our national educational needs.

Notes

1. Support for this research was provided by Mr. Eugene M. Lang, Chairman Emeritus of the Board of Trustees of Swarthmore College, and the National Center for Postsecondary Information. Special thanks are due to Professors Joan Kelly Hall and William Eggington for their patience, encouragement, and support. I am, of course, responsible for any limitations in this chapter.
2. Our operational definition of minority students includes and exceeds federal definitions. Title VII funding is restricted to students for whom English is not native (ENN), but we also include students for whom "standard English" is not native (SENN). Many African Americans, Asian Americans, and others from low income backgrounds have learned nonstandard English natively; their education is enhanced when they learn standard English as a second dialect.
3. SEN students are identical to MUSE students, that is, within the United States. However, the linguistic divisions described here can be applied to other English-speaking speech communities beyond the United States.

Discussion Questions and Activities

1. Discuss the concept of educational malpractice as presented in this chapter. How useful a term do you think it is (or is not) for understanding what happens in schools? In your previous experiences as a student have you ever been a victim of educational malpractice or do you know someone who has? What were the consequences for you and/or the student(s)? the teacher?
2. In this chapter, the author argues that all students can be classified into three linguistic groups: SENN, SEN and ENN. How well does this grouping represent students from your own educational experiences? In what group would you place yourself? In small groups share your opinion about the usefulness of these distinctions for addressing linguistic diversity in schools.
3. How much do you know about the different dialects of the U.S.? Choose one dialect to research, and with a partner or small group, find out as much as you can about its linguistic and other features. You might begin by browsing the text, *Handbook of the Linguistic Atlas of the Middle and South Atlantic States* (Kretzschmar, 1993) or the web site: http://www.emich.edu/~linguist/regional.html. Share findings with your classmates, and discuss the attitudes that are commonly held toward users of these dialects. How might such attitudes affect the educational achievement of students who are speakers of these dialects?

4. Examine different texts that are used to teach English to non-native
    speakers in programs with which you are familiar, or in which you
    hope to teach. What dialects are represented? What implications are
    there for learners of English? How should instructors choose which
    linguistic features (e.g. pronunciation, vocabulary words, syntactic
    structures, etc.) to teach? Survey current teachers of English about the
    choices they make in their teaching, their reasons for their choices,
    and their attitudes toward different dialects.
5. Baugh ends his chapter with a call for innovative educational
    reforms. What are some current schooling practices for SENN and
    SEN students that you believe need to be changed, and why do you
    feel change is needed? Share your experiences, as either a student or
    teacher, with effective educational practices. How might they be
    implemented in an English language program with which you are
    familiar?

Chapter 7

Transforming the Politics of Schooling in the U.S.: A Model for Successful Academic Achievement for Language Minority Students

S. Wong

To understand the politics of schooling practices one must begin with the following question: Who traditionally has been denied an education and excluded from schools? Until the 20th century, education was almost exclusively the domain of the elite. Even today, denying access to literacy and education has been a means of keeping people—whether indigenous peoples, African slaves or their descendants, women, factory and farm workers, foreigners, the colonized, or non-Europeans—in their places.

Underlying the American dream of success is the perception that education is a great equalizer. However, the idea that public education provides equal opportunity for all is a myth. This myth is pervasive in current discourse concerning the politics of schooling. In chapters throughout this book many controversial public policies are presented. In the subtext of the debates over the politics of schooling (whether bilingual education or test scores, English only, Ebonics, or World Englishes) lies a resentful accusation that the non-European, darker-skinned immigrants of today are being given special treatment that previous generations, who worked hard, sacrificed, and "pulled themselves up by their bootstraps," were not afforded. Are the immigrants of today being "catered to" or "coddled" and receiving special treatment that previous generations were not? What is the history of the politics of schooling? Are the new immigrants holding on to their home languages and refusing to assimilate, leading to militant nationalism, separatism, and "Balkanization"? Is there a gap between the academic achievement of immigrants today and those of previous generations? This chapter will explore the disparity between the myth and the reality of the politics of schooling in the U.S. It will discuss how educators in the field of Teaching English to Speakers of Other Languages (TESOL)/ Bilingual Education (BE) can reverse historic patterns of inequality, create new models to transform the politics of schooling, and support successful academic achievement for language minority students.

The Politics of Schooling: A Historical Perspective

American literature abounds with Horatio Alger stories of immigrants whose hard work, sacrifice, and *chutzpah* led from rags to riches. The myth of the American Dream of success lured generations of European immigrants to the port of New York City, Asian laborers to the gold mines and fields of California and Hawaii, and Latino workers to the railroads and industry in the Midwest. However, this American Dream of success never included the Africans who came to the shores of America as slaves and the indigenous people who populated the Pacific and Caribbean Islands and continent of North America prior to the arrival of the Europeans (Takaki, 1995).

A look at U.S. history reveals that from its inception, the United States was a multilingual nation (Wiley, 1996). First, there were thousands of indigenous languages. The struggle to preserve those languages before they became extinct is documented through the work of Franz Boas (1911) and other anthropological linguists. There are also records of missionaries who thought indigenous languages to be the "work of the Devil." They saw their mission of saving souls, "civilizing" indigenous people, promoting European culture, and teaching English to be closely intertwined. In Bureau of Indian Affairs boardinghouse schools, Indian children were taken away from their families and beaten for speaking their native languages.[1] The struggle to preserve indigenous languages continues today in Hawaii and through Indian-controlled schools on reservations (Leap, 1993; McLaughlin, 1994).

Another significant group that must be accounted for in the discussion of the politics of schooling is African Americans whose ancestors came as slaves in the early 17th century (Bennett, 1993). The Africans who came spoke a variety of languages, but these languages were forbidden and supressed. In the plantations of the South it was forbidden to teach slaves to read. It was forbidden because the slave owners knew that ignorance and lack of information would make it more difficult for slaves to run away. They feared the subversive character of literacy. Literacy and education could make slaves question their station in life. Acquiring literacy would enable slaves to develop critical thinking, to dream, to imagine a different life for their children. Like the history of many subjugated or marginalized groups, the history of slave literacy has been suppressed.[2]

African-American people's contributions to U.S. society, participation in history, and voices have been submerged in traditional textbooks. And yet there were slaves who learned to read. There is a record of slave literacy that is chronicled through slave narratives and African-American studies.

The first significant waves of immigrants from Asia were the Chinese (Takaki, 1990).[3] News of the California gold rush and the accompanying myth of the American Dream of success was spread to districts from the southern Chinese province of Kwangtung, who called California "Old Golden Mountain." While hundreds lost their lives building the railroads, the sad tales of those Chinese laborers who never made enough money to return to China to marry were overshadowed by the success stories of those few who returned to the villages to take brides. The news that Chinese were excluded from schools, were not allowed to testify in courts, had their homes burned down when they staked claims in the mines, were not allowed to own property, and were lynched in times of economic crisis never reached the villages. One can imagine how the myth of the American Dream was advanced in villages in Asia as middle-aged farm laborers who depended on others to write letters for them were presented in the villages by go-betweens as strong handsome, educated, and successful business men.

Asian-American contributions to the history of immigrant experience include the Japanese, who refer to the *Issei* (first generation), *Nisei* (second generation, the American-born children who along with their *Issei* parents were placed in the internment camps in World War 11), and *Sansei* (the third generation, who were a part of the "Asian-American" movement which emerged with the Third World Liberation Front Student Strikes at S.F. State and Berkeley in the late 60s). Korean Americans have contributed the term "generation and a half" to refer to the experience of being "not first generation and not second generation," being brought to the U.S. as children by their first-generation parents. Filipino men who came to work in the fields of Hawaii and the West Coast contributed to the development of the farm workers' movement. Miscegenation laws prevented them from marrying white women, and they were not allowed to go to school.

For Mexican Americans in the Southwest, the history of "immigration" begins with the land that was populated by the Aztecs, the Mayan, the Navajo, the Hopi, and other indigenous people and then conquered for Spain by Cortez. The story also begins with the history of the land that later became Mexico and still later became part of the U.S. through the Treaty of Guadeloupe Hidalgo in 1848 (Lima & Lima, 1998). This story includes the Mexican workers who were recruited to Chicago to build the railroads and to work in steel and the meat packing industries as early as 1916 and then, in times of economic crisis, were deported back to Mexico on the very railroad lines that they had built (Farr, 1994).

The formation of the Latino population continued with the Spanish American War and the territorial conquest of Puerto Rico and subsequent waves of immigration from Latin America and the Caribbean. While to the outsider the "Spanish-speaking" or Hispanic designation may seem to be the same, it includes many distinct regional dialects, nationalities, and ethnicities, as well as diverse racial, class, and historical experiences. The Cuban-American experience is very distinct from the Puerto Ricans'.[4] Lima and Lima (1998) point out that the official U.S. government racial-ethnic classification "Hispanic" can be seen as a response to the demands and political struggles of the Mexican Americans and the Puerto Ricans in the 60s:

> The State "recognition" of the role of the "Hispanics" in general in American life had the paradoxical result of creating a new invisibility for the *specific* demands of the *concrete* and *diverse* Mexican and Puerto Rican communities in the U.S. with their specific histories, questions and problems. (333)

The history of Latino "immigration" which continues to the present includes U.S. government expenditure of millions of dollars to fence and police the border, the *coyotes* who charge thousands of dollars to smuggle their human cargo, and the uncounted numbers of dehydrated bodies in the deserts that are never found. It also includes an immigration policy that uses "Braceros"—temporary farm laborers who have no rights to bring their families or to stay permanently in the U.S. and who have their permits revoked at the end of the season. Suerez-Orozco (1998) calls these "guest" workers "ghost" workers because they must materialize to do the dirtiest jobs for the upper classes at pay that no American-born worker would accept, yet they must remain invisible phantoms (voiceless and transparent), disappear, or be deported:

> When it became public knowledge that (California Governor) Pete Wilson and his wife had hired an "illegal alien" as a maid, his response was that he did not "remember her" and that he had "never seen her." (Suerez-Orozco, 1998: 301)

Interpreting rates of academic achievement for the descendants of enslaved, colonized, and indigenous people today cannot be separated from the historic patterns of denial of education and or use of schooling for subjugation. An a-historical view leads to blaming the victims of institutional inequity for low test scores and high drop-out rates, because they are genetically inferior, lacking in intelligence or motivation, or because they are morally deficient (lazy, untruthful, and devious).[5]

The Politics of Schooling: Social Stratification and Schools

To understand social stratification and schooling one must always be cognizant of the link between the history of exclusion and who is being excluded from education today. This section will discuss how differences in "tracking," "cultural capital," labeling, and bias in assessment lead to increased differences in the quality of education provided to children from diverse racial, linguistic, and cultural backgrounds.

Immigrants themselves cite "educational opportunities for their children" as one of the most important reasons they decided to leave their homelands to immigrate to the U.S. But in reality, how equal is public education? Jonathan Kozol (1991) in _Savage Inequalities_ points out that within the same school district there are different schools for the rich and the poor. Public schools in predominantly European-American, middle- and upper-middle class neighborhoods have state-of-the-art computer labs, manicured lawns, and well-equipped gymnasiums with clean locker rooms. Other public schools in poor neighborhoods for predominantly racial, linguistic, and cultural minority students have metal detectors, unsanitary and smelly toilets with no doors, leaky roofs and unsafe structures, outdated books, and no computers.

Tracking and social stratification

Tracking, in which students are assigned into different academic tracks or courses of study, assures that even if students from different socio-economic class backgrounds attend the same school, they get different programs. Children of higher economic status are disproportionately represented in the college preparatory academic courses and special programs for the gifted and talented. Working-class students and students from diverse racial, linguistic, and cultural backgrounds are disproportionately represented in secretarial, technical, industrial arts or shop, and special education courses.

Sociologists of education ask the question: Knowledge for whom? Is public education the great equalizer? Do public schools K-12 provide students of different races and language backgrounds an equal chance to graduate from high school? Are they given a foundation that prepares them for college? Sociologist Pierre Bourdieu conducted a study of the economic backgrounds of university students in France. His study found that few working-class students went to college (Bourdieu & Passeron, 1977). Bourdieu's study concluded that education _reproduced_ the inequities in society at large; that children of the more affluent were better served by education than the sons and daughters of poor and working people. He developed the concept of "cultural capital" that has generated interest among educators who want schools to be democratic equalizers. Understanding cultural capital can help us identify instances of systematic discrimination against students from poor and working-class backgrounds. Analysis of how schools work to maintain strati-fication is the first step towards developing institutional policies to transform them.

Public schools as they exist in the U.S. reproduce the inequities of soci-ety because the culture of schools reflects Western, European-American mainstream, middle-class or upper-class norms to assess student achieve-ment. Those who have "cultural capital" and are already a part of the culture of the school know the informal, unstated rules of the game. Consequently, they begin with a "head start." It is ironic that the com-pensatory preschool program for poor children is named "Head Start" because it is the upper-middle-class children with cultural capital who really have the "head start." Possessing cultural capital includes being read a thousand bedtime stories at home before entering kindergarten, being taken on vacations and to museums and zoos, and having toys that encourage construction and imaginative play.

Students with cultural capital speak the same language as their main-stream teachers. Students who speak minority languages or speak vari-eties of English such as African-American vernacular or World English speakers from Jamaica or Singapore speak in a way that is systematically not valued by the school (Smitherman & van Dijk, 1988). Systematic devaluing is reflected in tracking, labeling, linguistic and cultural deficit views, and bias in assessment and testing.

Labeling and linguistic and cultural deficit views

Reproduction of societal inequities is reflected in labeling. The term "Limited English Proficient" (LEP) is a negative label because it empha-sizes what second language learners cannot do and ignores the home lan-guage that they already know. The label not only stigmatizes students, marking them as different from the majority, but sets unfair expectations for rates of second language learning that are not applied to the majority monolingual students. When an Anglo child knows a few songs or colors in Spanish, it is seen as a great achievement, but when a Spanish-speaking child has made remarkable progress in second language learning, the standard she or he is measured by is the performance of the monolingual English child (Edelsky, 1991).

The label "at risk," which uses an infectious disease metaphor, places the blame for academic failure on the student. It ignores social and institutional policies which systematically allocate more educational resources (experienced teachers, better academic programs, buildings, computers, books) to schools for students whose families already have computers and books at home. School failure is a systematic problem whose locus should not be placed on the student but on the system (McDermott, 1987).

When a teacher says a child has "no language," the teacher is using a "cultural deficit label." The labels "culturally deprived" or "cultural or linguistic deficit" conceptually place the burden of academic failure not on institutional inequality in schools or the problems of poverty and economic deprivation, but on the students and their families' culture and language. Because linguistic stereotypes are subconscious, a teacher who is not trained in linguistics may not be able to identify the linguistic structure which triggered his or her reaction or even be conscious of his or her own linguistic bias (Luke, 1986). For example, a teacher may label a student who uses "double negatives" or who says "ain't" as lazy or ignorant. Sometimes a teacher may not be able to identify a different discourse structure or intonation pattern that marks a language minority student's speech, but merely gets a negative impression and labels the speaker as "rude" or "disrespectful."

Teachers' different expectations of discourse styles lead to communication mishaps in the classroom. For example, Michaels (1981) found that these differences caused white teachers to interrupt African-American children at inappropriate times during "sharing time" or to miss the entire point of an African-American child's story. In a related study European-American and African-American Harvard graduate students had widely divergent evaluations of an African-American girl's story about her grandmother. While African-American students found the story well formed, easy to understand and interesting, European-American students labeled the child's story as being "a terrible story, incoherent," suggested "family problems" or "emotional problems," and that the child "might have trouble reading if she doesn't understand what constitutes a story" (Cazden, 1988).

Negative labels lead to a downward self-fulfilling prophecy: teachers do not challenge students, students do not perform to high standards, and students are then tracked into non-academic, "watered-down" courses in which little learning takes place (Mehan, 1991).

Literacy is one of the most important measures of academic achievement. A vehicle used for tracking literacy both reflects social stratification and reproduces it. Social stratification begins in the first grade with students from the highest reading groups later being tracked into academic college preparatory courses in secondary schools and children from the lower reading groups later tracked into basic math and reading courses and industrial arts or technical classes. "Good readers" are guaranteed a place at the top, whereas "poor readers" have a greater chance of dropping out of school and are often blamed for their academic failure.

How are students assessed and divided into reading groups? Teachers evaluate children's ability using tests such as the Comprehensive Test of Basic Skills (CTBS), a standardized group-administered instrument, and the Woodcock Reading test (WRT), a standardized individual reading assessment measure. They also use informal inventories to assess emergent literacy such as letter and word recognition, familiarity with a title page or author, and knowledge of where books begin. Teachers without special training in assessing second-language reading proficiency may mistake lack of English proficiency for low intellectual ability (Grant, 1995). Teachers may mistake a child's fluent and "accentless" speech as an indication that the child no longer needs ESOL or BE and should be measured by native English-speaker norms (McLaughlin, 1992). In reality, it takes much more than two or three years to learn a second language (Collier, 1989).

After children are placed in the traditional three reading groups, they receive divergently different instruction. Those in the higher reading groups spend more time reading books and being given challenging materials and assignments while children in the lower reading groups spend time on the management of their behavior ("turn around, sit down, be quiet") rather than reading. Instead of having high expectations and working hard to challenge and motivate students, teachers use worksheets and provide a "watered down" version of the curriculum to children in the lowest reading groups. These patterns continue throughout school.

Testing and ESOL/bilingual students

ESOL teachers are constantly pulled between the requirement to "teach to the test" and the desire to prepare students for democratic citizenship, academic achievement, and a better future. In many institutions the politics of program support dictate that ESOL students must pass certain exams before they are allowed to pass to another grade, continue to study, or graduate. The trend towards state-wide testing in grades 3, 8, and 11 could have a negative impact on ESOL students if they are required to have a higher proficiency in English than their English speaking classmates are required to achieve in foreign language (French, German, or Spanish) proficiency exams. State-wide testing could lead to ESOL students receiving only certificates of attendance rather than being able to graduate from high school.

ESOL teachers have no choice but to do their best to help their students succeed in test-taking. At the same time, TESOL/BE professionals need to work within their institutions and through their professional associations and unions to influence which tests are used and how, and to develop appropriate instruments for second language learners that do not systematically disadvantage them. Advocacy is required to ensure that tests measure what they purport to measure: for example, that intelligence is not measured by English language proficiency or U.S. cultural knowledge to the exclusion of other languages and cultures (Cummins, 1986).

The patterns of tracking, labeling, and bias in assessment are systematic but not irreversible. ESOL/BE professionals can make a difference in the academic achievement of language minority students and the politics of schools. However, in order to transform patterns of inequality, it is important to understand how institutions operate and to work systematically to transform institutional policies and practices.

Changing Demographics: Challenges for the 21st Century

Of every 100 white kindergartners, 88 graduate from high school.
Of every 100 African-American kindergartners, 83 graduate from high school.
Of every 100 Latino kindergartners, 60 graduate from high school.
Of those same kindergartners, 25 whites, only 12 Blacks and 10 Latinos graduate from college.
Dr. W.E.B. DuBois said the problem of the 20th century is the color line. As we close this century, I think we can safely say that the problem of the 21st century will remain the color line, expanded in its definition by adding at least language and income.
David Hornbeck, Philadelphia Superintendent of Schools (1998)

In recent decades educational leadership has been raising serious questions about the changing demographics of the U.S. and its impact upon public education. English language learners from kindergarten to grade 12 have increased by almost 1 million in the U.S. during the last 10 years (August & Hakuta, 1997). At the same time, there are serious concerns about the academic achievement of racial, linguistic, and cultural minority students. According to a Congressionally mandated study (Moss & Puma, 1995), language minorities are particularly disadvantaged:

- They come from poor families and typically live in communities (mostly urban) with high concentrations of poverty.
- They receive lower grades, are judged by their teachers as having lower academic abilities, and have a higher drop-out rate.

Predictions are that by year 2050 European Americans will no longer be the majority in the U.S.; school districts across the country are becoming "majority-minority." The concept of a "minority" group will become obsolete; no group will form a majority (Garcia, 1994). If these predictions hold true, then the politics of education must be transformed to meet the needs of a diverse and potentially polarized future generation of "haves" and "have-nots."

Joe Lo Bianco (in press) refers to current institutional practices as *squandered bilingualism*: kindergarten children enter the school system speaking hundreds of languages and lose them by the time they leave school. As we enter the 21st century, skilled bilingual personnel are needed in every field and every profession. While school districts are charged with preparing students for democratic citizenship and participation in a global economy, many of the children who could be our future bilingual leaders are losing their home languages, losing respect for their parents, dropping out of school, and joining gangs. Their schooling has prepared them for nothing but dead-end, low-paying jobs at fast-food establishments. Is it no wonder that organized crime is able to attract and recruit young people? It is much more costly to keep a person locked up in prison than to keep that person in school. Yet a common response to crime is to lengthen sentences and build more prisons instead of schools.

A significant demographic trend is an *increase* in school-aged children living in poverty. Between 1980 and 1990 the number of poor school-age children increased by more than 400,000 to 7.6 million. Teachers can and must address poverty in their classrooms (Wong & Grant, 1995). Mainstream education colleagues may not be aware of the economic hardships and social pressures faced by their students. ESOL/BE educators must be advocates to raise awareness of their students' needs and economic realities. How can children learn if they are hungry, are working swing shift with their parents, or have severe dental problems? The economic and social conditions under which too many K-12 ESOL students live, the growing division between the "haves" and "have-nots," and increased racial, linguistic, and economic polarization are important challenges to the entire educational community.

Towards a Model for Transforming the Politics of Schooling

The first three sections of this chapter focused on the disparity between the myth and the reality of the politics of schooling in the U.S. by examining the following: (1) who was excluded from education historically; (2) the methods schools use to reproduce unequal power relationships in society such as tracking, labeling, and assessment; and (3) the changing demographics of increased linguistic diversity and poverty for

school-age children. This final section discusses the role TESOL/BE educators can play in transforming inequities in the politics and practices of
schooling and providing a model for the successful academic achievement of ESOL/Bilingual students.

The model includes three essential components for transforming the politics of schooling:

- Human resources: ESOL students, their families, and TESOL/BE
  professionals.
- Dialogic pedagogy.
- Curriculum for Democratic Citizenship, and Economic and
  Community Development.

The model of transformation must begin with human resources. (See
Figure 1: Human Resources.) Language minority students and their families, their home languages, and cultures bring a rich resource to other
students. Their diversity must be viewed as a *resource*, rather than a problem (Murray, 1992). The system of squandered bilingualism must be
replaced with a model of human resources that invests in linguistic and
cultural diversity, sees home languages and cultures as an asset, and sees
language minority students and their families as a precious resource.
In the global economy of the 21st century, bilingualism (and multilingualism) will not only be a valuable asset but a vital necessity. Bilingual
people are needed not only in education but every profession, including

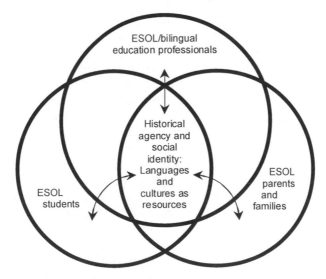

Figure 7.1 Human Resources
All figures in Chapter 7 designed by S. Teuben-Rowe

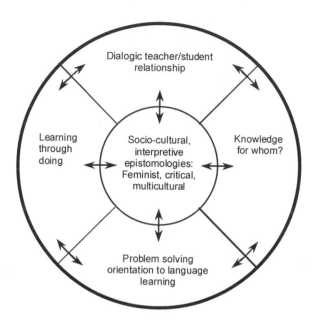

Figure 7.2 Dialogic Pedagogy

business, medicine, law, and engineering. In every academic field and profession, while English is an international language, knowledge of other international languages and intercultural communication is critical to overall success (Scollon & Scollon, 1995).

Central to developing human resources are creative partnerships between school districts and schools of education. Together they can identify community and school needs for bilingual personnel and then design a delivery system for on-the-job professional training to respond to the need. Priority must be placed on recruiting first-generation college students from diverse racial, linguistic, and cultural backgrounds. Research shows that partnerships between elementary, middle, and secondary schools and universities have been successful in increasing the numbers of minorities who graduate from high school and go on to college.

Colleges of education could attract skilled bilingual students by collecting data on the college's incoming students' foreign language proficiency (i.e. the future educational graduates of their programs—teachers, guidance counselors, administrators, educational researchers, and curriculum writers) and setting goals for student recruitment based on the needs of the school districts that colleges serve. Colleges could adopt the medical model of forgiving school loans in exchange for service in rural or inner city areas where there is a shortage of bilingual professionals. University–school district collaborative mentoring programs could train a whole new generation of bilingual professionals, community, and educational leaders, with cross-cultural sensitivities and community ties to new minority language communities.

Reversing history's wasteful use of human resources will require a tremendous reallocation of resources. Schools can *capitalize* on the multilingual resources represented by the hundred different languages spoken by incoming kindergarten children. Use of multilingual resources will not occur without a change in mission and educational leadership from the top. Successful minority recruitment requires creativity, planning, hard work, honest reporting, and evaluation. Professionals in TESOL/BE are in a unique position to advocate linguistic and cultural diversity because of their expertise in working with language minority students and their families. By including those who have been traditionally excluded, schools will not only be more culturally responsive to those who have been marginalized, but all students will have a stronger democratic, critical, and less ethnocentric knowledge base (Banks, 1993).

A second component of the model for transforming the politics of schooling is dialogic pedagogy.[6] (See Figure 2: Dialogic Pedagogy.) Paolo Freire, who used a dialogic approach to education in teaching Brazilian peasants how to read (1970), pioneered this component. In his approach, Freire was critical of "banking" models of education in which teachers "deposited" knowledge into students who were seen as passive receptacles. Freire's work in teaching adults literacy in their native language is invaluable in second language education in K-12 settings.[7]

As we see in Figure 2, the important feature of dialogic pedagogy is a teacher–student relationship that stresses mutual respect and dialogic sharing. Learning is both social and cultural (Vygotsky, 1978). Sociocultural approaches to the teacher–student relationship have used metaphors such as "apprenticeship" and "scaffolding" to investigate how children learn with the assistance of adults (Lantolf & Appel, 1994; Rogoff, 1990; Bruner, 1985). Language is not learned in isolation. Dialogic pedagogy facilitates expression of voices that have traditionally been excluded.

A second feature of dialogic pedagogy is its problem-solving orientation to language learning. Dialogic pedagogy encourages students to develop self-awareness of their language learning strategies and metacognitive processes, rather than reifying any particular set of material (i.e. vocabulary, grammar rules). It encourages an integrated approach to meaning, use, and form.

Third, dialogic pedagogy stresses learning through doing. Students learn and discover principles by applying them in real-life situations. Learning through doing encourages students to learn through observing, constructing, building, and designing. After engaging in activity, students reflect on their experiences through dialogue and writing, thus developing a reflective, self-critical attitude towards praxis (a dialectical process of theory, practice, and reflection).

Finally, dialogic pedagogy asks the question, "Who does knowledge serve?" Who is knowledge for? (Wong, 1993). Is it for the elite, for the privileged? Dialogic pedagogy serves the oppressed and the entire community rather than seeking the betterment of an individual alone. Dialogic pedagogy gives voice to those who have been previously silenced; it gives voice to new social identities (Norton, 1997) and new epistemologies (theories of knowledge or ways of knowing) that were not part of the traditional, male-centered, Western curriculum (Greene, 1988; Luke & Gore, 1992). By incorporating women's perspectives and cultures from Asia, Africa, the Americas, Australia, and the South Pacific, education is enriched and becomes more global.

A third component to the model for transforming the politics of schooling is a three-pronged curriculum that promotes successful academic achievement for (1) democratic citizenship, (2) economic development, and (3) community development. (See Figure 3: Curriculum for Successful Academic Achievement.)

The first prong of this curriculum for academic achievement is to prepare ESOL/BE students for democratic citizenship. Developing democratic citizenship may include helping middle and high school students, who are the future leaders of their communities, prepare for citizen tests. It may also include working with young American-born children who are the first in their families to become American citizens.

ESOL students or former ESOL students should be encouraged to develop their skills in public speaking and provide translation support for public meetings. ESOL curriculum that involves students in journalism and extracurricular activities such as student government and student clubs are important for democratic leadership training. An excellent example of ESOL student journalism from Montgomery County, Maryland, is Montgomery Blair High School's *The Silver International* sponsored by Mr. Joe Bellino.[8] Students tackle important topics (war, refugee experiences, poverty, and discrimination) as well as sports and student activities. ESOL student journalists learn much more than how to write an article. They also develop a sense of audience, voice, and community. They become student leaders in the process. Students also learn editing, layout, and desktop publishing, which is an asset in many lines

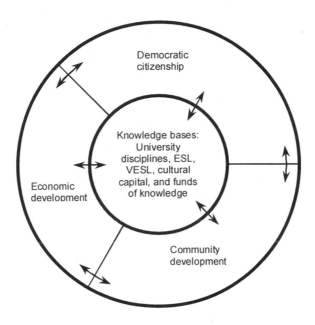

Figure 7.3 Curriculum for Successful Academic Achievement

of work including small businesses, corporations, non-profit organizations, and governmental agencies.

Curriculum projects in environmental justice, such as calling attention to toxic waste dumping in minority communities or workplace safety conditions, are important democratic issues that elementary ESOL students can tackle. Curriculum can include an investigative component, an advocacy component, and a community service component revolving around an issue such as a polluted area cleanup. By integrating dialogic pedagogy with curriculum for democratic and community development, ESOL students from K-12 can do something about poverty (Kempf, 1997). For example, students can work with children with special needs, make get well cards and visit the sick, perform for the elderly in rest homes, and create awareness about gender discrimination (McCormick, 1994); they can organize communities for change (Stephens, 1995).

The second prong of the curriculum for academic achievement is curriculum development to prepare ESOL/BE students for economic development. ESOL curriculum should help prepare students for skilled jobs in the global economy. High school Vocational English as a Second

Language (VESL) programs can involve partnerships between schools and businesses for economic enterprises. Curriculum development can include minority businesses developing projects that respond to local markets and niches. For example, there might be a market for fresh shitake mushrooms, around which a successful VESL agricultural program could be built. Air-conditioning repair, auto mechanics, or construction could all be outstanding VESL programs, depending on the interests of the ESOL students and professionals. A successful project for economics took place in Oakland, California. At the Oakland Airport, Castlemont High School students ran a specialty coffee stand that provided employment, invaluable on-the-job training, and business experience. The profit from the project was used by the school in two ways: as seed money for future student enterprises and as scholarships for students.[9]

The third and final prong of curriculum for successful academic achievement of ESOL/BE students is community development. Creating professional development schools, in which colleges of education work with school district schools for pre-service and in-service professional development, is an excellent way of developing ESOL/BE curriculum for community development. Some schools have social services, health clinics, and child-care programs on site. ESOL students of all ages can serve as student assistants or interns to those involved in the professional development school. Students can assist with translation and help social service providers serve the community in culturally responsive ways. For example, ESOL students grades 4-6 could help nutritionists investigate alternatives to dairy products for pregnant and nursing mothers who are not accustomed to drinking milk. High school ESOL students could help an AIDS prevention and treatment clinic do community outreach. Partnerships with local and national community organizations and civil rights groups could enhance the effectiveness of community development curriculum (McGroarty, 1998).

Curriculum to revitalize inner city communities could have a humanities and performing arts component. Research indicates that successful academic achievement for language minority students includes "more than just the basics" (August & Hakuta, 1997: 162). Drama, play writing, music, story telling, and multicultural literature are all important vehicles for community development and tap the strengths of ESOL/students and the emerging hybrid of mixed and hyphenated immigrant communities (Weinstein, in press).

Just as grocery stores in immigrant communities may cater to an African, Latin, or Caribbean cross-over market, ESOL/BE schools are a rich heteroglossic, diverse mix of ethnic culture and new identities in the U.S. Schools that incorporate the "funds of knowledge" from the community (Moll, 1990) are better able to revitalize communities and transform squandered resources into cultural capital.

One of the questions that continues to plague ESOL/BE professionals is: Why is there a lack of funding and support for ESOL/Bilingual programs, when the need for multilingual education is greater than ever? How can educational institutions respond to changing demographics when resources for programs that affect bilingual students are inadequate and the very existence of ESOL/Bilingual programs is threatened? To answer these questions, one must be mindful of the politics of schooling and how the history of exclusion and the patterns of tracking, labeling, and assessment impact public education. Without adequate funding and consistent support for ESOL/Bilingual programs, realizing the American Dream of economic prosperity and community involvement will not be a reality for most language minority students.

The intent of this chapter was to offer alternatives to the present dilemma that ESOL professionals and students face in the politics of schooling in U.S. society. Although the patterns of exclusion and inequality are systematic, the potential for ESOL/BE professionals to play a positive role is promising. Many ESOL/BE teachers were drawn to their field in the first place because of their commitment to internationalism, their respect for other people and other cultures, and their own experiences in language learning. Applied linguists and ESOL/BE educators have a history of advocacy and activism. Those who have lived in non-English speaking environments often have an empathy for language learners (either as English language learners themselves or as learners of other languages) and have a flexible multicultural orientation to problem solving.

Because of their experiences with people from diverse cultures, ESOL/BE educators can play a leadership role in designing pro-active models to support the learning of children and their families. They can forge new partnerships with community organizations with other professionals such as counselors, health care providers, nutritionists, social workers, law enforcement officials, and urban planners who see cultural and linguistic diversity as a resource and want to address the gap between the "haves" and "have-nots" through economic and community development (Boggs, 1998).

ESOL/Bilingual teachers can help mainstream teachers be more aware and responsive. They can help schools become more responsive to students and their families by insisting that schools get involved with the total life of the child. ESOL/BE educators can help other professionals be more aware of the need for translation and other language and cross-cultural issues. ESOL/BE educators and their students can serve as resources, for example, in identifying cultural and linguistic dimensions to community outreach and by recruiting leaders and active participants for school-community collaboration.

ESOL/BE professionals can also help develop curriculum for democratic citizenship and economic and community development that will enable students to succeed academically. Collaboration among ESOL/BE professionals in the development of content-based ESOL curriculum is a growing and important trend (Short, 1994). Research has shown that ESOL students succeed academically when teachers have high expectations of their students (Lucas *et al*, 1990), classroom practices reflect the cultural and linguistic background of students (Pease-Alvarez *et al*., 1991), parents are involved in education, (Delgado-Gaitan, 1990), and a supportive atmosphere exists for learning and strong leadership for school-wide change (Nieto, 1992).

Another important role for ESOL teachers within schools is to help ESOL students and their families have access to information; access to information is power. It may include ensuring that parents know that translation is available for important meetings or asking that information concerning college bound programs, summer enrichment, and after-school programs be translated. For ESOL teachers, advocacy often involves bridging cultural as well as linguistic barriers. For example, immigrant parents may be very concerned about the academic achievement of their children but, unlike upper-middle-class parents with cultural capital, may not "push" for their children to be in the classes with the best teachers (Wong & Teuben-Rowe, 1996).

ESOL/BE professionals may also find that they need to advocate for ESOL students to be eligible for academic programs and to have access to computers and school activities. For example, in some high schools, ESOL students are not eligible to take foreign language classes. In some middle schools, ESOL students are not eligible for magnet enrichment programs. Counselors may steer ESOL students away from college preparatory courses. Career days may not include language minority professional role models.

One of the most important lessons that ESOL/BE teachers can learn is how to use the resources around them to be effective social change agents. Often educators overlook the fact that ESOL students, their families, and ESOL professionals are a powerful human resource. With a concerted effort and a clear plan for transforming the politics of schooling, ESOL/BE professionals can replace the systems and structures of inequality with creative strategies of inclusion. By utilizing the dialogic approach and developing curriculum for democratic participation and economic and community development, ESOL professionals can create new spaces for change and develop new models for the successful academic achievement of language minority students.

Notes

1. Many deaf children in boarding schools were also physically punished for using American Sign Language.
2. Literacy for slaves was similar to literacy for oppressed people in other countries and other historical contexts. In teaching literacy to landless peasants in Brazil, Paolo Freire connected teaching of the "word" with the "world." In New Zealand, while the indigenous Mori initially were interested in learning to read English, once the missionaries developed a written form of the Mori language and translated the Bible into Mori, it was forbidden to let the Mori have access to written materials in English (Smith & Elley, 1997).
3. This historical sketch provides a few examples of exclusion from the author's family history. See Ronald Takaki's (1990) *Strangers from a Different Shore* for a comprehensive history of Asian Americans. See Don Nakanishi and Marsha Hirano-Nakanishi's (1983) *The Education of Asian and Pacific Americans: Historical Perspectives and Prescriptions for the Future* and Don Nakanishi and Tina Yamano Nishida's (1995) *The Asian American Educational Experience: A Sourcebook for Teachers and Students* for issues facing Asian Americans in education.
4. For a phenomenological investigation of being a generation and a half Cuban American see Maria del Carmen Torres-Queral's *Living on the hyphen: An exploration of the phenomenon of being Cuban-American.* Unpublished dissertation. The University of Maryland, College Park, 1998.
5. A classic example of academic discourse which blames the victim is Nathan Glazer and Patrick Moynihan's *Beyond the Melting Pot* (1963). Glazer and Moynihan compared rates of achievement of the American Dream for successive waves of immigrants to New York City. In comparing the Irish, Italians, Jews, and Puerto Ricans, which they contrasted to the African Americans, they attributed the lack of success of African Americans, not to the pervasiveness of racism or the history of involuntary slavery, but to the black matriarchy, a "deformed" family structure.
6. Dialogic pedagogy is also called critical pedagogy (Pennycook, 1994), critical literacy and participatory education, or participatory curriculum development.
7. For an in-depth treatment of participatory curriculum development in ESOL see Elsa Auerbach, Chapter Eight.
8. *The Silver International.* Published by Montgomery Blair High School ESOL students, 51 University Blvd. East, Silver Spring, MD 20901 (301) 649-2800. Joe Bellino, faculty sponsor: jbellino@mbhs.edu.
9. Personal communication with Jean Quan, Member of the Oakland Board of Education and Chair of the National Council of Urban Boards of Education.

Discussion Questions and Activities

1. How can teacher expectations make a difference in the achievement of language minority students? Are there "college bound" tracks and classes in schools in your area? How many ESOL/BE students are involved? How are labels like "LEP" a self-fulfilling prophecy? What

are labels that are used to refer to English language learners in schools in your area? What labels have you heard that are positive? What are some ways that ESOL/BE professionals can be advocates for ESOL students in their schools?

2. As ESOL teachers we have to "teach to the test," because it means life chances for our students. At the same time, because tests and systems of assessment are systematically biased against language minority students, we need to work to change the tests. Investigate the testing practices at a local school. How do they impact on language minority students at that school, in your district, your state? What are ESOL professionals doing to prepare students for the tests? What can ESOL professionals do to advocate for fairer testing and assessment in your local context?

3. What are examples of the effects of poverty on students in your area? What can/should you do? How do you address the problem of being poor in a school where some students are affluent? How do you address the problems of poverty in a mainly low-income school? What can elementary students do to address poverty? Middle school students? High school students?

4. How can ESOL teachers involve all students in participation in the democratic process? What are some issues that you would like to address with your students through a curriculum for democracy? How can collaborating with ESOL students and their families develop community and school leadership and support ESOL professionals' own leadership development? What can teachers do when they hear students make derogatory comments about other students who are "different"—stereotypic or derogatory comments about people who are religious minorities or racist, sexist, or homophobic comments?

5. Jonathon Kozol calls differences in funding per student allocated to public schools in poor communities and more affluent communities "savage inequalities." Labeling, tracking, and assessment policies also systematically discriminate against racial, linguistic, and cultural minority students. Other policies include who is identified for "gifted and talented" as opposed to "learning disabled," hiring, and assignments of experienced teachers. Make a list of other practices that are part of the patterns of inequity. What can ESOL/BE professionals do to address these inequities and transform schools? What kinds of innovative and visionary curriculum could address community and economic development?

Additional Questions and Activities

1. How much do you know about bilingual education? What programs are available in your local schools? In schools around your state? To find out, contact your state department of education. Prepare a summary of your findings for your classmates. For national information, explore the web site of the National Clearinghouse for Bilingual Education at: http://www.ncbe.gwu.edu/

2. Discuss how English language teaching can be viewed on the one hand as social empowerment and, on the other, as cultural hegemony. What are the consequences of these views for you as a teacher of English? For your students?

3. Discuss specific ways in which and reasons why education can be considered one of the most successful ways of destroying or retarding language. Include specific examples from your own experiences. How might this be so for language minority children and adults in schools?

4. Name two methods of English teaching that you are familiar with. What are some underlying values and assumptions about teaching and learning embedded within them? Which sociocultural group(s) do they seem best suited for? Why? In general terms, how are teaching and learning sociocultural activities? How does the "exporting of methods of language teaching" occur? Give examples. What are some possible social, cultural or political consequences of the exportation of teaching methods?

5. Interview eight adult community members who are and eight members who are NOT associated with schooling (i.e. they are not administrators, teachers, or students) on their knowledge of and attitudes toward "bilingual education." Write a report of your findings that includes your reflections on their significance. How do the beliefs of each group compare to each other? To your own beliefs?

6. Participate in the daily school life of a student (any age, any grade, any program, from kindergarten to adult education) who is from a linguistic group that is different from yours. Spend at least 15 hours with this person, shadowing her or him through various school activities, interviewing her or him about her or his attitudes toward schooling. Keep a journal of your experiences, thoughts, observations, etc. Write a summary of what you learned about the person's culture(s), about the role of schooling in helping and/or hindering her or his academic progress, about your own attitudes toward working with those who differ from you and about some of the relevant issues related to linguistic diversity and schooling.

7. Gather curricular materials used in the English language program with which you are most familiar. What linguistic groups are most frequently represented in them? Provide examples from the materials. What are some implications for you as a student? As a teacher? For the students who use these materials? In your opinion which groups should be represented in English language textbooks? Why?
8. What are some schooling practices that you believe structure inequality (officially and unofficially) for linguistic minority students in educational institutions? How can teachers challenge harmful institutionalized language policies and still help students attain proficiency in standard English? How "doable" are they in the institutions with which you are most familiar?
9. In your opinion, what makes a language "standard"? "Non-standard"? Does what counts as a "standard" language vary across contexts or are there invariable features that make a language "standard"? How have notions of language standards changed over time, if, indeed, they have? Survey several teachers of different subject matters, different age groups, and different educational contexts on their perspectives of language standards. How do their perspectives compare? What implications can you draw from your findings for the education of language minority students?

Additional Reading and Resources

August, D. and Hakuta, K. (eds) (1998) *Educating Language-Minority Children.* Washington, D.C.: National Academy Press.

Bailey, G. and Manor, N. (1987) Decreolization? *Language in Society* 16, 449–473.

Baker, C. (1993) *Foundations of Bilingual Education and Bilingualism.* Clevedon: Multilingual Matters.

Baker, C. and Jones, S.P. (1998) *Encyclopedia of Bilingualism and Bilingual Education.* Clevedon, England: Multilingual Matters.

Brisk, M.E. (1998) *Bilingual Education: From Compensatory to Quality Schooling.* Mahwah, N.J.: Erlbaum.

Bull, B., Fruehing, R. and Chattergy, V. (1992) *The Ethics of Multicultural and Bilingual Education.* Teachers College Press.

Canagarajah, S. (in press) *Resistance in English Language Teaching: Ethnographies from the Periphery.* Oxford: Oxford University Press.

Chambers, J. (1983) (ed.) *Black English, Equity, and the Law.* Ann Arbor: Karoma Press.

Culhane, J. (1992) Reinvigorating educational malpractice claims: A representational focus. *Washington Law Review* 67 (2), 349–414.

Ferguson, C.A. and Heath, S.B. (1981) *Language in the U.S.A.* New York: Cambridge University Press.

Garcia, O. and Baker, C. (eds) *Policy and Practice in Bilingual Education.* Clevedon: Multilingual Matters.

Gee. J. (1990) *Social Linguistics and Literacies.* London: Falmer Press.

Hoover, M., Lewis, S., Politzer, R., Ford, J., McNair-Knox, F., Hicks, S. and William, D. (1996) Tests of African American English for teachers of bidialectal students. In R.L. Jones (ed.) *Handbook of Tests and Measurements for Black Populations*, 1 (pp. 367–381). Hampton, VA: Cobb and Henry Publishers.

Irujo, S. (1998) *Teaching Bilingual Children: Beliefs and Behaviors*. Boston: Heinle & Heinle Publishers.

Ladson-Billings, G. (1992) Culturally relevant teaching: The key to making multicultural education work. In C. Grant (ed.) *Research and Multicultural Teaching: From the Margins to the Mainstream*. London: Falmer Press.

Luke, A. (1986) Linguistic stereotypes, the divergent speaker and the teaching of literacy. *Journal of Curriculum Studies* 18 (4), 397–408.

Morgan, B (1998) *The ESL Classroom: Teaching, Critical Practice, and Community Development*. Toronto: University of Toronto Press.

Mufwene, S. (1994) *Africanism in Afro-American Language Varieties*. Athens: Georgia State University Press.

Omi, M. and Winant, H. (1986) *Racial Formation in the United States: From the 1960s to the 1980s*. New York: Routledge & Kegan Paul.

Pennycook, A. (ed.) (1999) Special issue: Critical approaches to TESOL. *TESOL Quarterly* 33 (3).

Sadker, M. and Sadker, D. (1994) *Failing at Fairness: How Our Schools Cheat Girls*. New York: Simon and Schuster.

Serpell, R. (1997) Literacy connections between school and home: How should we evaluate them? *Journal of Literacy Research* 29 (4), 587–616.

Weinstein, G. (in press) (ed.) *Learners' Lives as Curriculum: Six Journeys to Immigrant Literacy*. McHenry, IL: Center for Applied Linguistics/Delta Books.

Section 3
Possibilities for Action

Having considered the various social, cultural, and political dimensions of the teaching of English as an additional language in Sections One and Two, in the chapters in Section Three we move into discussions on possibilities and opportunities for action not just in classrooms but in other professional contexts as well.

In Chapter Eight, Auerbach lays out a particular approach to English language teaching that incorporates the principles of "participatory pedagogy." After first defining such terms as "participatory," "teacher-centered," and "learner-centered," Auerbach discusses the six principles constituting her approach as well as both the contextual and pedagogical conditions for learning that must be considered in the design of a participatory learning community. In the discussion she presents a number of creative ways for building a non-traditional learning environment in the classroom. The role of the language teacher in such an environment, Auerbach claims, is not to solve problems. Rather it is to pose problems and facilitate critical reflection and, in doing so, use both the challenges of and obstacles to the creation of participatory communities as possibilities for growth for themselves as well as for the students.

Chapter Nine is also concerned with reflective practice, but turns our attention on to teacher practice. Here Cutri examines the spiritual moral dimensions of classroom language policies and makes the case that spiritual morality can—indeed must—play a role in the education of teachers of language minority students. After first defining and comparing "secular morality" to "spiritual morality," Cutri provides a detailed description of the characteristics of a spiritual moral approach to understanding classroom policies and practices. In light of these characteristics, she discusses the significant role that teacher beliefs play in creating conditions for learning in their classrooms. Only by articulating their beliefs and becoming engaged in a spiritual morality, Cutri argues, can teachers fully acknowledge, understand, and become involved in the social, economic, and spiritual interdependency of people in a diverse democracy.

Chapter Ten takes us to a discussion of language teacher preparation programs. Here, Grabe, Stoller, and Tardy outline the disciplinary foundations of what they call an "applied linguistics" approach to English language teacher preparation. The first part of the chapter contains descriptions of the major elements of four disciplines that the authors argue provide key resources for the preparation of language teachers: linguistics, psychology, anthropology, and education. In the second half of the chapter they present a case study in which they examine the reflections of a graduate of an English language teaching program on the usefulness of her studies to her teaching. While they do not explicitly address the social, cultural, or political dimensions of teacher preparation knowledge, they create the possibility for readers to do so.

In Chapter Eleven, the final chapter of this section, Forhan and Scheraga provide a fairly detailed plan of what can be considered "practical professional knowledge," i.e. what one needs to know in order to be an informed, active citizen of his or her professional community. As part of the plan they define advocacy and present a strongly argued rationale for "getting involved." Throughout the chapter they present a variety of ideas for action, several of which are illustrated with examples of activities in which they or their colleagues have been involved. While they do not ignore the difficulties that can arise, Forhan and Scheraga do not dwell on them. Rather teachers are urged to actively pursue the myriad possibilities and opportunities for "making a difference" in theirs and others' professional lives.

Chapter 8

Creating Participatory Learning Communities: Paradoxes and Possibilities

E.R. Auerbach

Before reading this chapter, take a few minutes to jot down your ideas about these questions:

- *What do you think makes a classroom participatory? What would an ideal participatory learning community look like? What characterizes it and how would you achieve it?*
- *What are obstacles to creating participatory learning communities?*
- *What do the terms "teacher-centered" and "learner-centered" mean to you? In your view, how (if at all) do they relate to the notion of participatory education?*
- *Now think about real second language classrooms in which you have been a student, teacher, or observer. How was that classroom similar to or different from the models you described above? Why was it different? How were goals set? How was content selected? How were classroom processes determined? How was learning evaluated?*

After you've considered these questions individually for a few minutes, discuss and compare your responses as a group. You may want to list the responses on a blackboard for future reference. What are some of the issues that this discussion raises for you?

My guess is that there is a full range of responses to each of these questions within your groups. In terms of the first question, the range probably includes those who see participatory learning as active student participation in classroom activities, others who see it as student involvement in curriculum development, and still others who see it as action for social change. Regarding the second question, I would guess that some of you see learner-centered pedagogy as being closely linked with participatory learning, while others may have been uncomfortable with the question itself. In any case, I would bet that debate about this question was heated—that your values surfaced quickly as you discussed it. In terms of the third question, my guess is that there was quite a divergence between the ideal you described and the realities you have experienced.

This chapter will present my views on these questions based on 15 years of practice as an ESOL teacher and teacher educator primarily in adult ESOL and literacy contexts. What I say should be taken as just that—one person's views based on one set of experiences and inter-actions in one set of contexts. As you will see, I think each of us needs to arrive at our own stance through a combination of reflection and action in specific contexts, learning from what others have done (their theories, research, and practice) while at the same time developing, trying out, revising, and reflecting on our own experiences with our students. Thus, a key ingredient to developing a participatory learning community is being open to learning from our practice, from our students, and from our mistakes. Every context is different and every group is different.

But while I would say that there are no generic prescriptions for creat-ing participatory learning communities, I'm not ready to end this chapter quite yet: I do think there are several things that teachers need in order to work toward participatory learning communities. The first is a concep-tion or understanding of "participatory" and the rationale for fostering this kind of pedagogy. In essence this is an ideological stance. The second is an overview of a process for fostering a participatory learning commu-nity and a sense of the factors which will shape that process. The third is an understanding of how to respond to difficulties as they arise (which they inevitably will). In this chapter, I will present my own stance and outline some of the processes and practices that follow from it. My hope is that you will use this chapter as a tool in making your stance explicit (by resisting some aspects of what I say, questioning others, and hopefully sometimes agreeing). The process of making one's own stance explicit is critical because, whether we recognize it or not, it will inevitably guide classroom decisions.

Defining Terms: What Is Participatory Pedagogy?

To me, the teacher is a central driving force in creating a participatory community. If you were one of the people who said that a participa-tory community is learner-centered, this may seem like a contradiction: how can the teacher's role be central in learner-centered pedagogy? I would go so far as to say the opposition between learner- and teacher-centered pedagogies is a false one: all classrooms are "teacher-centered" to the extent that it is the teacher's conception of education that shapes how the learning community develops. Clearly teachers have their own goals, their own understandings of effective L2 pedagogy, and, most importantly, they have power. To deny this is both irresponsible and disingenuous: students know it and teachers act on it whether or not they acknowledge it. The real question is how teachers use this power and why they use it the way they do—what guides their decision-making. Thus, the first task of teachers is naming their stance; in what follows I present mine.

Even though I believe that "learner-centeredness" is a false construct, I think it is necessary to differentiate between the terms "participatory" and "learner-centered" because they are so often equated. In my view, these approaches are informed by different ideologies, have different goals, and lead to different classroom practices. The notion of learner-centeredness often stems from an ideology of self-actualization or individual empowerment. It is based on a view of Second Language Acquisition (SLA) that focuses on individual learners and their mental processes and ignores the social context of L2 acquisition and the relations of power in which it is embedded. Further, it assumes that learners know what they want and what is "best" for them, that giving learners choice is *in itself* empowering, and that the teacher should follow their lead. What often follows this view is the idea that learners can and should determine every aspect of curriculum development from setting their own goals to selecting content and learning processes to evaluating their own learning. In some cases, this conception of "participatory" gets reduced to "participation." The teacher's role in this view is to tailor curriculum to students' perceived needs. This is a view that can promote an ideology of individualism, and in some ways could even be said to work against community-building. In fact, as Toohey (1998) argues, individualizing practices can actually contribute to the construction of stratification and the perpetuation of inequalities within classroom communities.

An alternative view argues that participatory education is not just about greater learner participation, but about a particular kind of participation, namely participation as the practice of democracy. Originally developed in work with peasants and slum dwellers in Latin American, Asian, and African contexts, the key premise of this model is that marginalized people will be able to affect change in their lives only through critical reflection and collective action. Paulo Freire (1970), a key theorist of this approach, argues that both the content and processes of education can either reinforce or challenge the powerlessness of marginalized people. When the teacher is seen as the expert whose task is to transmit knowledge, to fill learners with new information or skills, and when their own knowledge is excluded, learners are left silenced and powerless.

Participatory education aims to empower learners by putting their experiences and knowledge at the center of the pedagogical process. The teacher's task is to draw out this knowledge and extend it with learners. Through dialogue and collective learning, learners gain a critical understanding of the social conditions that marginalize them; this understanding becomes the basis for strategizing for change.

As such, participatory pedagogy differs from learner-centered approaches in at least three ways: in its aims, in its view of the relationship between curriculum processes and content, and in its conception of teacher–learner roles. Where advocates of learner-centered education often posit learner involvement in curriculum processes as an end in itself, participatory educators see learner involvement as preparing them to challenge inequities in the broader society—to become active participants in making their world a better place. Curriculum content is critical in this struggle: it must come from and go back to the social context of learners' lives. Through dialogue, participants both validate their own knowledge and jointly construct an understanding of the social conditions that shape individual experiences. The curriculum emerges through a cyclical process of investigating the context of learners' lives, codifying critical themes from their lives into curriculum content, critically analyzing the themes, acquiring skills, taking action, and evaluating the whole process. In this view, content and process work together.

Because the struggle for a more just social order cannot be restricted to the struggle of individuals, participatory education posits transforming relations among learners and between learners and teachers. New roles inside the classroom lay the groundwork for challenging inequalities outside the classroom: through sharing and comparing experiences, reflecting critically on them, adding new knowledge, and developing collective strategies for change, learners move toward challenging the conditions that have left them powerless. Thus, the teacher has an active role in this process which is explicitly guided by an ideological stance. As Freire says:

> The teacher's authority… is indispensable to the development of the learner's freedom…. If my political-ideological belief is democratic, liberating,… the contradiction I experience with students' freedom is reconcilable…. That, however, does not mean that the educator stops being an educator and stops teaching or that the learner stops being a learner and stops learning. What the educator needs to do, if he or she is truly and coherently democratic is to "take good care" of his or her authority by exercising it. And the best way a teacher can take care of his or her authority is to respect the freedom of the students. (1996: 163–64)

So this is a wonderful paradox inherent in participatory pedagogy: accepting one's power as a teacher entails enabling students to exert their power. Once teachers come to realize that being a co-learner and accepting authority are not oppositional, the way is open for them to explore participatory learning. Explicitly articulating one's ideological stance and embracing one's authority as a teacher go hand in hand with fostering collective dialogue, mutual learning, and democratic decision-making among students. The central ingredient, as Bartolome argues, is political clarity on the teacher's part: "It is not the particular lesson or set of activities that prepares the student [for democratic participation]; rather, it is the teacher's politically clear education philosophy that underlies the varied methods and lesson/activities that she or he employs that make the difference" (1994: 179). The dance of teachers and students as they negotiate their respective goals, expectations, and understandings is central to participatory ESL.

Aiming High: Principles for Participatory Practice

Making the transition from participatory pedagogy as it has been conceptualized and practiced in Asia, Africa, and Latin America to ESOL pedagogy in English-dominant contexts is by no means a seamless process. Many questions arise: To what extent are the social conditions of ESOL learners similar to those of the "marginalized" with whom this approach was developed? Is the term "marginalized" even relevant in characterizing the social identities of ESOL learners? Is challenging marginalization an appropriate goal for ESOL? None of these questions has easy answers. On the one hand, it is important for teachers to recognize the danger of simplistically constructing all ESOL learners as "oppressed"; on the other, it is important to acknowledge the complexity of their identities as non-native speakers of English and the ways these identities may position them as outsiders. By virtue of sharing neither the culture nor the language of the dominant social groups, ESOL learners face challenges that make principles of participatory education particularly relevant for their language learning. My argument in this chapter is that exploring and building curriculum around those aspects of learners' realities that position them as outsiders can be a basis on which to construct participatory learning communities. The principles of participatory education for language learning that I think are most relevant are outlined here:

- *The starting point is the experience of the participants; their needs and concerns should be central to curriculum content.* For language education to be relevant, what goes on inside the classroom must relate to students' lives outside it; thus, the starting point is the concrete experience of the learners. Unlike other approaches where language forms and functions are the organizing principle, in a participatory approach, content is the core of curriculum development and the content revolves around critical social issues which learners are struggling with in their lives.

- *Everyone teaches, everyone learns.* Students are seen as experts on their own reality, and, as such, invited to believe in themselves. This means investigating, validating, and extending what they can and want to do rather than stressing what they cannot do or imposing what experts think they should be doing. The focus is on learners' strengths, not their inadequacies. The teacher is not the one with answers, but the one who facilitates students' discovery of their own answers, contributing his or her expertise while learning from the students' about their reality. As such, teachers are problem-posers, not problem-solvers.

- *Classroom processes are dialogical and collaborative.* The collective knowledge of participants develops through dialogue and sharing. The teacher catalyzes reflection on students' everyday reality. As concerns are identified, the teacher re-presents them to the class and guides students through an exploration process. This collective reflection de-personalizes problems, provides support, and becomes the basis for action.

- *Individual experience is linked to social analysis.* Participants look at their personal situations in light of each others' experiences, examining the causes for problematic conditions. Individual experiences are recontextualized. For example, learners talk not only about the difficulties of finding apartments, but why there is a housing shortage, why some landlords prefer to rent to immigrants and others prefer not to, as well as strategies for finding housing and challenging housing discrimination.

- *The acquisition of skills and information is contextualized.* Participatory education neither downplays nor overemphasizes skill-building; rather than being taught in isolation or as ends in themselves, skills and information are taught as a means in the process of addressing issues of importance to students. As skills and information are integrated with reflection and analysis, they become appropriated as new knowledge to be used in service of action for change.

- *The content goes back to the social context.* The goal of participatory education is to enable participants to critically understand their realities so they can make changes in their lives. This means that reality is not seen as static or immutable; learners can do more than adapt to it. Language learning is not the end in itself but rather a means for participants to shape their reality.

All this sounds great—lofty ideals for transformative classrooms! But, as anyone who has struggled to implement these ideals can tell you, putting participatory ESL into practice is not easy. Both teachers and students may have deeply ingrained beliefs that are at odds with the principles outlined here. Teachers may not know how to move toward participatory practices or may confront institutional and contextual obstacles that undermine their efforts. Ideal participatory classrooms probably do not actually exist; they are always in the process of becoming. What is important is a vision that takes into account the constraints and possibilities, and a sense of direction, with ideas for how to get from here to there. In the next sections, I will look at some of the factors that must be considered in negotiating constraints and possibilities.

Taking Stock: Contextual Factors

Classrooms do not exist in a vacuum; the possibilities within any classroom are shaped in important ways by factors outside of it. These contextual factors may be physical (like the location of the instructional site in relation to the learners' communities or its physical condition) or institutional (like funding, administration, curriculum mandates, or working conditions). They may include factors like the relation of the teacher to the learners' communities or the reasons that learners are participating in the program. Whether the site is accessible to learners (located within their community or on a bus route) and in a safe place may be critical in creating a cohesive learning community. Beyond physical accessibility and safety, however, the relationship of the institution/learning site to the learners' communities has important implications. How do learners see the institution? What are the power relations within the community and how is the institution positioned in relation to them?

Whether learning takes place in a church, a public school, a day care center, a community-based educational institution, a multiservice center, a union hall, or a workplace significantly shapes who participates, what their expectations are, and how they participate. It is often more convenient for staff to centralize classes in one location; it facilitates logistics (like photocopying) and means teachers do not have to transport books and materials. However, in adult education, turf is a critical issue for students, partly because of transportation (cost, distance, and time), partly because of effort (it is harder for students to mobilize themselves to do something difficult if they have to travel to an alien place), but mostly because of familiarity and comfort. Students with little prior education often feel like strangers in school settings. If they are on their own turf, students have one less reason for apprehension about learning. In addition, issues important to students will emerge more readily in an atmosphere where they feel a sense of ownership.

Several examples from literary projects in Boston illustrate this point: residents in a housing development wanted ESOL classes held within the development rather than at a learning center a few blocks away because they felt that the classes would be on their "turf" (even though the actual distance was the same). Participants in one family literacy project did not want to attend classes at the local public school because of negative associations with schooling and a sense of being outsiders at the school, while parents in another neighborhood did want to have classes located at their children's school because they felt it would give them a greater presence and increased power in the school. It was difficult to recruit literacy students to classes at an adult education site because the site was seen in the neighborhood as a "school" (and literacy students were intimidated about going to school); it was much easier to set up literacy classes at a multiservice center where community residents came for legal assistance, health care, etc., because the site was seen as a neighborhood center.

What happens in a workplace program can also be shaped by its physical location: locating an on-site program in the lunchroom where supervisors drop in and out may inhibit dialogue and authentic communication about workplace issues; alternatively, locating the program in a union-hall may influence who does or does not participate. A class in a well-furnished conference room or training center may send participants the message that their learning is valued; likewise, child-size chairs or classes in basements reinforce messages of marginalization.

Possibilities for collective action to address learners' concerns are shaped in turn by whether the learners come from a single community (neighborhood, workplace, and housing development) with a built-in organizational base or from disparate communities. Since content comes from the social context in a participatory approach, it is easier to find common issues if the students come from and work in an immediate shared context: issues relating to the community of the housing project are more likely to become content if classes take place there. For this reason, participatory learning communities often emerge not in educational settings, but in community development or political action contexts (e.g. women's organizations or tenants' rights groups). For example, tenant activists set up ESL classes when residents they were working with identified language needs in advocating for better housing conditions. The point here is that the possibilities within the classroom are shaped by external factors that should be taken into account in setting up programs and implementing them. It is critical to become familiar enough with the learners' community to know the significance of different places in their lives. This means being willing to be flexible and, if necessary, moving the location as you learn more about the community; sometimes you have to go to students instead of expecting them to come to you. Further, context and content can be linked to promote language acquisition once classes have been set up. For example, learners' sense of safety and comfort getting to a site or at a site can become content for dialogue and action as classes develop. In one class, students who were afraid to come to class at night set up a buddy system as a result of classroom dialogue about the issue.

Another contextual factor is the relationship between the teacher and the communities of the learners. Because participatory education starts with participants' experiences and social realities, it is helpful if teachers have some shared understanding of these experiences and realities. This means that the traditional notion of "expertise" is extended to include not just formal training in second language theories but cultural, linguistic, and social knowledge based on lived experience. Many participatory programs thus involve learners in the hiring process and sometimes hire teachers from "non-traditional" backgrounds who may not have formal credentialing, but who come from backgrounds similar to those of students.

The nature of institutional expectations and support also shapes pedagogy. What is the attitude of the learning site toward participatory learning, emergent curricula, and participant activism? Support for teachers, the amount of learning time, length of teaching cycles, pay, and funding are concrete factors that may facilitate or impede the creation of participatory learning communities. For example, funders may mandate a limited number of hours of instruction per week and a specified length of time that a student may participate in classes. Classes that meet for only a few hours a week for a few months undermine these possibilities: it takes time to gain trust, build confidence, redefine roles, and engage students. They may want to stay in the same class for several cycles precisely because the classroom has provided a supportive context for learning.

The question of who decides a program's goals is another key factor in determining its potential for moving in a participatory direction. Do funders concerned with welfare reform, job readiness, family literacy, or health issues determine goals? If, for example, students are only participating in order to receive benefits or if funders mandate a particular kind of content (e.g. preparation for minimum wage jobs), participant resistance may be an inevitable (and healthy) response. Whether the program aims to prepare students for particular roles in the social order or enables them to set their own agenda is critical: externally mandated curricula and predetermined outcomes work against negotiating goals and content with participants.

What these tendencies mean is that an aspect of creating participatory communities is advocating for the conditions that foster them. Teachers, like students, may need to become activists on their own behalf in order to create an environment in which participatory learning is possible. In some cases, becoming an activist means being involved in governance issues at the program level, and advocating student involvement in program governance as well. Teachers may need to strategize with other like-minded teachers and work with their students as allies. In other cases, this may mean going outside the program and taking up struggles that relate to policy. In Massachusetts, for example, adult educators and learners regularly lobby at the State House. This ongoing struggle to affect funding, working conditions, and governance is key in moving toward participatory learning communities.

Setting the Tone: Pedagogical Factors

Once entering the door of the classroom, introducing participatory learning may go against everything that students (and teachers) expect. ESL learners have their own ideas about what counts as language learning, and having a democratic classroom may not be one of them. They often expect rote learning and drill. To some extent classroom learning styles is an issue for any teacher who embraces communicative language teaching. However, when the approach advocates respecting learners and involving them in decision-making, the dilemma may seem even sharper. What is a responsive, non-traditional teacher to do if her students want traditional teaching? Or if her students say as one teacher reports, "The teacher should be like a President. In America, Democracy; in the classroom, no"? (Auerbach, in press). When students favor a traditional, teacher-directed classroom, it is important to remember that often they feel this way because it is the only model they have been exposed to; they do not know the alternatives. In order to address this dilemma we need to both respect student wishes (so as not to impose a model they are uncomfortable with—which, ironically, would reinforce a "teacher-knows-best" dynamic) and to give students experience with concrete alternatives as a basis for making informed choices. Thus, another paradox in participatory education is that in order to create a non-traditional learning context, it may be necessary to leave plenty of space for the traditional (wading rather than diving in).

A first step in this process of creating a participatory atmosphere is setting the tone—creating an atmosphere where students feel respected and comfortable. In this section, I'll briefly present some guidelines for setting the tone, listing strategies for making students feel that their ideas, experiences and knowledge are valued.[1] Of course, a delicate balance must be struck between inviting students to be open and respecting their privacy: it is important not to put them on the spot. Drawing students out without being invasive requires sensitivity on the teacher's part. Again, the purpose of participatory learning is not to get students to reveal personal information or problems, but rather, to find common social concerns. The sharing of experiences leads to a greater sense of the relationship and underlying commonalities between individual experiences.

The first "rule," thus, is never to ask direct, personal questions but to leave students a way out of talking about issues that are too loaded or sensitive for them. For example, a teacher might teach the phrase, "I'd rather not talk about that" early on. Another strategy is to start by asking questions in the third person, in an impersonal way (e.g. by showing pictures of newcomers and asking, "Why do you think *they* want to study English?"). Another useful phrase is "Do you know anyone who___?"; this allows students to talk about themselves behind the mask of talking about a third person. Teachers should allow space for non-participation and respect students' silence.

If teachers formulate and ask all the questions or set all the "rules," the traditional power relations of the classroom are reinforced. Letting students decide what they want to ask gives them some control to monitor the issue of invasiveness. For example, students can generate questions that they want to use to find out about each other. This simple modification of a traditional introduction activity allows them to determine what they feel comfortable about asking and answering. Likewise, students can explicitly formulate their own guidelines for handling personal information in class.

Another strategy for setting a tone of respect for learners' knowledge is immediately using student input as the basis for classwork. For example, after eliciting students' reasons for wanting to study English, the teacher can type them up as a class text with exercises for the next day's lesson.

It is important to be sensitive to the messages sent by physical arrangements—seating, wall décor, and equipment. Teachers can try varying seating arrangements (traditional teacher-fronted arrangements, circles, small groups, etc.) and invite students to reflect on the dynamics created by each. When possible, teachers can involve students in decorating the classroom. Explicitly analyzing the effect of variations in physical space with students and involving them in decisions will give them a sense of "turf" and control.

Lessons that elicit information about students' homelands (e.g. exercises which start "In my country …") are one of the most positive ways to develop students' sense of comfort. Simple grammar and vocabulary exercises that leave space for students to fill in information about their own cultures, beliefs, and practices can enhance classroom learning.

A misconception about problem-posing education is that it focuses only on heavy, loaded issues. Students want their classes to be fun, enjoyable, relaxing; teachers making sure there is time for talking about things that aren't "heavy" is critical. Teachers can set the tone by laughing at themselves and pointing out their own mistakes. Ironically, making room for what is not important creates the space for people to bring up what is important. Teachers bringing in pictures of their own families or talking about their own concerns (a baby who wakes up three times at night, problems with landlords, a flooded basement) can open the door for students to share their pictures and stories.

Students and teachers both need to feel safe in the classroom and often traditional roles are the most comfortable for everyone. Teachers can acknowledge students' expectations; teachers should not feel that they have to be constantly innovative, breaking the rules in every lesson. The key is not scrapping all the tried and true ways, while at the same time still taking risks. This means mixing traditional forms (grammar exercises, fill-in-the-blanks, etc.) with less familiar forms. Lessons can be set up so that the teacher provides a familiar structure, but content comes from the students.

The sharing of experiences can help students and teachers move from one model to another. Teachers can invite students to examine their feelings about learning methods, ranging from formal, in-school experiences, to informal, out-of-school learning. As students consider their past education, they develop an awareness of what did and did not work for them. One way to elicit this kind of dialogue is by using photos of differing learning contexts (formal and informal); students can discuss ways of learning and expand their view of what counts as education.[2] They can also write about their own memories of learning to read and write after reading published stories by others on these topics.

While good teaching always entails sensitivity to classroom dynamics (participant structures and turn-taking), traditionally the teacher is the one who tries to address problems when they arise (e.g. uneven participation by certain cultural groups, men doing most of the talking, and tensions around certain topics). In participatory education the issues are posed back to students as content for dialogue and language work so that they can be involved in noticing, analyzing, and addressing the issues. This can be done by inviting students to research issues: Who sits where? Do certain students always sit in the back? Why? Is there tension between particular groups? How often does each student talk? Do certain students or groups of students dominate? What would happen if different seating were tried? Bringing classroom issues back to students for discussion, reflection, and decision-making reinforces their sense of control and takes the teacher out of the position of authority.

Students can be invited to lead a class in which they teach others something that they are good at (hair braiding, cooking a national dish, and relaxation exercises). This role reversal serves several purposes: it provides an authentic context for communication; it causes students to think about what they know and are good at; it provides a forum for cultural sharing; it prompts a reconceptualization of who has knowledge in the classroom and promotes the exchange of knowledge; it invites students to think about what helps people to learn; and, it is fun.

Finally, students can be invited to critically analyze classroom activities and be asked to discuss which activities they enjoy, which they feel they learn most from, and what the advantages and disadvantages of different types of activities are. They can be invited to investigate the impact of different learning/teaching strategies (e.g. explicit correction vs. modeled corrections, grammar drill vs. content-based dialogue). Teachers do not need to uncritically tailor tasks to students' perceptions but rather use the evaluations as a way of fostering metacognitive awareness.

Scratching the Surface: Ways to Identify Issues for Curriculum Content

Because the content in a participatory approach centers on experiences of learners, the curriculum emerges through interaction with them. It is based not on needs assessment done before instruction begins but on collaborative investigation of critical issues affecting learners. In traditional models, students undergo some sort of assessment such as a test or interview that often aims to identify students' "needs." Needs are often defined in terms of deficiencies, skills or competencies that students lack, but which experts have determined are necessary to meet socially or institutionally defined standards. Participatory education problematizes this notion of needs assessment: rather than testing or measuring skills in relation to specified externally defined outcomes, teachers explore participants' strengths, interests, concerns, and expectations with them. Further, not only individual, but community issues are considered as well. Assessment is ongoing and integrated with instruction; it is a continual process of uncovering what is important to participants and connecting these issues to language instruction.

In participatory learning, teachers may face the following challenge: students may refuse to take authority, instead proclaiming, "You're the teacher—you decide." Two strategies that may be more productive in discovering relevant content are active listening and structured exercises designed to elicit student preoccupations, strengths, and interests. The most powerful way of finding students' concerns is being on the lookout for issues that emerge spontaneously. This means being tuned into the conversations that occur before and after class, changes in mood (when students appear distracted, unusually quiet, sad, or nervous), reasons for absences, and times when students suddenly burst into their first languages. Casual questions such as, "What made it hard for you to come to class yesterday?" can elicit information about problems that students are struggling with. Again, it is important to be sensitive about issues identified in this way: students may not feel comfortable about sharing them with the class; at the same time, however, what appears as an individual problem very often touches others in the class as well. In this case, the teacher's task is to find the underlying issue that can be generalized to others and to present it in a form that applies to the whole group without singling out the individual.[3]

Structured activities that create space for student input serve several functions. First, they satisfy students' desire for "real" lessons (as opposed to open-ended or spontaneous discussions). Second, they provide authentic contexts for English use, and third, they elicit issues in an indirect way. The following activities demonstrate how providing a concrete, powerful trigger or catalyst for student response works.

Presenting a published photo story of the life of an immigrant family often triggers animated responses. One especially useful text is a booklet called *Our History Book* that comes from *English at Work: A Tool Kit for Teachers* (Barndt, 1991); it is a simple but powerful model for students' own stories because it focuses on familiar issues.

Students can combine drawing and writing activities in describing their life journeys; this activity entails making a time line (or some kind of graphic representation) of the important events in one's life, discussing it with a partner and/or writing something about it. Again, this form leaves room for choice: some students may emphasize the graphic aspect while others may develop the writing.

Students can be invited to bring in an object that is important in their lives to share with classmates. These objects often prompt students to tell stories that are windows to their lives—who they were in their home countries, what is important to them, significant experiences. The fact that the exercise centers on a concrete and familiar object facilitates language use and often enhances proficiency.

Themes can also be elicited in the context of doing traditional-looking grammar activities. The advantage of these exercises is that they satisfy students' preconception of what they are supposed to do in class. A fill-in the blank or substitution format allows student content to be inserted in a controlled structure. _I need, I want, I like, I can, I can't_ charts can be used to elicit student concerns in the context of working on infinitives, gerunds, and modals. Simple present tense exercises combined with the vocabulary of feelings can provide a rich context for finding student responses to different situations.

Another way to integrate an ongoing system for finding themes is by instituting activities that occur on a regular basis each day or week. These can range from a daily ten minute period when students talk about anything they're thinking about to Monday reports on the activities of the weekend. Calling these "Good News/Bad News" can open the way for students to include not just social activities but also concerns and issues (Nash _et al._, 1992). Teachers can post newsprint on the wall for students to report ideas, events, or questions as a kind of posted journal. Newsletters can become reading texts, and writing activities can be evaluation tools.

One of the ways that needs and concerns can be identified with students is by encouraging them to become researchers of their own lives. This means that they ask questions, collect data from their environment, analyze and reflect on the data, and then decide what (if anything) to pursue. Specifically, when this kind of research focuses on language and literacy use in the home, community, and workplace, it can become both a needs assessment tool and a tool for finding themes. By carrying out investigations about daily life, students often identify issues of concern. Logs, charts, or lists are simple tools to guide research. Students can record things under the following topics: _everything that made you happy, sad, or angry in one day; every time you need to use English in one day; every time you had a problem using English in one day._ They might investigate language choice or language use—who uses which language with whom in various contexts or situations. In the process of exploring this question, themes about family dynamics and rules may emerge. Participants can investigate neighborhood issues using simple exercises like, "What do you see when you look out your window?" which, in turn, can prompt discussion of safety, crime, drugs, and play space for children.

Students can be asked to take pictures of significant places, things, or people in their lives as a way of identifying what's important to them. For example, students can take turns borrowing a camera and taking pictures of things that are important for their community. These pictures can become a catalyst for dialogue and student writing. Students can be asked to respond to photographs from sources like _National Geographic Magazine_, UNICEF calendars, or books with photos from their home countries.

Students can be given choices about what they want to respond to and asked minimally guiding questions such as, "What does this picture make you think of?" Photos that represent different angles of a similar situation can trigger critical analysis.

Asking students to draw maps of their communities indicating significant places is a way of identifying some of the social dynamics in their daily lives. A community map is a simplified drawing which shows sites like banks, schools, bars, parks, health centers, factories, bus stops, and laundries. After drawing these maps, students can discuss where they go often, where they never go, where they feel welcome, where they use English vs. their L1, who in their families go to which places and where students and their families would like to go. Issues about inclusion and exclusion, the challenges of getting around, their unmet needs in the community, and services that are or are not available may surface.

Readings can be used to elicit student reactions and related experiences or as models for students' own writing. Culture specific forms like proverbs or folktales are especially powerful in this regard because they are simple, familiar, and yet allow for rich interpretation. Texts by other learners can also be a catalyst for student writings.

Themes can also emerge from student writing, either unexpectedly or as a result of a catalyst activity. Journals are an important way to get a sense of what is happening in students' lives. Open-ended quick writing exercises can also lead to the uncovering of themes. They might be asked to write about something that is making it difficult for them to do their homework, something they dream about, themselves five years ago, today, and in five years, etc.

The participatory process does not stop when students' concerns have been identified. Both what is learned (content) and how it is learned (processes) shape students' perceptions of their own possibilities and prepare them for particular ways of acting in the outside world. This means that the ways in which issues are explored must actively involve learners in bringing their own knowledge to the learning process. Of course, the kind of follow-up for any given theme will depend on an interaction between the teacher, the topic, and the students. What teachers need, thus, is not a set method or sequence of activities, but what Barndt (1991) calls a "tool kit" of techniques, procedures, and activities. The essence of the concept of tools is that students' experience can best be explored through the use of concrete representations of that experience that provide a focus for language work, dialogue, social analysis, and strategizing for change. As such, tools are much more than the traditional paper and pencil activities: they are often visual, non-verbal instruments that generate active responses, thinking, and dialogue.

The dual functions of tools—both developing language and exploring themes on a conceptual level—go hand in hand and cannot be divorced. If either aspect is ignored, the fundamental premise of a participatory approach to ESOL (that language/literacy instruction should help people to address issues and make changes) is undermined. If a meaningful issue is reduced to mechanical follow-up exercises that focus only on skills, the original motivation for working on language and literacy is lost. Students get the message that content from their lives has little value except as a pretext for language practice. By the same token, if issues are left at the level of discussion, and no explicit attention is paid to language work, students may feel that their linguistic needs are being ignored. Since for many talk does not count as legitimate language instruction, they may feel that they are not getting their money's worth. Thus, the tools structure the link between the development of language/literacy and analysis/action; they invite the kind of discussion which pushes people to think through complex issues and which challenges them both conceptually and linguistically.

Tools serve the additional function of providing a framework for increasing student participation in curriculum development. As students feel more comfortable, they become increasingly involved in the process of producing materials themselves; teacher-created tools become models for student-created tools. Thus, the use of tools may move from published materials to teacher-produced materials (e.g. codes or teacher-written texts), materials collaboratively produced by teachers and students (e.g. language experience stories), and student-produced materials (writings, photo-stories, videos, etc.).[4] The students' role in the production of materials may become increasingly active as they become more comfortable with changing roles.

An example of the development of a participatory learning community that developed through the exploration of a powerful theme in learners' lives is documented in Kathy Boudin's article, "Participatory literacy education behind bars: AIDS opens the door" (1993). She writes about the transition from a decontextualized, skills-based literacy curriculum to a curriculum in which incarcerated women explored the issue of AIDS through reading, vocabulary work, writing, and eventually the production of a video. In this case, the tool, the video, was a context for the development of participants' literacy and critical reflection, as well as becoming a vehicle for education and dialogue among the wider prison population. As such, the participatory process resulted in a concrete action beyond the classroom.

Use of the first language in the ESOL classroom provides one example of how an issue arising from the teaching context can become content around which to develop both critical thinking and language. Use of students' first languages can be a source of tension among both teachers and students. Teachers often hold the belief that "English Only" should be the rule in ESL instruction. They may be torn between demanding that students use English as much as possible and realizing that students often are most engaged when they are able to express their ideas in their L1 or help each other through use of the L1. Yet, when teachers allow L1 use, students themselves often react against it, seeing it as exclusionary in mixed language groups or an impediment to learning. Tensions between students may arise, with some feeling that it wastes time or creates bad feelings, and others seeing it as a necessary support. These dilemmas, in turn, lead back to the question of the teacher's role: should teachers make rules about language use and enforce them? Because the underlying issue is not just a pedagogical one, but an ideological one as well, I would argue that what's critical in addressing them is not so much the decision that ultimately gets made but rather the process for making the decision. As Freire (1970) suggests, central to acquiring the skills and confidence for claiming more power outside the classroom is a shift of power inside the classroom.

But asking students their opinions is not enough; this does little to extend their capacity to analyze the issues. I think the key here is creating a context that enables them to make informed, critical decisions. What this means is that the arguments (both for and against L1 use) need to be addressed with learners. For example, the teacher can write a dialogue in which students disagree about whether L1 use should be permitted in an ESOL class. Then, through a series of structured questions, the teacher can draw out participants' opinions about the functions of L1 use. They can move from simplistic "yes" or "no" positions to more nuanced ones which look at the conditions and contexts in which L1 use is and is not productive and why. Certainly, teachers can contribute their own knowledge and opinions in these exchanges, but what is important is a shift toward critical understanding and shared authority. Students can learn to structure arguments, provide evidence, and, depending on the level, may write essays to support their stances. Through this kind of analysis, students can arrive at their own rules for language use in the classroom. The teacher moves from being a problem-solver or arbiter of tensions to a problem-poser or facilitator of critical reflection. The pedagogical bonus is that students develop metacognitive awareness of language learning strategies; the classroom management bonus is that it takes the teacher off the hot seat. Most importantly, students gain a greater sense of control over their own learning. This process can model a way of addressing other issues of classroom dynamics as well as issues from students' lives outside the classroom.

Embracing the Challenges: It Ain't Easy

The question of language use is only one of the seemingly endless dilemmas that teachers who aspire to creating participatory learning communities face. There are always tensions, reversions to traditional roles, struggles about how to deal with hot topics, and conflicting political analyses or goals. There is a never-ending stream of questions: How can we engage in critical analysis with "low level" students? Is it ethical to promote critical analysis? What if students are not interested in social change? What if students in the group have differing concerns and there don't seem to be common themes? In fact, these teaching issues never really cease: whenever we answer one question, another pops up. We never seem to "arrive" in this process. But, the fact that participatory classrooms are always in the process of becoming may actually be good news: struggling with these questions and challenges keeps teachers watching, listening, experimenting, reflecting, and reinventing our practice. The bottom line is that learning has to be ongoing and collaborative for teachers as well as learners. Three key factors provide the fuel for this process of creating participatory learning communities.

The first is making space for student resistance—inviting students to express their discomforts either with the content or the processes of instruction. The surest way to make any theme or activity wither on the vine is to impose one's own analysis or to expect unanimity of response. It is critical to expect and welcome resistances to what you (as the powerful teacher) are orchestrating—including resistances to participatory learning itself. Once resistances have been named, they can become the object of collaborative reflection and dialogue. These resistances provide a window on student experience, a forum for dialogue about learning strategies, a context for analysis of social and pedagogical issues, and a guide for subsequent curriculum development. The point is that the resistances yield rich insight and content for both students and teachers.

A second factor in keeping the participatory fires going is embracing a stance of inquiry. Because participatory curriculum development aims to be responsive and emergent, it demands that teachers investigate their practice and learners' contributions in an ongoing way. This process is fully congruent with current perspectives on professional development which maintain that effective teaching is not achieved through the implementation of a teaching technology but rather through critical responsiveness to learners. Training in specific classroom methods, behaviors, or techniques in itself does not prepare teachers for the complex reality of the classroom; it is the ability to discover needs and decide how to act on them that makes good teachers. Thus, what teachers need is not a prescription for what to do and how to do it, but rather investigative skills and a framework for making decisions (Gebhard *et al.*, 1990). This framework can best be developed in the context of dialogue and analysis with a community of knowledgeable peers.

Thus, a third factor in creating participatory learning communities is insuring that you are part of your own community of like-minded teachers. Teachers, like students, need a context in which to see their individual experiences as part of a larger whole, to recontextualize them: this means finding allies, other practitioners with whom you can share problems, strategies, successes, fears, joys, and challenges. Some of my graduate students, for example, have continued to meet on a regular basis after getting their degrees so that they can maintain a sense of community and sustain the vision they developed while in school. This is critical not only for support, but also for growth: through articulating issues arising from practice and inviting dialogue about them, teachers can gain a deeper understanding of classroom dynamics, develop new teaching strategies, and work together to address common problems that may arise from institutional or political contexts. If teachers come from the same workplace, they may take up challenges related to working conditions (like, for example, asking for paid teacher development time in which to learn from each other).

As I have reread this chapter, it struck me how often I talked about contradictions, challenges, ironies, and paradoxes: it seemed that I kept coming back to the ways in which participatory education seems to trip over itself and to confront its opposites. I started by talking about the perspective that participatory pedagogy does not mean fostering participation for its own sake. I went on to talk about the need to accept one's authority as a teacher by respecting and fostering students' authority. I then said that the reality is that ideal participatory classrooms never really exist; they are always in the process of becoming. In the section on pedagogy, I argued that in order to create a non-traditional learning context, it may be necessary to leave plenty of space for the traditional. I went on to talk about the need to be careful not to silence students while at the same time respecting their silence, as well as the need to find ways into student experience while also leaving students *ways* out of talking about their experience. I noted that not over-emphasizing important issues can allow important issues to emerge. I argued that the challenges or obstacles in building participatory communities are exactly what makes them move forward and grow. I talked about inviting resistances to participatory education as part of the participatory process. So this is what I have learned in writing this chapter: the ways that participatory pedagogy seems to demand space for its opposite may actually be the most critical factor in creating participatory learning communities. These paradoxes are not something to be feared or wished away: they are to be expected and even welcomed!

Notes

1. Further explanations and examples can be found in *Talking Shop* (Nash *et al.*, 1992) and *Making Meaning, Making Change* (Auerbach, 1992).
2. See "Learning Pictures,"*Talking Shop* (Nash *et al.*, 1992) for fuller descriptions.
3. An example of finding curriculum content through this kind of conscious listening can be found in "Barbara and Ana," *Talking Shop* (Nash *et al.*, 1992).
4. Detailed descriptions and examples of tools can be found in Chapter Five of *Making Meaning, Making Change* (Auerbach, 1992).

Discussion Questions and Activities

1. How does the author distinguish between "learner-centered" and "participatory" pedagogy? Do you agree with her distinctions? Why or why not? What are your discomforts or questions about the participatory approach as it is characterized in this chapter? What aspects of this approach do you find useful? Why? Look back at what you said before reading this chapter. What would you add to, modify, or reassert after reading this chapter?
2. What kinds of approaches to additional language learning have you experienced as a language learner? A language teacher? What were the advantages? The disadvantages? How have your experiences shaped your beliefs about language pedagogy? Share your reflections with your classmates.
3. What do you see as missing from this chapter? What factors affecting participatory learning communities have been neglected or omitted? What else (beyond what is in this chapter) do you already do or could you imagine doing to create a participatory learning community?
4. Visit an English language program for adults in your community. Talk with as many instructors and students as you can to get a sense of their beliefs and assumptions about language learning. Ask one or two instructors if you can observe their classes. Write up a summary of your interviews and a description of your observations to share with your classmates. Based on the data collected from your interviews and observations, discuss the approaches to learning that are part of the program, as well as the social, communicative, and other consequences that appear to result from learners' participation in this program. How successful a program do you think it is? Make sure you substantiate your opinion!
5. This chapter addresses primarily English language programs for adults who are in subordinate positions in the U.S. socioeconomic context. To what extent or which aspects of this approach might

apply to other groups of learners (e.g. highly educated learners, children) or other contexts?

Chapter 9

Exploring the Spiritual Moral Dimensions of Teachers' Classroom Language Policies

R.M. Cutri

Political, empirical, and pedagogical efforts to equitably educate language minority students have not successfully curbed the anti-immigrant, anti-indigenous minority, and anti-bilingual/ESL education trend that persists as the 1990s draw to a close. This trend's consequences increase in light of demographic information indicating the growth of the language minority student population in the United States (Macias, 1999; Carrasquillo & Rodriguez, 1995; Chapa, 1990). Goodlad (1990a) asks the question: "To what lengths should teachers go to reach the diversity of students in their charge?" (23). Certainly, teaching is far more complex than it has ever been (Fenstermacher, 1990). Bull, Fruehling, and Chattergy (1992) describe the state of today's U.S. public education and assert that "the citizens of the United States are more uncertain than ever about what the ideal of unity in diversity should mean and about how our schools should help to achieve it" (3). On a daily basis, teachers in schools ranging from rural to urban settings teach today's diverse students and confront their personal role in how U.S. schools promote or hamper the ideal of unity in diversity.

The complexities involved in equitably educating language minority students exceed a strictly political or pedagogical level of policy making. These complexities raise ethical issues and involve the moral dimensions of teaching in a diverse democracy. However, policy makers, administrators, and teachers rarely consider the moral dimensions of bilingual/ESL education. Rather, policy makers and educators usually remain steadfastly focused on the technical aspects of education and programmatic debates about bilingual/ESL education (Palmer, 1998; Krashen, 1998). In this chapter, I push beyond the technical and programmatic foci and explore the spiritual moral dimensions of making classroom language policies. First I distinguish between a secular and a spiritual morality in schools and society. After developing the construct of the spiritual moral dimensions of bilingual/ESL education, I then examine the influence of teachers' beliefs on their individual classroom language policies. Finally, I explore how a spiritual morality can help teachers examine their beliefs and the moral dimensions of making classroom language policies.

Moral Dimensions of Bilingual/ESL Education

Mention of the words "moral" and "spiritual" demands that definitions of both concepts be established. In this section and the next, I offer a working definition of morality and examine versions of secular morality. In upcoming sections, I provide a working definition of spirituality and explore a spiritual morality. Writing about the moral dimensions of schooling in general, Goodlad, Soder, and Sirotnik (1990) center their understanding of what is moral in education around the issues of "professionalism in teaching," "the proper role and function of American public education," and "the inherent moral and ethical relationship between those who teach and those who are taught" (xi). Specifically addressing multicultural and bilingual education, Bull, Fruehling, and Chattergy (1992) define ethical issues in multicultural and bilingual education as considerations of what people should do:

> These are *ethical*, not factual questions. They ask what people *should* do from among the actions that the facts make possible—what responsibilities people have toward one another, what freedom they should exercise, how they should make decisions that affect themselves and others, what role tradition should have in people's lives. They demonstrate that the ideal of unity in diversity has a moral and not just a pragmatic meaning. (4)

I define the moral dimensions of bilingual/ESL education as relationships between diverse people in public education settings that are guided by a set of associated principles of equity. Principles of equity stress fair and appropriate treatment of all people. Equity thus differs from equality as its focus exceeds creating simple parity. This definition prepares us to explore the construct of a secular morality.

A secular morality

In the long run, all U.S. society will suffer economically and socially if the large population of language minority students in the United States does not adequately learn English and master academic content. This economic and social interrelatedness illustrates the secular moral dimensions of bilingual/ESL education in a diverse democracy (Cutri & Ferrin, 1999).

In other words, it is a secular morality motivated by utilitarian goals of a fair, well-functioning society. It is such social and ecomonic interdependency that can motivate all educational stakeholders (students, teachers, administrators, family, and community members) to recognize and accept their moral responsibility toward educating language minority students. An example of such social and economic interdependency recently motivated business communities to promote bilingualism because their co-operations faced shrinking pools of biliterate employees (Reveron, 1999). The business community isn't the only one to address issues of diversity as they relate to social and economic interdependency.

Contemporary educators, like their predecessors at the beginning of the century, turn to the secular moral dimensions of teaching in efforts to improve schooling and social conditions (Goodlad *et al.*, 1990; Banks, 1991; Zeichner, 1993; Haberman, 1995; Durkheim, 1961; Dewey, 1938; Counts, 1932). The schooling and social conditions they combat include today's inequitable distribution of wealth and disparate access to knowledge and education (Goodlad & Keating, 1994; Kozol, 1991). Contemporary secular moral approaches to urban and multicultural education are grounded in the secular morals of equity and social justice and the belief that improving schooling will contribute to improving society. These approaches emphasize the sociopolitical components of linguistic, cultural, and socio-economic difference, consider diversity a resource, and advocate examining and critiquing personal and institutionalized racism as a means of improving society and schooling. Contemporary conceptions of the secular moral dimensions of schooling in today's diverse society manifest themselves in different models of political morality.

Liberal scholars concerned with the diversity and social and economic interdependency of today's schools and society have turned for direction to various political models of moral decision making (Goodlad *et al.*, 1990; Darling-Hammond, 1997; Barber, 1997; Kozol, 1991; Bull *et al.*, 1992). Bull, Fruehling, and Chattergy (1992) define a political morality as an ethic that concerns the ways that societies make decisions and also asks what societies should do. Models of political morality address social and economic interdependency within a society. Different models of political morality are guided by different principles indicating the public good.

Critical pedagogy offers its own version of a political morality. Critical pedagogists call for rigorous intellectual engagement with issues of politics, oppression, and social justice. They summon teachers to identify the presence and implications of the historical, cultural, economic, and political factors that underlie their own beliefs, attitudes, and pedagogy and seek to radically transform society along more equitable lines (Giroux,

1992; Darder, 1991; Cummins, 1995; Wink & Almanzo, 1995). However, one must ask whether an intellectual commitment to this process is enough to sustain people through the messy and oftentimes painful course of establishing equitable schooling and social conditions for all people.

Though supportive of the goals of these various political models, I argue that by themselves these constructs do not sufficiently sustain people at profound emotional levels in their struggle to plan for language minority students' equitable education. Working for the equitable education of language minority students means contending with the strong tides of politics and emotions surrounding anti-immigrant, anti-minority, and anti-bilingual education movements. A secular moral commitment based on social and economic interdependency or based on an intellectual commitment to a political morality does not adequately motivate and sustain people. A spiritual morality offers another approach to language policy promoting equitable public education in a diverse democracy.

A spiritual morality

I define spirituality in educational settings as (1) a quality of personal reflectivity and acknowledgment of a power higher than one's self (Mayes, 1998), (2) a compassionate desire to connect with other people and one's self that contributes to a sense of a mission for a greater good (Palmer, 1998), (3) a motivating and sustaining force for social action (Wexler, 1996), and (4) a holistic consideration of people.

Mayes (1998) references Brown, Phillips, and Shapiro's (1976) integrative notion of four levels involved in teaching: the intrapersonal, which addresses feelings and self-concept; the interpersonal, which focuses on interrelations between teachers and students; the extrapersonal, which emphasizes critiques of the politics and economics involved in teaching; and the transpersonal. What is the transpersonal level? Mayes (1998) defines the transpersonal as

> the level of one's hopes (and fears) for oneself and others in a cosmic context. It is that ontological foundation of Being on which we build the meaning structures that scaffold our lives. It is, in short, what we ultimately live for and how we view ourselves *sub specie aeternitatis.* And finally it is (if we believe in such things) the transcendent goal of our pilgrimage on this planet. (Mayes, 1998: 6)

A secular morality based on social and economic interdependency and various models of political morality address the extrapersonal level of teaching, but they stop short of a transpersonal emphasis. Mayes (1998), however, suggests that a transpersonal commitment can form a durable foundation of one's commitment to a political cause. Similarly, a transpersonal commitment to equitably educating language minority students requires us to move beyond the relatively safe and comfortable parameters of seeking an exclusively secular morality. A commitment to bilingual education rooted in an overarching spiritual morality includes and energizes a critical awareness of political processes, social and economic interdependency, and social justice.

Scholars who acknowledge the spiritual dimensions of humans' participation in society and schooling insist that social and education theory must attend to these spiritual dimensions (Wexler, 1996; Purple & Shapiro, 1998; Palmer, 1993; West, 1990; Buber, 1965). Thus the morality they propose to guide teaching is not strictly secular. In this movement toward spirituality in social theory and education, the spiritual is conceived as motivating and strengthening social action (Wexler, 1996).

A moral commitment to bilingual education grounded in such spirituality has the potential to reach people in at least three ways. First, this type of ontological or spiritual morality can address individuals' desire for personal well-being by highlighting the interdependency of our society and economy. Second, by emphasizing the goal of social justice, a spiritual morality can activate people's sense of equity. And third, a spiritual morality can draw strength from spiritual motivation and commitment. The purpose of the remainder of this chapter is to explore the possibilities offered by a spiritual morality specifically in the context of teachers' individual classroom language policy decisions.

Teachers' Individual Classroom Language Policies and Beliefs

Language policy creation and implementation does not occur in a vacuum. Factors from various levels—federal, state, district, school—influence teachers' individual classroom policies regarding language diversity and interactions with language minority students. One crucial influence on teachers' individual policies and interactions are their own beliefs about language diversity and language minority students. Teacher credentialing agencies and researchers have begun to acknowledge the influence of teachers' beliefs and assumptions about language minority students on their interaction with them (Commission on Teacher Credentialing (CTC), State of California, 1992; August and Hakuta, 1997). California's multicultural/bilingual credentialing standards (the CLAD/BCLAD credentials) state that candidates must have adequate opportunities to learn and develop, in addition to other skills, the following:

Multicultural competencies to examine racism and to evaluate personal attitudes toward people of different cultural, linguistic, racial, ethnic, socio-economic backgrounds. (CTC, 1992)

Goodlad (1990b) also stresses the power of teachers' beliefs:

And because even sincere educational purpose can be corrupted by misguided beliefs about learning potential, our educators in this nation of minorities must also believe in the ability of all to learn; and they must hold steadfastly to this belief in their work. (44, italics in original)

However, such attention to how teachers' beliefs and attitudes influence their individual classroom language policies and interactions with language minority students is not widespread at either the pre-service or in-service levels of teacher education. Additionally, how to facilitate such examination of beliefs remains curricularly and pedagogically unclear. In the upcoming section of this chapter, I demonstrate how the construct of a spiritual morality can offer direction for belief examination, particularly in the context of teachers' individual classroom language policies. However, before pursuing this discussion, I must finish establishing a working definition of classroom language policy and orient our discussions within the literature on teachers' beliefs.

In the United States, language planning and policy decisions for educational settings take place at the federal, state, and local levels. These policy decisions involve issues such as primary and second language use, development, and/or maintenance as well as program models that facilitate these various goals. Federal policy impacting language in educational settings, such as Title VII of the Elementary and Secondary Education Act and Supreme Court decisions, set the tone at a national level. However, the U.S. Constitution delegates most educational decisions to the state level. Therefore, state policies regarding language use and instruction in educational settings are very influential. Districts and schools also determine policy for program models that impact primary and second language use, development, and/or maintenance. Ultimately, it is the teacher who implements federal, state, district, and/or school language policies at the classroom level.

Teachers' individual classroom language policy decisions occur in the context of presiding external policies. Their individual classroom policy decisions are also influenced by teachers' own beliefs and assumptions regarding language minority students, how second languages and content are learned, and the role of public education in a diverse democracy. Díaz-Rico and Weed (1995) describe teachers' individual language policy decisions as follows:

> Teachers have a significant influence over the daily life of students in their classrooms. They can actively create a climate of warmth and acceptance for language minority children, supporting the home language while fostering the growth of a second language. Conversely, they can allow policies of the school to benefit only the language majority students by accepting the exclusive use of the dominant language, and permitting majority language students to gain through the social and cultural reward system at the expense of those students who speak minority languages. This day-to-day influence and reaction of teachers amounts to a language policy. (261)

Díaz-Rico and Weed illustrate how teachers' language policy decisions at the classroom level involve both (1) the influence of their individual beliefs about language minority students and related issues and (2) their reactions to external policy guidelines and mandates.[1]

Within their discussion of the role of teachers in language planning and policy, Díaz-Rico and Weed describe another important characteristic of teachers' individual classroom policy decisions. First they acknowledge that language policy decisions occur both formally and informally, and they state that "the central idea of language planning is that actions and decisions are deliberate" (1995: 262). This type of deliberate decision making relates to the type of professional behavior that scholars assert must characterize teachers' practice (Goodlad *et al.*, 1990a; Goodlad,1990a; Teemant *et al.*, 1999). These scholars contend that in addition to making professional decisions deliberately, teachers must base their decisions on current knowledge bases and recognize the influence of their own beliefs and assumptions. The deliberateness with which teachers make classroom decisions corresponds to their ability to identify and articulate the knowledge base and beliefs that inform their decisions. However, most teachers are not able, nor are they educated, to perform the metacognitive tasks of identifying and articulating the rationales behind their classroom practice (Korthagen & Kessels, 1999).

Research on teachers' beliefs concludes that teachers indeed act on their beliefs, but usually cannot explicitly identify nor articulate those beliefs upon which they are acting (Richardson, 1997). Bullough and Gitlin help clarify this phenomenon with their distinction between "public theory" and "private theory." They define public theory as "expert talk" or that which is traditionally taught in teacher education programs as theories of education (1995: 3). Conversely, private theory is

> grounded experientially, and is represented by personal, idiosyncratic, biographically embedded, and often implicit concepts and understandings by which individuals make life meaningful. (3)

This private theory powerfully impacts teachers' policy and practice decisions, and, as Bullough and Gitlin define it, does not inherently lend itself to explicit articulation and identification of influences. Elaborating on the biographical component of private theory, Bullough and Gitlin explain:

> As a beginning teacher it is in good measure through you—and your values, beliefs, and knowledge of young people and about content and how to teach it—that students will either engage or disengage from learning. (14)

The influence of teachers' values, beliefs, and knowledge on whether or not students engage in learning is reminiscent of what Díaz-Rico and Weed describe as the impact of teachers' language policy on students in their classroom. Bullough and Gitlin (1995) and Díaz-Rico and Weed (1995) illustrate how teachers' beliefs influence their classroom policies and practices and consequently students' engagement or not with learning. Despite the insight and significance of these findings, the fact remains that most teachers do not articulate their private theory or identify and critique their beliefs and assumptions about language minority students. Now, let's examine the impact of unexamined teacher beliefs on classroom language policies.

Implications of unexamined beliefs for teachers' classroom language policies

Teachers who do not identify their fundamental beliefs about language minority students, how language and content are learned, and their role in public schooling in a diverse democracy often participate in standard schooling practices without examining them. In other words, teachers who do not examine their own beliefs often take schooling practices for granted and do not question their origins, but rather accept their appropriateness without much question (Sirotnik and Oakes, 1990). In this unquestioning mode, practices such as tracking, segregation, and over-identification of language minority students to special education programs become the acceptable, appropriate norm. Sirotnik and Oakes (1990) assert that in this unquestioning mode, teachers do not address essential moral dimensions of teaching. Questions promoting such moral inquiry might include: "Do I believe that these normative school practices are truly what is best for students?" Without engaging in such moral inquiry, teachers can assume that their classroom language policies simply reflect the appropriate status quo and have no significant moral implications.

In addition to evading the moral dimensions of teaching, teachers whose beliefs remain unexamined also leave themselves subject to forces they may or may not agree with. The first of these forces is their own un-examined beliefs and assumptions about language minority students. The majority of teachers sincerely care about the students under their stewardship and want to do the best things for them. However, many teachers are unfamiliar with language minority students and their needs and strengths. This lack of knowledge about language minority students and how best to teach them frustrates teachers and usually leads to either of two conclusions: (1) the teacher concludes that he or she is an inadequate teacher, or (2) the teacher concludes that there is something wrong with language minority students that is beyond a regular teacher's capabilities to deal with. The first conclusion may motivate the teacher to seek additional education, or it may result in resentment toward language minority students. The second conclusion compromises language minority students' access to content knowledge and language development by assuming that these students enter school with significant deficits preventing their learning. Both conclusions detrimentally affect students and teachers on affective/social and cognitive levels and inevitably impact classroom language policies. If teachers were to examine their own beliefs about language minority students and how language and content are learned, and then were to gather information on these topics, they would probably not reach these same conclusions.

Teachers who do not examine their fundamental beliefs about language minority students and who do not acquire information about educating language minority students also leave themselves open to forces of ever changing external policies. A historical review of federal bilingual/ESL education policy clearly demonstrates the disparity of approaches to bilingual/ESL education. For example, one set of amendments to the Title VII legislation supports native language instruction and the development of social and academic English skills (1984), and the next set of amendments, a mere four years later, does not (1988). This type of vacillation illustrates why Casanova (1995) poses the question: "Bilingual Education: Politics or Pedagogy?" (15). Such vacillation may not be as extreme in the state and local level policy changes, but oftentimes state and local policies do send teachers conflicting messages. For example, California's multicultural and bilingual teacher credentialing standards reflect the most current knowledge about how to best educate culturally and linguistically diverse students, but California's present restrictive state law regarding bilingual/ESL education contradicts some of the information teachers learn in their multicultural and bilingual credentialing process. These examples are not intended to imply that a solid knowledge base about how to best teach language minority students does not exist. Indeed it does (August & Hakuta, 1997; Thomas & Collier, 1997).

Rather, these examples demonstrate that this knowledge base does not always translate into policy decisions. Politics dominate bilingual/ESL education and often lead to unproductive "effectiveness" debates between program models or debates over related social issues (Crawford, 1995; Krashen, 1998).

Teachers whose fundamental beliefs about language minority students and the teaching of language remain unexamined may find themselves scrambling to meet the demands of whatever policy currently reigns. In this condition, teachers are either tossed to and fro in a sea of changing politics and policies, or they become recalcitrant and proceed with whatever classroom language policy and practice they have always used and consider policy mandates and research as fickle, unfounded intrusions. In either case, teachers are not encouraged to morally deliberate about their decisions regarding their classroom policies and practices with language minority students.

Using an informed knowledge base to examine your own beliefs and external policies and forming moral conclusions about your beliefs and external policies is not an easy or comfortable task. Most teachers are not trained to examine their own fundamental beliefs or to consider the moral dimensions of teaching (Richardson, 1997; Bullough and Gitlin, 1995; Goodlad, 1990b). Additionally, even if teachers are trained to do so, these tasks do not fall within most people's comfort zone of thought and action. Given these situations, it is not surprising that most teachers do not engage in these tasks on a regular basis. As a result, teachers' classroom language policies and practices usually remain unarticulated, uninformed by current knowledge bases, and devoid of moral deliberations. Teachers proceeding with such classroom language policies and practices should not be merely written off as unprofessional, uncaring individuals. Rather, as scholars and advocates for language minorities and teachers, we must challenge ourselves to figure out how to better engage teachers in these considerations.

A spiritual morality and teachers' classroom language policies

In an earlier section of this chapter, I described the characteristics of a spiritual morality. In this section, I revisit these characteristics and demonstrate how they can inform teachers' classroom language policies. I contend that considering the spiritual moral dimensions of bilingual/ESL education urges teachers to identify their fundamental beliefs about language minority students and related issues and supports their efforts.

Examining one's fundamental beliefs requires teachers to be personally engaged in their profession and reflective as opposed to remaining distant and objective. Most teachers, and most people for that matter, usually do not consider a person's intimate beliefs and private theories as appropriate topics for consideration by teachers or students in public school settings (hooks, 1994). Yet, the impact on language minority students of teachers not examining their fundamental beliefs nor their implications on their classroom language policies is too great to ignore.

Spirituality is also considered a taboo in traditional education. However, its potential to spark intimate and engaged reflection is great. Individuals' intimate beliefs usually remain private and unconnected to public concerns such as the education of language minority students. Explicitly considering the spiritual dimensions of one's profession inherently involves considering one's intimate beliefs.

In the section describing a spiritual morality, I identified three ways a spiritual morality engages people. I now revisit those three items and relate them specifically to teachers' individual classroom language policies. First, a spiritual morality highlights our interdependency as human beings participating in shared social and economic practices. Like a secular morality, a spiritual morality acknowledges the utilitarian dimensions of human relations. However, contemplating the spiritual nature of human beings can prompt individuals to consider human relations as having even more significance than purely utilitarian ends.

Considering the spiritual moral dimensions of working with language minority students may help teachers not only acknowledge the social and economic interdependencies they share with students, but also the essentially human experience that they share with them. Too often teachers who are overwhelmed and overworked slip into patterns of considering language minority students and their parents merely as demographic statistics and participants in various programs. This coping technique on the teachers' part may help them to feel less frustration and disappointment. However, this pattern also prevents teachers from experiencing the excitement, success, and personal growth that can come from working with and learning from culturally and linguistically diverse people. Individual classroom language policy that results from failing to consider the shared human experiences between teacher and language minority student will not promote cognitive, social/affective, or linguistic growth on the part of anyone involved.

Second, a spiritual morality can activate people's sense of equity. In secular terms, we often think of equity as synonymous with "justice, fairness, and impartiality" (Microsoft Word, 1998). Yet, a spiritual morality elevates the concerns of justice, fairness, and impartiality to another level. Within the context of a spiritual morality, justice includes elements of mercy, fairness takes on elements of grace, and impartiality is transformed into a compassionate consideration of multiple perspectives. Our secular definitions of mercy and grace connote pity and civil condescension, but those are not the connotations a spiritual morality elicits from these terms. Rather, the mercy and grace encouraged by a spiritual morality encompasses compassion, generosity, and humility. Teachers who consider equity in these terms develop individual classroom language policies that exceed a concern for teaching techniques aimed at efficiency alone. Certainly, these teachers still maintain high quality teaching techniques, but implement them with an intention and a demeaner characterized by clemency.

Third, a spiritual morality draws upon people's spiritual motivation and commitment to a cause, rather than only calling on their intellectual concerns. Developing and implementing individual classroom language policies respectful of the spiritual moral dimensions of bilingual/ESL education is difficult. These tasks often require teachers to modify or disregard altogether some of their previously held beliefs and assumptions regarding language minority students and schooling practices. Individual classroom language policies guided by a spiritual morality may come into direct conflict with external policies about bilingual/ESL education. Teachers facing peers, administrators, and community members not in agreement with them will need to articulate the rationale behind their classroom policies. These rationales must include not only reference to the ethics guiding their policies. Teachers must also be able to explain how their policies are supported by research on how children learn a second language and content.

Teachers basing their individual classroom language policies on a spiritual morality will need moral courage to carry out their efforts. Moral courage draws on sources beyond merely the intellectual or even emotional level. Moral courage originating from a spiritual morality harnesses the power of intellectual and emotional commitment and combines it with a source of resolution and duty.

Individual classroom language policies guided by a spiritual morality call upon teachers' intimate beliefs and private commitments while simultaneously connecting these beliefs and commitments to the public concern of equitably educating language minority students. This connection pushes beyond the realms of objectivism which Palmer (1998) defines as "fearful of both the knowing self and the thing known, distances self from world and deforms our relationships with our subjects, our students, and ourselves" (54). Classroom language policies based on a spiritual morality move beyond such fear and distance and allow teachers to acknowledge the humanity that pervades their relationships with language minority students. This acknowledgment of the humanity of both teachers and language minority students stresses the social, economic, and spiritual interdependency of people in a diverse democracy.

Notes

1. In their definition, Díaz-Rico and Weed obviously express their own opinions about what teachers' individual classroom language policies should promote.

Discussion Questions and Acitivities

1. Explain what Cutri means when she refers to the moral dimensions of bilingual/ESL education, and reflect on what the moral dimensions of bilingual/ESL education mean to you.
2. What are the characteristics of a secular morality and what are its limitations in Cutri's opinion?
3. What are the characteristics of a spiritual morality and what are some of its limitations in your opinion?
4. Identify at least two of your beliefs about language minority students and describe how these beliefs are reflected in your informal and formal classroom language policies.
5. Cutri argues that considering the spiritual moral dimensions of working with language minority students helps teachers to

    (1) recognize the interdependency and humanity that they share with their students,

    (2) activate their sense of equity, and

    (3) draw upon their spiritual and intellectual commitment to bilingual/ESL education as sources of moral courage.

    How do you think considering the spiritual moral dimensions of working with language minority students can help you to accomplish these things?

Chapter 10

Disciplinary Knowledge as a Foundation for Teacher Preparation

W. Grabe, F.L. Stoller and C. Tardy

Many teacher development programs have designated linguistics as the academic discipline underlying teacher preparation. We believe the development of language teachers through professional programs requires an applied linguistics perspective, rather than a "linguistics applied" approach. Unlike certain narrow definitions of applied linguistics (i.e. as some subset of linguistic theorizing), it is actually an interdisciplinary field that is practice based rather than theory driven. That is, applied linguistics seeks ways to resolve and improve upon language-based problems in real-world settings. Learning and teaching second languages represents one such setting. At issue, then, is how to use the resources of a range of disciplines to address learner difficulties in language classrooms and to enhance teaching practices.

This perspective on applied linguistics and language teacher development does not imply that applied linguistics is atheoretical. Rather, this orientation draws on relevant principles across a range of perspectives to solve language-based problems that are, for the most part, complex, involving people with their own skills and motivations in combination with distinct learning practices, social contexts, and multiparty interactional dynamics. No one set of disciplinary knowledge could possibly provide the resources to develop realistic solutions to problems encountered in language classrooms. Instead, applied linguistics and, by extension, teacher development programs, must draw on resources from disciplines beyond just linguistics to prepare future language teachers for the multidimensional challenges of the profession.

In discussions of the most important and relevant disciplinary knowledge, there is always the danger of generating a list of topics that covers dozens of fields and leaves the reader with only a vague sense of the direct impact and value that specific fields of knowledge provide to the teacher. We therefore limit our discussion to four disciplines—

linguistics, psychology, anthropology, and education—that contribute major disciplinary knowledge to teacher development. Because these fields are complex in nature, it is not our goal to provide a blueprint of each discipline in this chapter. Rather, in the sections to follow, we outline topics from these disciplines that create the foundation for active, reflective, critical, and adaptive teachers. We recognize, at the same time, that disciplinary knowledge cannot be packaged neatly; it is certainly not the case that a single set of disciplinary foundations, discussed in a single chapter, can be established that apply equally to all teachers. Thus, our goal is a more general one of proposing arguments for the types of knowledge that we think will support more thoughtful and reflective teachers, teachers who are better prepared to meet the varied needs of students in a wide range of instructional contexts. Although the disciplinary knowledge set forth below does not guarantee stellar language teachers, we believe that exemplary teachers are more likely to develop with this array of supporting knowledge. It should be noted, however, that novice teachers often question the relevance of so-called disciplinary knowledge (sometimes in the form of entire courses) that is not explicitly pedagogical in nature. It is therefore the responsibility of teacher educators to help prospective teachers understand the value of the disciplinary foundations presented here.

Disciplinary Knowledge: Linguistics

Linguistic knowledge is central for language teachers. Teachers need to understand how language provides both the means and the medium for learning and understanding. An informed teacher should be aware that (a) language serves communicative and social purposes; (b) language structure and form provide ways to shape communication effectively; (c) language processing abilities underlie all learning; (d) school-valued written language is quite distinct from informal spoken language (as well as informal written correspondence); and (e) language varies to reflect social, cultural, ethnic, and regional groups of speakers.

A field such as linguistics offers many competing views on the nature of language structure, its functions, and its patterns of variation; not all linguistic perspectives will be equally relevant for teachers, and it is the responsibility of teacher educators to promote the most relevant aspects of linguistics to prospective teachers rather than aspects that are most theoretically current (or of personal research interest). In this section, we discuss briefly five areas of linguistics that allow the language teacher to make informed reflective decisions about instructional curricula and learners' progress. These areas include descriptive grammar, phonology, sociolinguistics, discourse analysis, and psycholinguistics.

Most language teacher preparation programs today include at least one introductory syntax course, usually consisting of a basic introduction to transformational grammar or a more current version of generative grammar. In Great Britain, Canada, or Australia, students often become acquainted with systemic functional grammar as an alternative system. In either case, teachers-in-training often exit the course with little idea as to how such knowledge can be used for teaching or for understanding patterns of language use in the classroom. In both cases, theoretical formalism and terminology bury many potentially useful insights. Because both approaches focus on theoretically interesting systems rather than teaching the rules of usage alongside the structures of the language, prospective teachers often question the relevance of syntax courses for teacher development purposes.

Having said this, there is nonetheless a need for teachers to understand the forms and structures of language as a system and as social expectations. The teacher must move beyond native (or native-like) intuitions and understand

- how language structure works as choices within a system,
- how language structure constrains and opens up communications,
- how these constraints and opportunities vary in spoken and written language,
- how structures of language serve to control the flow of information,
- how structures and usage rules reflect social preferences and institutional expectations, and
- how language structures themselves are the medium for conveying all types of content knowledge in addition to language knowledge, and that the learning of such knowledge is usually assessed through these same language structures.

A teacher who does not understand these fundamental principles will not be able to engage students in ways that can lead to student autonomy, empowerment, and reflective awareness of their learning. Teachers who comprehend the role of language form in learning will be able, in contrast, to demystify the learning and evaluation process at cognitive and social levels.

Of course, to provide teachers with such an understanding of language form and structures is not an easy task. To be particularly meaningful, instruction and training must be centered around tasks and activities that reveal (a) the system's underlying language structures, (b) the options open to the language user to convey intended information most appropriately, (c) the impact of usage rules in terms of social evaluation of learning outcomes, and (d) the integration of language structure and language use for communicative purposes of all kinds. In addition, prospective teachers must learn to observe and evaluate these structures, uses, and options in pedagogical materials (e.g. textbooks) and in students' written and spoken language. Such an awareness, when transferred to students, genuinely provides the possibility for student empowerment and autonomy.

A second area of linguistics that provides teachers with resources for language instruction is phonology, the system of sounds used and recognized by speakers of a language. Phonology can enhance teachers' understanding and performance in a number of ways. Three areas in particular deserve comment: dialect variation, letter-sound correspondences for early reading, and pronunciation.

Descriptive articulatory phonology offers a basic explanation for the sounds used in a language and the phonological processes that generate dialect variation and changes in a language. Understanding how languages can change and how dialects vary in their phonological rules provides teachers with insights into the pronunciation patterns of learners in a classroom, as well as an explanation for the consistent difficulties that language students experience in speaking (and possibly in reading). Such knowledge for teachers reveals ways in which students from different dialect varieties of a language may be severely disadvantaged when they are asked to produce standardized, school-valued pronunciation—particularly when teachers are unaware of dialect influences—and, as a result, label students as learning disabled or in need of special education.

Language teachers, whether engaged in literacy or basic language skills instruction, benefit from some grounding in letter-sound correspondences, since students who are learning to read in an alphabetic language need to develop letter-sound correspondences to make the alphabetic system work. This ability involves matching the letter system to the sound system of the language. To do this effectively, both teachers and students need to know that the sound system in English is comprised of approximately 44 sounds that correspond to 26 letters and letter combinations. Phonics can be relatively ineffective in many classrooms because teachers begin with the letter and combination-of-letters systems, without ever presenting the system of sounds in the language that opens up the alphabetic principle. In many cases, teachers do not know how many phonological sounds exist in a language such as English.

Teachers of beginning second language students or students with pronunciation difficulties need to understand student problems that may stem from interference from first language (L1) sounds and processes, second language (L2) sounds or processes that do not exist in a student's L1, or some combination of phonological differences between the L1 and

L2 and a fossilization of pronunciation. Creative instructional practices that teach the phonological system to students depend on teachers' solid foundational knowledge of L2 phonology.

A third area of linguistics, sociolinguistics, provides many opportunities to make relevant connections to effective teaching practices and learner needs. Sociolinguistics, which is the study of how language varies systematically due to differing social contexts, raises teacher awareness of the patterns of language use observable in classroom settings and indicates social-context influences on learning and learner behavior. These insights can be incorporated into curriculum planning through projects and activities that promote cooperation, tap student expertise, and lead to critical awareness of the social force implied by differing ways of using language. Subtopics in sociolinguistics that support teacher development include dialect and register variation, social group variation in language use, communicative competence, literacy development, language and disadvantage, language policy and planning, and multilingualism. Space does not permit a detailed explanation of why these areas are included, but a few major themes are offered to indicate their relevance for teacher development.

Dialect and register variation raise awareness of how language varies due to both social group (based on ethnicity, social class, gender, age, religion, and so forth) and the setting in which language is used (e.g. in legal settings, doctor–patient interactions, social services interactions, and professional academic settings). The study of variation reveals that people use language in distinct ways depending on social influences, purposes for communication, and specific physical settings and interactants. Such knowledge is critically important in evaluating students' language needs, structuring lessons, and understanding how students perform and how well, or how poorly, they function in various instructional settings.

Other subfields of sociolinguistics—literacy development, language and disadvantage, language policy and planning, and multilingualism—provide informational resources that help teachers understand student backgrounds, curriculum policy decisions, the status of linguistic minorities, and the difficulties that many L2 students encounter when learning institution-valued literacy skills in a second language. These issues not only heighten teacher awareness of students' needs, but also empower teachers to initiate changes in policy and practice. For example, teachers can use knowledge based on sociolinguistics to change classroom practices to be more inclusive and to enhance student empowerment and learner autonomy.

The study of discourse analysis, sometimes seen as part of sociolinguistics, helps teachers understand the ways in which spoken and written discourse are used in classroom contexts (i.e. in classroom discourse). To appreciate the complexities of spoken discourse, prospective teachers should be introduced to conversational analysis, interlanguage pragmatics, and conversational style. Understanding how conversation can be structured, how interactions are influenced by cross-language contexts, and how individuals and social groups have differing styles of interaction all indicate ways that communication can be carried out in classroom settings, and why, or why not, spoken interaction assists instruction and student learning.

Through written discourse analysis, prospective teachers examine register variation among texts, genre differences in materials used in classes and created by students themselves, and the processes and products of student writing. Tools for examining written discourse allow both teachers and students to reflect on the ways that written language varies and is distinct from spoken language. They also help teachers and students grasp how written discourse is organized and structured to serve communicative purposes effectively, and when and why written communication may be relatively ineffective.

The study of classroom discourse illuminates discourse patterns that actually occur in classroom settings, including how teachers talk to (and with) students, how teachers structure the use of spoken language in the classroom, and how students interact with each other under varying conditions. Teachers can also explore the written texts that are used in classroom settings for learning purposes, for reference use, and for free reading. Understanding issues of text complexity, genre variation, informational flow, and learning from texts leads teachers to reflect on the role of written discourse in classroom contexts.

The key issue for studying spoken and written discourse is that prospective teachers learn how information is conveyed through textual organization and structure. The insights gained by teachers can be shared with students and explored as part of group projects and content-area reading and writing. Language students are then able to reflect on how language both conveys and, at the same time, structures information. Discourse analysis applied in this way empowers students to examine texts critically and to understand the role and impact of socially valued forms of knowledge.

Another linguistic subset, psycholinguistics, examines the cognitive processing of individuals. It offers fundamental insights into how language is understood, produced, and learned. Psycholinguistics explores issues of bilingual processing and acquisition, as well as cognitive aspects of second language acquisition. Psycholinguistics, when focused on teacher needs and instructional relevance, has much to offer to teachers, providing fundamental knowledge about learning processes, explaining how reading and writing abilities develop, and raising awareness of individual variation in learning.

Psycholinguistic research on language comprehension reveals how students learn to read and write, and points out the important roles of word recognition, working memory, text comprehension processes, and vocabulary. Research on language production processes reveals how students generate written texts and why they make spoken errors under rapid processing constraints. Of course, understanding how individuals learn their first and second languages is essential knowledge. For this reason, current second language acquisition research on task-based and content-based learning, and L1 research on learning from text comprehension, represent major sources of information with potential for teacher reflection.

Disciplinary Knowledge: Psychology

Aside from linguistic foundations for language teachers, there are important concepts and issues developed in psychology that offer insights into the learning process and its evaluation. From psychology, teachers can learn the role of motivation and attitudes in learning. They can also learn about the importance of individual learner differences; the various cognitive processes that learners engage when comprehending, using, and learning language; the ways that knowledge is learned, enhanced, stored, and used; and the differences between children and adult learners and between first and second language learning. Perhaps most importantly, psychological theories of learning offer perspectives on how students learn and what teachers can do to assist learning.

The field of psychology, particularly cognitive psychology, generates a number of topics and principles that have direct relevance for language instruction, curriculum planning, and teacher reflection. Research on basic cognitive processing highlights the abilities of the fluent language user, including purpose for processing, speed of processing, automaticity, working memory activity, inferencing, and comprehension formation. One relevant issue that emerges from this knowledge is how such an efficient system evolves for the L1 speaker and how such a system can be developed for the L2 learner. Many of the same issues arise when one considers the processing demands of bilingual language use.

A second major contribution from psychology centers on the role of motivation and attitudes as central criteria for learning. Recent discussions of motivation have focused on the role of intrinsic motivation—how it forms and contributes to learning. In addition to discussions of the roles of interest, self-esteem, and attributions for success and failure in learning, the recent research on optimal experiences, better known as the theory of "flow," offers new insights into language learning through its discussion of motivation, persistence, challenge, content complexity, goal specification, and opportunities for success. Its applications to educational contexts include curriculum planning, materials development, insights into student performance on learning tasks, and teacher reflection on student attitudes toward learning.

A third major area of psychology that informs teaching and learning is research on assessment in learning. Psychology is the source discipline for assessment and evaluation of performance outcomes, attitudes toward learning, and various alternative assessment procedures. Psychology typically focuses on issues related to the validity, reliability, and appropriacy of assessment practices.

A fourth key area of psychology is research on learning and learning theory. Psychological research presents essentially three complementary views on learning processes, each of which offers insights into language learning. Neo-Piagetian theories, Vygotskyan theories, and associationist learning theories all suggest important principles for learning and a reflective teacher would want to explore how curricula incorporate persuasive principles from each approach. One of the most interesting extensions from basic research on learning has been the development of research on expertise—how individuals learn to perform at high ability levels, whether at chess, in surgery, in sports, or in language use. Because learning a second language to a level of high proficiency can be viewed as a type of expertise, this field raises many interesting ideas for language learning, teacher reflection, and curriculum assessment.

Disciplinary Knowledge: Anthropology

Another disciplinary knowledge area, anthropology, offers complementary insights into the teaching–learning process by raising the awareness of cultural and social variations among groups of people and the miscommunications that can arise when different cultures and social groups meet. Among the field's most important contributions to teacher preparation are principles of communicative competence, cross-cultural communication, and the Whorfian hypothesis and linguistic relativity. The concepts associated with these areas can influence how teachers view their students and how well teaching methods respond to student needs. Anthropology (along with social psychology) can also introduce prospective teachers to the attitudes that people adopt with respect to other cultures and their expectations and assumptions about how others will perform.

The concept of communicative competence (not to be confused with communicative approaches to teaching) is of central importance to virtually all views on language teaching and student learning. Such a perspective on our abilities to use language effectively for a variety of purposes suggests a number of goals for any language curriculum, regardless of specific tasks and organizing principles. The theoretical notion of communicative competence has motivated not only instructional practice and curriculum efforts but also assessment practices. Language-specific aspects of communicative competence surface when one examines variation in language use across cultures and social groups.

Cross-cultural communication studies offer a number of insights into the efforts being made by students as they attempt to cope with not only new language knowledge, but also expectations for how to use the language knowledge appropriately in new cultural contexts. Patterns of successful communication and miscommunication point out sources of hidden differences between first and second languages. Such insights can help explain learning difficulties and can also be a source of instructional activities designed to help language students understand the subtle differences across languages.

A well-known hypothesis from anthropology (and from psychology more recently) that addresses issues in cross-cultural communication is the Whorfian hypothesis, which suggests (in stronger and weaker forms) that one's L1 constrains ways of thinking about events in the experiential world and leads persons using their L2 to express their perceptions of information and experiences within the categorical systems provided by the L1. Although described in various ways and commonly regarded as unimportant in many teacher development programs, this hypothesis has undergone a recent resurrection and is currently drawing considerable attention.

Disciplinary Knowledge: Education

In addition to anthropology, education offers insights into many of the same issues raised by psychology, although from different perspectives. Educational research explores learning theories, assessment practices, motivation and attitudes among learners, and teaching practices that result in effective learning. From a more pedagogical perspective, education offers teachers ideas for creating meaningful learning opportunities for students, innovating in classroom contexts, adapting instruction to meet learner needs, and developing lessons that reflect thoughtful syllabus planning and well-articulated curricular goals.

Two of the major supports provided by education involve curriculum design and needs analysis. An exposure to alternative curricula can help prospective teachers develop a critical awareness of the relative strengths and weaknesses of each type, and the ability to adapt different designs for diverse educational settings. Needs analysis, a central component for curriculum planning, represents an area of critical importance for language teachers. Although it is often the case that student needs are established from district and state guidelines rather than from direct assessment of student abilities and needs, teachers need to understand the interplay between district-mandated needs specifications and the ongoing needs analyses that teachers can conduct to fine-tune approaches to whole-class and individualized instruction. The juxtaposition of these two perspectives provides prospective teachers with many opportunities for questioning, reflection, and critical appraisal.

Two other important education-based notions are action research and innovation. Action research allows teachers to engage in systematic classroom-based inquiry to understand their own teaching practices and their students' learning processes. By means of an introduction to action research and associated procedures, prospective teachers are exposed to ideas for gathering and analyzing data, coming to manageable conclusions, and implementing change as a response to action research results. An exposure to innovation research, therefore, fits nicely with discussions of action research. Innovation research is an area that studies changes with positive outcomes. In educational contexts, innovations can involve improvements in areas such as teacher planning, teaching and assessment, tasks and assignments, student output, student collaboration, classroom management, and student engagement with text materials.

Educational research on effective instructional practices represents another area of importance for teacher development. Although much of this research does not address L2 students or L2 settings in particular, there are many concepts stemming from it that are relevant for L2 curriculum planning and classroom instruction. For example, the extensive work on reading strategies, vocabulary instruction, rereading activities, and extensive reading approaches all offer ideas for planning and adapting L2 reading courses.

A final set of notions that the field of education offers for L2 teacher development includes emphases on attitudes and motivation and perspectives on assessment practices. Although there is some overlap with work being done in psychology, in education these topics are explored more from the perspective of the practitioner. Thus, issues of student attitudes and motivation center less on understanding motivation per se and more on how to engage students, support their learning, develop their self-esteem, and build learner autonomy. Similar goals apply to assessment practices, especially with respect to alternative assessment approaches (e.g. the use of interviews, record keeping, observations of specific tasks and group activities, portfolios, project performances, and student self-reports).

Integration of Disciplinary Knowledge into Teacher Preparation Programs

To this point, we have examined four disciplines that provide key resources for language-teacher education. However, the simple integration of disciplinary foundations into teacher-education curricula is not sufficient for teacher-development purposes. Accordingly, we do not prescribe a single formula for the integration of this disciplinary knowledge into teacher preparation programs. Some of the topics introduced here may become the focus of a single course that explores one academic discipline and its implications for language teaching; other topics may be skillfully woven together in a Foundations of Language Teaching course that demonstrates the interconnections among the topics and their relevance for the language classroom. Whether these topics become the emphasis of one course or components of a set of courses is not important; what is more critical is the manner that disciplinary knowledge is presented to prospective teachers. Training programs should equip teachers with problem-solving capabilities enabling them to adapt disciplinary resources and concepts to match the needs of students in diverse educational settings. Teachers-in-training need to understand the value of the disciplinary knowledge presented and need to develop critical-thinking abilities to make informed decisions as they use these resources. For this reason, the disciplinary knowledge deemed important for teacher development must be seen as flexible and adaptable for many uses.

To provide a wider perspective on these issues, we include a case study of a teacher-in-training who successfully completed a master's degree (M.A.) program in Teaching English as a Second Language. At three points in her training, she reflected on the types of knowledge bases that were most helpful and why, for reflective teaching practices. The case study provides a practitioner perspective on the issues of disciplinary knowledge and offers insights into the processes of teacher education. The courses in which the subject was enrolled did not cover all the disciplinary knowledge presented earlier in this chapter however, we believe that the case study reveals interesting insights about the value of disciplinary knowledge.

The aim of the case study was to determine the extent to which the content from nine teacher-training courses (four pedagogically explicit methodology courses and five pedagogically implicit foundations courses) transferred to lesson planning and classroom teaching. The participant in the study (who will be called Kathe for the purposes of this discussion) was enrolled in a two-year M.A. program. Like some peers, the participant had had some English as a foreign language (EFL) experience before beginning her graduate course work, and she taught as a teaching assistant while enrolled in the graduate program.

The case study was initiated at the end of the Kathe's first year of graduate study, when she went abroad to teach EFL for the summer. The study continued when she returned to the university to complete her second and final year of graduate course work. The study commenced again three years after the subject had received her MA. By that time, she had completed three years in the workplace, teaching and developing courses and materials in an English for Specific Purposes program abroad.

The first stage of the study involved the identification of transferable content from five completed courses:

Methodology Courses	Foundations Courses
ESL Methods	Introduction to Linguistics
ESL Curricula/Materials Design	English Grammar
	Research Methods

After having completed these five courses, Kathe went abroad to teach a summer EFL course. During that time, data were collected by means of brief daily journal entries (entered by the participant herself) that documented content from one or more of the five completed training courses she had completed and used in planning and implementing her EFL lessons.

The second stage of the study occurred after Kathe had completed four additional courses:

Methodology Courses	Foundations Courses
Testing Language Skills	Second Language Acquisition
TESL Practicum	Sociolinguistics

In this stage of the study, data on transferable content were collected by means of a post hoc analysis of 19 weeks of detailed lesson plans that Kathe had designed and implemented for an English for Academic Purposes course that she had taught. She examined lesson plans to identify elements (i.e. teaching and assessment techniques, pedagogical approaches, concepts related to teaching and learning) that she perceived to be linked to content from the nine training courses that she had completed. It should be noted that the participant agreed to single out practices (in journal entries during the first stage of the study and in lesson plan analyses during the second stage of the study) that were new to her, stemming from graduate course exposure. Although some of the knowledge might have been implicitly understood beforehand, because of past educational and teaching experiences, it was assumed that specific entries were not understood in an explicit and reflective way before graduate course work.

The third stage of the study, three years later, involved Kathe's reflections on the extent to which her M.A. course work had impacted her teaching and professional development. Unlike the earlier stages of the study, during this stage she could not specify exact sources for her teaching actions and ideas with any degree of confidence. What she discovered was that most of her teaching-related activities, and corresponding decision making, represented an amalgamation of what she had learned from her M.A. courses, from classes she had taught while a graduate student, from experiences in her current job, and from colleagues, journals, and conferences. Kathe claimed that knowledge resulting from these different sources has given her the confidence to rationalize why and how she does things as a teacher, the security to make decisions as a teacher and course developer, and the ability to participate actively in the profession (e.g. giving presentations, writing articles, and carrying out research of her own). Because Kathe could no longer identify the graduate courses from which stemmed current classroom practices, what we report here are findings from the first two stages of the study.

An analysis of first- and second-stage case study data (i.e. journal entries and post-hoc lesson plan analyses) revealed that Kathe perceived that all nine training courses had some direct link to her teaching actions and decisions, although the amount and type of transferable content varied. As might be expected, the methodology courses had more direct links to actual teaching than the foundations courses. Yet, all nine courses contributed to Kathe's understanding of general teaching and learning principles and strategies. The majority of courses heightened her linguistic awareness in addition to her understanding of communicative competence. For the purposes of this chapter, we limit our discussion to the specifics of transferable content from the foundations courses only.

An analysis of data reveals that the introductory course in linguistics helped Kathe develop a more sophisticated understanding of language and L2 learner needs. Although they were not explicitly addressed in the course, she made logical extensions from course content to a variety of teaching and learning strategies. For example, from the unit on morphology, she gained insights into vocabulary teaching and learning strategies and felt confident designing vocabulary lessons that included an introduction to roots of words and affixes. From phonology and phonetics, she gained knowledge that assisted her in diagnosing students' pronunciation needs, designing lessons to introduce students to the manner and place of articulation of different English sounds, and giving students feedback on their oral performance. Likewise, knowledge of minimal pairs suggested the need to train L2 students in distinguishing between similar phonemes. From a unit on psycholinguistics, Kathe learned about the processes of learning to read and write and felt empowered to create meaningful reading and writing lessons and restructure lessons from mandated texts to assist students in developing their literacy skills. Her exposure to discourse analysis introduced her to the more abstract notion of discourse competence and the more concrete idea of using signals of discourse organization to teach writing. The introduction to interlanguage helped Kathe understand her students' performance and progress. Although the participant gained a greater understanding of English syntax from the English Grammar course (see below), she began to appreciate the complexities of language learning and teaching the Introduction to Linguistics course, where she was exposed to the notions of grammatical competence and other components of communicative competence (i.e. discourse, sociolinguistic, and strategic competence).

Although the focus of English Grammar was not strictly pedagogical, Kathe was able to draw connections between course content and actual classroom teaching, primarily in the area of grammatical competence. Upon completion of the course, she believed that she had a heightened understanding of English grammar (e.g. passives, conditionals, modals and auxiliaries, comparatives and superlatives, participles and gerunds, relative clauses), which allowed her to explain to students, for example, when to use English articles and when and why different tenses and aspects are used. In addition, she felt that she was better able to diagnose students' grammatical problems, provide meaningful feedback on students' written and spoken performance, and devise grammar exercises as a result of the course. Kathe also claims that part of her understanding of sociolinguistic competence (e.g. the relationship between modals and politeness) stemmed from this course.

Despite frequent debates among teachers-in-training regarding the applicability of research methodology to classroom teaching, journal entries and lesson plan analyses revealed that the participant was able to apply notions of research methods to her classroom teaching. Kathe attributed her confidence in operationalizing theoretical constructs for both teaching and assessment to the Research Methods course. In addition, she felt that she could better comprehend and benefit from published research, which could then be applied to classroom teaching. As an example, Kathe identified studies on register variation that examined characteristics unique to academic writing, lecture notes, and business telephone conversations as being particularly applicable to her teaching.

In the course on second language acquisition (SLA) in which Kathe was enrolled connections between course content and classroom teaching were rarely made explicit. Examples of transferable content from SLA, thus, are less tangible than the transferable content from, for example, Introduction to Linguistics. However, the participant was able to apply certain aspects of course content to teaching. In relation to general strategies for teaching and learning, she reported that she developed a deeper understanding of the role of motivation, attitude, and acculturation in language learning and was able to apply this knowledge to the classroom in a number of ways. For example, she understood that some, but not all, of her students' mistakes could be attributed to first language transfer and that students' progress in English could be related to their degree of exposure to and involvement with the L2 community. To address these concerns, the subject made a conscious effort to integrate meaningful in-class and out-of-class language-use opportunities into her instruction. In addition, course discussions on the dynamic state of interlanguage helped her understand why L2 student errors may disappear and then reappear and why the rates of student progress may fluctuate. Exposure to the concepts of monitoring and the affective filter helped her train students to monitor themselves while giving oral presentations, completing written assignments, and participating in teacher-student conferences.

The survey course in sociolinguistics influenced Kathe's teaching in a variety of ways, but the greatest impact was in the area of sociolinguistic competence. Exposure to sociolinguistic issues related to language variation, appropriacy, politeness, paralinguistics, body language, and conversational analysis raised her awareness of the need to address sociolinguistic competence in the classroom and the challenges that students face in their development. As a direct outcome of the course, the subject was able to introduce her students to conventions for communicating appropriately in various situations (e.g. a formal debate, an informal discussion, service encounters, a formal letter, an academic paper). In addition, she taught her students how to analyze their own conversational style in English (e.g. number of turns, ways of entering a conversation), how to understand the relationships between forms and functions of English speech acts (e.g. I'm sorry, excuse me, pardon me), and how to comprehend various sources of linguistic crosstalk (e.g. prosody, cultural taboo).

Although single case study findings like those summarized here are limited in their generalizability, this case study offers insights into the transferability of disciplinary foundations to lesson planning and teaching. Findings suggest that foundation courses contain content that transfers directly to lesson planning and teaching, although each training course is likely to influence a trainee's teaching in different ways and to varying extents. They also suggest that it is not necessary for courses to focus explicitly on pedagogical issues for them to be of value to trainees; rather, courses with a less explicit pedagogical focus can, in fact, be applicable to language teaching.[1]

Conclusion

In this chapter we have explored the types of disciplinary knowledge needed as a foundation for effective, informed, and reflective language teaching practices. We focused on the importance of knowledge from four academic disciplines—linguistics, psychology, anthropology, and education—and attempted to illustrate the ways in which that knowledge could prepare prospective teachers for the challenges of the language-teaching profession. Although most teacher-education programs do not currently integrate all the topics presented here into their curricula, many have interspersed much of this knowledge into the various courses that make up their teacher-education programs. Unfortunately, it is this disciplinary knowledge that many teachers-in-training are most resistant to. Teacher educators must strive to help new language professionals understand the value of this knowledge and the critical role it will play in making sound pedagogical decisions, planning classes, developing materials, delivering instruction, evaluating student progress, and conducting meaningful action-research projects to improve one's teaching. Language teaching, as anyone who has been in the classroom knows, is a complex endeavor. It is our strong feeling that an exposure to and an understanding of knowledge from a range of disciplines provides teachers with the tools to address those complexities effectively and meet the multifaceted needs of their students.

Notes

1. Follow-up studies should be conducted with less experienced trainees, more experienced trainees, pre-service teachers, and in-service teachers, in different types of teacher education programs, to clarify the extent to which teacher-education course content transfers to L2 lesson planning and classroom teaching. The field of L2 teacher education stands to gain from the insights resulting from such studies.

Discussion Questions and Activities

1. The authors have outlined topics from linguistics, psychology, anthropology, and education that they think are important for teacher development. Identify one topic from each field that you

think is critical and provide a rationale for your choice. What particular aspects of the different disciplines do you think will prove most helpful to you for making pedagogical decisions, planning classes, developing materials, delivering instruction, evaluating student progress, and conducting meaningful action research projects? Explain your choices.

2. The case study presented in this chapter started out as an action research project. What are the strengths of the case study? What are the weaknesses? What kind of action research project might you engage in to understand better the value of disciplinary knowledge in your teaching?

3. Consider the topics listed below. In small groups, order them from most (1) to least (12) important for a language teacher. Be prepared to explain your decisions.

> the concept of flow
> the role of attitudes and motivation
> the role of dialect variation
> school-valued discourse
> societal multilingualism
> cognitive processing abilities
> literacy skills
> Whorfian hypothesis
> assessment practices
> communicative competence
> needs analysis
> innovation

4. In small groups or pairs, search the internet to gather program information from several institutions, both here in the U.S. and abroad, that offer a master's degree in TESOL. Compare their programs of study to yours. Discuss your findings. How might programs for those interested in teaching English as a foreign language compare to programs for those interested in teaching English as a second language? For those interested in teaching adults to those interested in teaching children? If you had the opportunity to design your own TESOL master's program, what would it look like, and why?

5. How might the notion of disciplinary knowledge, as defined in this chapter, be understood as political knowledge?

Chapter 11
Becoming Sociopolitically Active

L.E. Forhan and M. Scheraga

Just Do It!

> I lost my mother in October, but she's still whispering in my ear all those things mothers whisper and wonder if they're getting through to us. Yes, mom, you really got to me when you reminded me over and over again, "If you want something done right, do it yourself." "If you want something done, give it to a busy person. It'll get done." "You're only a victim if you allow yourself to be a victim." And the one time I heard her brag about me: "The reason Mona gets so much done is because while other people are thinking about it, she just goes out and does it."
>
> It's time to just go out and do it! (Mona Scheraga)

Introduction

Those involved in professional activities related to the teaching of English to speakers of other languages have long recognized the importance of advocacy, of becoming sociopolitically active as ESOL professionals. We recognize the importance of such advocacy because authorities make decisions that impact upon the quality of the programs that we teach in and the conditions of our employment in these programs. Similarly, decisions are made which affect our students and the members of the communities from which they come. For an ESOL professional, becoming sociopolitically active is a process of participating in decisions that affect us within our profession and that affect our students in their daily lives. Advocacy for the ESOL professional means informed participation in decision making; it means lending one's voice to the chorus of voices which shapes our understanding of the issues pertinent to our work and our students' lives and which impact upon the policies related to those issues. Such participation means working to retain and strengthen what is good and effective in our programs and policies. It also means working for change where improvement is warranted, i.e. to better the learning experiences of our students, to promote safety and dignity in the communities where they live, and to improve our own employment conditions.

Becoming sociopolitically active doesn't happen overnight; nor is it a one-shot experience. It is an ongoing, organic process of growth and development, of learning about the issues, of learning how decisions are made pertinent to those issues, and of developing skills that will enable us to participate effectively in those decision-making processes. Becoming sociopolitically active is a process of growth and development within the individual, an evolution of insight and skill-building which for some of us occurs in the very early stages of our professional lives, while for others may not happen until much later.

It can also be a process of group growth and development. Professionals can evolve a collective body of knowledge and skills emerging from the experience and expertise of professional colleagues or the members of a professional organization.

Most ESOL teachers, materials writers, and program administrators did not enter the profession with any thought of becoming involved in advocacy, and yet repeatedly they have realized the importance of becoming sociopolitically active and have become engaged in either professional advocacy, political advocacy, or both. How does this happen? How is it that as we strive to become insightful and effective teachers or materials writers we find ourselves getting involved in sociopolitical activities? What explains this phenomenon?

Sociopolitical Concerns

The first part of the answer can be stated quite simply: concerns. Concerns drive the process. As teachers, we want our students to succeed, to achieve their English language goals as effectively as possible, to receive high-quality instruction in legitimate programs. We want them to learn in environments where they will have numerous, meaningful opportunities to explore and practice using English and where simultaneously, they will be affirmed in terms of their own cultural and linguistic backgrounds. We want them to live in communities where they will be safe and where they will have adequate support as they make the transition from being non-English speakers to being successful English language communicators, able to participate meaningfully in their "new" communities. As professionals, we are also concerned about our own employment conditions: about job security, pay, benefits, workload, and opportunities for ongoing professional development. And finally, because we do not exist in a professional vacuum, we are concerned about our ESOL colleagues, both those who work "down the road" and those who work across the globe. We do not work in isolation from each other—we are part of a profession. We share what we know and try to learn from one other so that we can continue to add to our knowledge and skills.

In 1993, TESOL's Sociopolitical Concerns Committee surveyed TESOL members at an open meeting to identify the concerns they felt ought to be sociopolitical priorities within the profession. The responses were numerous and diverse, and they reflected a broad range of issues, some restricted to people's immediate professional circumstances, others grounded in the broader political arena; all were relevant within the context of the profession.

What follows is a sampling of those concerns:

- the need for accuracy in assessing adult literacy;
- the need to make membership in TESOL accessible to ESOL teachers from developing countries;
- requests for a formal TESOL statement on the language rights of the hearing impaired;
- concerns of widespread exploitation of ESOL teachers in terms of excessive hiring for part-time assignments and failure to create full-time continuing positions;
- concerns that a considerable number of ESOL teaching positions do not offer salaries commensurate with the local standard of living;
- the need to include AIDS education in content-based ESOL materials and curricula;
- concerns about discrimination against non-native speakers of English in ESOL hiring practices and in offering graduate assistant-ships in masters and doctoral-level TESOL programs;
- the need for K-12 ESL standards in U.S. public school;
- concerns about the growing "English-Only" movement in the U.S.;
- concerns about the dismantling of bilingual education programs for public school students with limited English proficiency.

Becoming informed about our concerns

Because of the fundamental relationship between understanding an issue and committing oneself to related advocacy, education is a critical element in any meaningful sociopolitical activity. You should never advocate for or against something if you don't understand it. Nor can you ask colleagues or community members to become involved in something that they don't understand. Obviously, there is a basic and ongoing need for information. We need to inform ourselves, and we need to get information out to others. For some of us, educating is a logical and effective form of sociopolitical advocacy. We ask questions and try to find out where to get accurate, reliable information. We do the research and enlist others to work with us, and then we share our findings. We share what we're learning with our colleagues at work. If we belong to an organization of ESOL professionals, we disseminate information by writing articles for the organization's newsletter, by giving presentations and conducting workshops at professional conferences, and by serving as issue-related resource people at both professional and community event information booths. We also share information with the members of our communities by writing editorials for local newspapers. And finally, we extend our role as educators by talking to legislators and other decision-makers, providing them with information and letting them know what decision we would like them to make.

Effective advocacy

Because they are both real and serious, concerns are usually what motivate people to become sociopolitically involved on a personal level. In terms of collective advocacy, however, our concerns are but a first ingredient. The second element in our entry into the sociopolitical arena as ESOL professionals is the ability to see the relationships between our professional goals and broader policy decisions, i.e. policies in our places of work and in our professional organizations; legislation at local, regional, and national levels; and practices affecting our colleagues and neighbors globally. Once we see the relationships between our professional lives and broader policy decisions, our desire to participate in the processes of making those decisions catapults us into activism.

Effective advocacy is not restricted to experienced, well-established professionals, but embraces all, including veterans and new members of the profession. Similarly, effective advocacy is not restricted to top-level administrators or officers of professional organizations. Rather, it depends upon the broad-based, active dedication of teachers, materials writers, researchers, and program administrators who are able to see the impact of existing practices and proposed changes upon their lives and on the lives of their colleagues and students and who subsequently choose to take part in preserving and strengthening those practices or in initiating change.

The Many Faces of Advocacy

Just as a powerful chorus consists of a rich blend of many different voices, advocacy—the things that we do to preserve what is strong and positive or to change what is less than desirable—takes on a wide array of faces. The particular appearance of a sociopolitical activity is determined not only by the nature of the issue at hand, but by the synergy of the individuals who are involved in advocacy pertinent to that issue: by their understanding of the issue, the creativity of their ideas, and the depth of their effort in addressing it. What follows is a series of case studies of various advocacy experiences. Before proceeding however, we wish to present a disclaimer: the writers of this chapter feel that it is important to acknowledge the limitations of the material being presented here. The suggestions and models are almost entirely U.S. based, leaving a serious gap in our understanding as a profession of what advocacy means in other cultural contexts. Much of what has been learned about effective ESOL advocacy in the cultural context of the U.S. may well be inappropriate and thus unproductive or, worse, counterproductive in other parts of the world. For the many ESOL professionals working or preparing to work outside of the United States, our hopes are twofold:

(1) That this chapter may serve as a point of departure, a catalyst for different models of sociopolitical insight and skill-building that can be effective because of their relevance to a given cultural context.
(2) That the sociopolitical limitations of this chapter will serve to encourage presentations and publications providing information and specific models for effective advocacy in the myriad of cultural contexts in our global community.

Face #1: New York State TESOL and funding restrictions

Members of NYSTESOL (New York State TESOL) became concerned about proposed legislation to reduce educational funding throughout the state. Of particular concern was the impact that such reductions would have upon programs for students with limited English proficiency. NYSTESOL members worked actively, writing articles, editorials, and letters to legislators. They also facilitated workplace and conference discussions to inform colleagues and fellow citizens about the serious repercussions of these proposed cutbacks.

Somewhere in the midst of these activities, another idea emerged: NYSTESOL would sponsor a media event—something constructive, something educational, something that would focus positive attention on the importance of the issue. NYSTESOL decided to host an educational brunch. High-profile state legislators were invited as the guests of honor. Many attended the brunch, which provided the legislators the opportunity to learn more about the educational and social dimensions of the proposed cutbacks. The brunch also acquainted these officials with the ESOL professionals in New York State and provided a valuable opportunity for them to learn something about the work that we do and the learners that we serve.

Face #2: Counteracting negative stereotypes

While enlisting the full force of a professional organization proved to be a very effective advocacy strategy for educators in New York, there are other ways to have a meaningful impact on decision makers. In Yakima Washington, an individual ESL instructor at Yakima Community College was also worried about proposed educational funding cutbacks. Her worries deepened as she became increasingly aware of the negative stereotypes regarding students with limited English proficiency being propagated by supporters of the cutbacks. These stereotypes included the "facts" that ESL learners were unmotivated, indolent, not genuinely interested in learning English, and just looking for government handout. In short, that "they" were a waste of taxpayers' money. She knew firsthand these images did not come close to describing her hard-working students and wanted to find a way to address both the deception of the stereotypes and the importance of society providing educational support to these students. This teacher's action plan did not involve a group of professional colleagues; it involved her students.

She started out by having the students read articles about the proposed funding cutbacks. Follow-up discussions explored the repercussions of such cutbacks and then probed for ideas for action. The students decided to write letters to local officials, to introduce themselves, to tell the lawmakers why their English classes were so important, and to invite the officials to come and visit the class. One official accepted the invitation and spent an afternoon with the class, becoming acquainted with the students, hearing from them about their studies and their lives, and seeing some of their work. This was followed by a student presentation on the local community access TV station; the ESOL students spoke in English for themselves, explaining how they were learning the language and why it was important for them to do so.

This class advocacy project was valuable in so many ways. It provided the students with an opportunity for real, personally meaningful English language use. It empowered them to advocate for themselves, and it enabled local officials and members of the community to move beyond stereotypes, to see the ESOL students as individuals with names and faces, with accomplishments and dreams.

When addressing matters of educational funding or other legislative issues that impact upon the educational or societal experiences of our students and their families, effective ESOL advocates realize that they have to find ways of being heard by those who make decisions. Both group and individual efforts are necessary. Even if you are an active part of an effective group project, it is important that your legislators hear your individual voice as well. Legislators want a sense of how broad-based the particular stance on an issue is. For them, knowing the position of your professional organization is one thing; discovering that 10 or 50 or 100 individuals have written or telephoned or emailed encouraging that same position is something else again.

Workplace Advocacy

For ESOL professionals, advocacy emerges not only with respect to issues of public policy, but with respect to conditions in the workplace and to the effectiveness of our professional organizations. As professionals, our primary goals are

(1) to be effective teachers, materials writers, and program administrators, and
(2) to strive for ongoing professional growth (i.e. to keep up-to-date with research and practice, and in so doing, to continually improve upon what we do).

If you have to juggle two or more part-time teaching jobs simultaneously in order to make ends meet, it is highly unlikely that you will have the energy or the time to devote to becoming a better teacher. If the trunk of your car serves as your office, it is hard to imagine that you will have effective conferences with your students, that you will be able to develop and maintain material files, or that you will be able to communicate and collaborate with professional colleagues. In terms of workplace advocacy, ESOL professionals have long grappled with the following issues:

(1) Underemployment (i.e. the lack of permanent, full-time positions);
(2) Low pay;
(3) Lack of benefits;
(4) Lack of professional standards (e.g. the hiring of unqualified instructors); and
(5) Discrimination against qualified ESOL professionals who are non-native speakers of English or who are speakers of what is seen to be a non-standard dialect of English.

These are some of the numerous issues that have affected ESOL professionals within the workplace. They are serious and have had a profound impact upon the quality of the work that we do, upon our potential for professional growth and development, and upon the quality of our personal lives.

Face #3: Employment conditions survey

As is the case with issues of public policy, before we can effectively address a workplace issue, we have to understand it; we have to be accurately informed. To this end one professional organization, PennTESOL East (ESOL professionals from eastern Pennsylvania), conducts a survey every two years to gather data on the employment condition of its members. As the 1992 Survey Summary explained,

> Information about salary, benefits, and access to full-time jobs is compared to social characteristics of the respondents, such as gender, age, etc. The survey gives us a look at salary levels and other factors from the point of view of teachers rather than employing institutions.

Such an analysis is valuable, for it not only provides straightforward data on employment conditions, but suggests causal factors pertinent to those conditions. The 1992 survey gathered data on areas of professional expertise (i.e. higher education, elementary/secondary education, adult education), gender, age, number of years of teaching experience, educational credentials (i.e. an ESOL graduate degree), employment status (i.e. full time or part time), whether part-timers wanted full-time employment, number of teaching hours per week, salary, benefits, and whether or not respondents were unionized. Once this information was gathered, the Sociopolitical Concerns Committee of PennTESOL East analyzed the data and prepared a summary that was disseminated to the full PennTESOL East membership. In addition to providing the survey results, they articulated reasons why these conditions needed to change.

> There are also important professional advantages in having one job, rather than several part-time jobs. Some part-time teachers are not invited to participate in normal, traditional professional matters, such as curriculum development, textbook selection, work on committees, etc. We believe that long-term professional teachers who work part-time should have the right to exercise their professional judgment in teaching and governance decisions in the same way that full-time faculty do. We believe we need to encourage programs in our area to do better. We want to go on record that we expect institutions to use full-time positions whenever there is enough work available to fill them.

PennTESOL East distributed this information to its members who, with an informed understanding of the employment situation in their region, worked together on the development of a set of guidelines for professional standards to be followed by ESL programs at all educational levels throughout eastern Pennsylvania.

Face #4: An adjunct manual

As this important workplace advocacy was underway in Pennsylvania, ESOL professionals in the State of New York, equally concerned about the seriousness of underemployment in the profession, were completing work on a manual, "What Can Adjuncts Do? Recommended Actions and Selected Papers on the Situation of Part-time Faculty in Post-Secondary Education." Drawing upon the experience and expertise of ESOL professionals from throughout the United States, the manual examines the general situation of part-time instructors in higher education, presents an update of ongoing work in the area of professional standards, provides copies of official resolutions and position statements on part-time employment from TESOL affiliates and individual ESOL professionals, and makes recommendations for specific actions. The manual has been an important tool for advocacy throughout the United States, not simply in terms of the factual information that it contains, but in terms of its service in clarifying the pedagogical and professional ramifications of underemployment and in identifying issues that have to be raised if this problem is to be effectively resolved.

Face #5: The power of one

While successful advocacy is very often a collective undertaking, it is important to remember that strong movements sometimes begin when just one individual makes a stand. This is what happened in 1991 at the annual international TESOL Convention and Exhibition. At the end of every annual convention there is a general business meeting, open to all members of the organization. During the meeting, as attendees were invited to bring forth new business, a member of TESOL, Mr. Narendra Parmar, made a statement regarding the widespread practice of stipulating "native speaker" in the recruitment and hiring of ESL teachers in the United States and in U.S.-run overseas programs. Mr. Parmar explained that he found the term "native speaker" to be discriminatory, demeaning, and quite difficult to define. He pointed out that it was most discouraging that TESOL published such job notices in its placement bulletin and that it permitted recruiters in its own employment services area of the convention to openly discriminate against TESOL members. Mr. Parmar spoke alone, not as the representative of an institution or of a professional organization, yet his message filled the hall and set immediately into motion very serious work which resulted in an official TESOL Statement on Non-Native Speakers and Hiring Practices, reform of the internal hiring practices of TESOL as an international organization, and a reform of TESOL's policies regarding job postings in its placement bulletin and at its conventions.

Mr. Parmar's solitary voice sounded a wake-up call to all of us; he put the spotlight on discriminatory practices within the profession and perhaps more importantly moved ESOL professionals to re-examine our own assumptions about English language teaching, to ponder what it is that makes a "good" English language teacher, whether native-speakers are better teachers than non-native speakers, or whether one need be a native speaker to be an authentic speaker. His concerns have raised serious questions about language fluency and about the very nature of effective language teaching.

Face #6: Addressing international economic and professional disparities

Many ESOL professionals utilize the programs and services of their professional organizations (e.g. newsletters, journals, manuals, workshops, seminars, and conferences) to become better teachers, to collaborate with other authors, to strengthen curricular documents, or to develop special projects. However, throughout the world there are innumerable ESOL professionals who benefit rarely, if ever, from the information, services, and expertise of TESOL, Inc., or other ESOL professional organizations. This is because these individuals work in countries where currencies and salaries do not mesh even remotely with the common expenses of membership in a professional organization such as TESOL, Inc. In the mid-1990s, a U.S. Peace Corps officer reported that at that time the average salary for an English language teacher in the Ukraine was $4.00 per month (yes, your dollars!) and that the highest paid Ukrainian English language supervisor earned $40.00 per month. With the price of individual TESOL membership dues above $40.00 annually, it is easy to see that membership would not be accessible to our ESOL colleagues in the Ukraine. There are far too many other ESOL professionals throughout the developing world in particular who are in the same circumstances as teachers in the Ukraine. Because they cannot afford basic membership dues and postage costs, they do not benefit from the flow of ideas and information available from the organization. They do not receive the newsletters and journals, they rarely if ever attend conferences, and seldom enjoy the benefits of consultant visits.

ESOL professionals have long been aware of these disparities. Many who can afford membership in a professional organization have been involved in making the benefits of organizational membership, especially opportunities for professional growth and development, more accessible to low-income colleagues. In some cases TESOL affiliates have established "sister" relationships with ESOL programs (or individual professionals) in another part of the world. Such relationships have taken a variety of forms and usually include sharing published materials. For example, every few months, the affiliate might put out a call to all members to donate professional newsletters and journals for a mailing to the "sister" organization abroad. Periodically, the organization might put out a call to members to donate duplicate copies in their possession of current texts, tapes, reference materials, and other teaching-related resources and, again, send off a parcel to ESOL colleagues who may rarely be able to afford new materials.

One organization that has been both exceptionally dedicated and creative in terms of making opportunities for professional development accessible to all in the profession is NELLE, Networking English Language Learning in Europe. Founded in the summer of 1988, NELLE (pronounced "Nellie") is an umbrella association, not for individuals, but for organizations in Europe (including eastern Europe) concerned with English language teaching or with language teaching in general. NELLE came into being out of the concerns:

(1) That in much of Europe there were no professional organizations for English language teachers in private language schools, in adult education, or in in-company training programs.
(2) That existing organizations for other types of English language teachers were operating in isolation from each other.
(3) That little was known about professional standards and about pay and other employment conditions in English language teaching throughout Europe.
(4) That most English language teachers had little opportunity to meet one another and that many worked in complete professional isolation.
(5) That often the national and international teachers' associations didn't or couldn't cater to teachers' needs in a local context.

In response to these concerns, NELLE was founded:

(1) To create a European umbrella for the active networking of all existing English Language Teachers' Associations.
(2) To support the establishment of new local English Language Teachers' Associations and to help these young associations put their aims into practice.
(3) To actively promote networking and cooperation among existing teachers' associations in an effort to eliminate professional isolation and to build a framework for professional growth and development.
(4) To promote and organize a broad range of professionally related events: conferences, workshops, and special interest group meetings to encourage cooperation among English language teachers.

NELLE's first four conferences, held in Osnabruck, West Germany (1989); Maastricht, Netherlands (1990); Prague, Czechoslovakia (1992); and Innsbruck, Austria (1994) reflect NELLE's philosophy "that a truly international European organization should not be seen to have its roots in any one major country" (Sebbage, 1993). By 1990, the third conference brought together 230 ESOL colleagues "from 17 countries across Europe as far apart as Spain, Romania, and the Baltic States, not to mention Russia, the British Isles, and North America" (Sebbage, 1993).

NELLE's commitment to inclusion, to building bridges among ESOL professionals, and to eliminating contexts of isolation is significant in its proactive approach. NELLE's very structure, which does not allow membership by an individual, is designed to encourage teachers to form themselves into teacher associations. NELLE assists non-organized English language professionals with the groundwork of forming a viable association and promotes professional interaction among associations previously existing in isolation of each other. In addition to these accomplishments, NELLE advocates actively for creative cost-sharing as a tangible way of enabling members of local teacher associations to participate in workshops, conferences, and other professional events. Some NELLE models for cost sharing include organizing a "workshop tour" series throughout a particular region of Europe as a way of attracting and being able to afford desired speakers, researchers, teacher trainers, and interested publishers. Arranging a "workshop tour" allows small professional associations to share costs and to benefit from the accessibility of good presenters. NELLE has also promoted cost sharing at some events by scheduling them in locations where ESOL professionals without financial support for travel costs would not have far to travel. Finally, in making conference and workshop arrangements, NELLE has served as a sort of "roommate service," helping to match up ESOL professionals from the following two groups:

(1) those who do not receive support for their professional development and most likely would not be able to afford to attend the conference;
(2) those who receive generous financial support for professional development and would like to share those resources with fellow colleagues.

Face #7: Textbooks and stereotypes

In the summer of 1995 a group of 12 EFL teachers, teacher trainers, and teacher supervisors from Israel, Gaza, and the West Bank gathered at Ohio University in Athens, Ohio, for a five-week program of professional development and collaboration. Some in the group were Moslem, some were Jewish, and others Christian. All had come together to find ways of improving themselves professionally and of improving English language teaching in the region. In the course of the five weeks that these educators spent together, a great deal of fine, rigorous work was done, one part of which involved work on an in-depth project that could be put into use back home. The 12 participants were invited to design their own projects and were invited to work individually or in groups. All but one chose to work in groups, and as often happens in forming task-oriented groups, it was personal interest rather than gender, age, religion, or political affiliation that drew people into one group or another.

Two of the groups chose different dimensions of peace education as the focus of their projects, one involving language learning as a context for exploring conflict resolution, the other examining the role of textbooks in reinforcing negative stereotypes. Members of the second group revealed that in their home region EFL texts generally illustrated negative concepts with an image representing someone from the other culture. So, for example, a child's textbook in Israel might portray a thief as a Palestinian, while the thief in a Palestinian child's book would likely show an Israeli. The teachers explored the prevalence of this practice (very prevalent!) and the impact that it had on the attitudes of students and teachers alike with regard to members of the neighboring culture. Members of the group indicated that the effects of these images were powerful and negative and that they contributed significantly to reinforcing feelings of mistrust. The group then drew up a proposal to be put before education officials, materials writers, program administrators, and teachers advocating for the elimination of all stereotypical illustrations and examples in textbooks at every level. The ESOL professionals who worked on this project understood that such basic change would not come overnight. They were equally aware of the expenses involved in rewriting textbooks, but they did not change course, for they felt that at the core, the issue was very important and that if the first step was only to generate serious discussion, that itself was an essential part of the process.

Developing Advocacy: Where Do You Fit In?

Becoming professionally active

As you enter and become active in the profession, find out whether there is a professional organization in your locale. If there is, learn as much about it as you can: its purpose, structure, activities, and how one becomes a member. ESOL professionals worldwide have come together in an amazing array of configurations to form professional associations as an important way of exchanging ideas and information which enable them to become more insightful and creative teachers, more skilled at authoring effective textbooks and related ESOL materials, better at developing and revising curriculum. It is important that you connect on a regular basis with others in the profession—with those who, like you, are just launching their careers as well as with those who have long been teaching, writing, and directing programs. ESOL professionals have a tremendous wealth of expertise and experience to offer one another, and regardless of whether the association is large or small, it is invaluable to connect, to share ideas and concerns, and to explore solutions and strategies together.

ESOL professionals have formed innumerable organizations geared to meet the needs of a specific locale, e.g.:

- Linguistic Association of Teachers of English at the University of Moscow
- English Language Teachers' Association Stuttgart
- PennTESOL East
- Three Rivers TESOL
- National Association of Teachers of English as a Foreign Language in Ireland
- TESOL-Italy
- JALT (Japanese Association of Language Teachers)

They have also reached across state and national boundaries to form associations providing greater breadth and depth of opportunities for professional interaction, e.g.:

- MidWest TESOL
- InterMountain TESOL
- IATEFL (International Association of Teachers of English as a Foreign Language)
- NELLE (Networking English Language Learning In Europe)
- TESOL, Inc. (Teachers of English to Speakers of Other Languages, Inc.)

As you become connected to a broader pool of professionals and as you begin learning from them how they teach English to children, help adults develop literacy skills, teach academic English, or get textbooks and software published, you will discover a deepening of your understanding of what language is and of what it means to teach English to speakers of other languages. You will also become familiar with various issues that impact upon the work that you do. As you become aware of the issues that affect you and your students, you will very likely want to have some input into the discussions and decisions pertinent to those issues. This means becoming sociopolitically active!

Getting started: Roll up your sleeves and throw away the myths!

Getting started is the slowest stage of many a task, including the task of becoming sociopolitically active. In spite of the fact that we are well-educated professionals, most of us may not be particularly knowledgeable about policy making and may feel quite intimidated by the prospect of trying to figure it out. It's really not very different from the feelings that entry-level students have when they consider whether or not they've got what it takes to learn a whole new language. Their worries sometimes overwhelm and immobilize them, and yet step by step, with encouragement and perseverance, they dismantle their fears and begin to enjoy the experience of communicating successfully within a community that is no longer alien. As we embark upon the journey toward advocacy, it is important to recognize the worries and the myths that can hinder us from taking that next step.

According to the Joint National Committee on Languages—an information clearinghouse on U.S. federal legislative efforts affecting ESL and bilingual funding—the 10 myths that most commonly hinder individuals from getting involved and acting upon their concerns can be stated as follows:

(1) "Normal" citizens cannot affect politics (i.e. you have to be someone "important" to successfully participate in decision-making).
(2) Politics is confusing (i.e. if we don't already know how something works, we can't find out).
(3) You need money to be effective in politics.
(4) My opinion won't count.
(5) They won't read my letter anyway.
(6) I don't know to whom to write (i.e. there's no way to find out).
(7) I don't have the time to get involved.
(8) I don't need to get involved; it doesn't affect me, my family, or my community.
(9) I don't know the issues and I don't know how to find out.
(10) I want to get involved, but I don't know where to start.

These are misconceptions, ideas that are often held to be truths, but which are not grounded in fact. If you want to begin the process of becoming sociopolitically effective, it is very important to recognize these myths and study their flaws. Think about the situations that you know about personally where a single individual (or a small group of individuals) DID affect politics. Think about policy-making at your place of work or in the community where you live. How can you find out who makes decisions at that level and how those decisions are made? What resources are available to help you gather this information? Are there librarians or staff at local newspapers or radio/TV broadcasting stations who can steer you in the right direction? Can you think of any examples of people who were successful in making or preventing change in spite of the fact that they didn't have significant financial resources? Work your way through the myths, using your personal experiences to dismantle as many of them as possible. If there are colleagues or classmates who, like you, would like to begin the process of becoming sociopolitically active, work together to uncover the flaws in the myths and to remove these obstacles from your path. Freeing ourselves from the myths is empowering for it enables us to see ourselves in a new way. Once you are free from the constraints of the myths, you are free to find out whatever it is that you want to know. You are in motion: learning, sharing information, building your skills, transferring skills to others, realizing that your voice matters, that "two and two and fifty make a million," and that you can make a difference.

Becoming an Effective Advocate: What Individuals Can Do

As an ESOL professional your personal interest—not simply in the quality of your teaching, but in the quality of your program—is critical. Equally important is your genuine interest in the living conditions and social environment that your students and their families face in your community. It is usually your own personal interest and your curiosity that will steer you in a particular direction, motivating you to find out more about a situation or a current issue.

Once you are interested, take action. Start by informing yourself: ask questions, read, listen, and then ask more questions. Find out as much as you possibly can, and if the matter is controversial, find out as much as you can about opposing viewpoints. This is very important; knowing how "the other side" sees the issue helps you to clarify your own position. It indicates questions that you may not have asked, but ought to, and down the road may strengthen your ability to articulate your perspective in the face of opposition.

As your understanding of the issue deepens, add your voice to those who are discussing or debating positions. Write letters to local newspapers; write, call and meet with decision-makers; share information and ideas with others (professional colleagues, members of your community). Stimulate them to think. Catalyze them to act. Throughout all of this, be sure to welcome the questions and concerns of others. They may need time to work through the process of informing themselves, just as you did. They may need to work through concerns and raise questions that seem obvious to you; but if those concerns and questions are genuinely welcomed and if you are helpful in responding, they too will deepen their understanding of the importance of the issue at hand.

Remember there is strength in numbers and therefore, it is of great importance to use your interest and your skills within a broader framework, through your professional organization. As issues emerge that are of importance to you and as you become informed about those issues, get the word out to colleagues throughout your affiliate. Talk with your affiliate newsletter editor about the significance of an issue; offer to write an article about it. Identify others who can also write articles. Propose issue-related presentations and discussion sessions at meetings and conferences of your professional organization. Help identify presenters (including yourself!) and offer to facilitate debates, panel discussions, and round tables. Propose that there be advocacy skill-building workshops at organizational conferences as an ongoing part of regular conference programming, and as your own advocacy skills develop, offer to facilitate those workshops.

If your professional organization doesn't yet have a sociopolitical concerns committee, meet with your affiliate leaders and work toward starting one. Put out a call through your newsletter or an affiliate mailing to identify members of your organization who are interested in serving on the advocacy committee and get the ball rolling. If your professional affiliate already has a sociopolitical concerns or advocacy committee, get involved. Let your affiliate and advocacy leaders know that you are interested in working on a particular issue or in developing your advocacy skills in general. Find out what needs to be done and ask how you might contribute. Find out about projects that others are doing and whenever possible, offer to help with something that you've never done before; it's an invaluable way to develop new skills.

As an individual, encourage your professional organization to address advocacy in terms of

(1) Issue-specific activities (e.g. underemployment in ESOL, the English-Only movement, cutbacks in educational funding, etc);
(2) General advocacy skill-building (e.g. learning how to get reliable information about current issues, getting reliable information about related decision-making processes, identifying and effectively communicating with key decision-makers, organizing effective letter-writing campaigns [snail-mail or email], successfully involving others outside the professional organization to work with you);
(3) Building and strengthening your affiliate's advocacy network. (Ideally, you want every member of your professional organization involved.)

Remember, sociopolitical action is organic; keep yourself active and your affiliate in motion!

Effective Advocacy: What Professional Organizations Can Do

If your professional organization wants to participate effectively in the discussions and decisions that affect the membership and the people they serve, it is essential to establish a strong, vibrant sociopolitical network, one that not only extends into the far reaches of your organizational membership, but also branches outward to connect with ESOL professionals and other educators in the wider global community.

The first step in strengthening your organization's voice is to set up an advocacy committee as an official part of your organizational structure. While this committee might consist of a few current leaders, it is equally reasonable that members of the organization not already committed to responsibilities of leadership be asked to take on these new duties. What is important is not whether one is or isn't a current office holder in your organization, but whether that individual has the commitment and the communication and organizational skills to facilitate

(1) identifying sociopolitical concerns;
(2) prioritizing those concerns;
(3) developing an advocacy network throughout the organization;
(4) promoting advocacy skill-building among all organizational members;
(5) extending the advocacy network beyond the boundaries of the local professional organization.

Some affiliates refer to their advocacy committees as sociopolitical concerns committees, others as advocacy teams. It is not important what you call it; what is important is that your organization recognizes first, that it has a voice, and second, that it is imperative to use that voice to participate in the discussions and decisions related to the lives of its members and those they serve. As you seek members for your advocacy committee, individuals who have shared their concerns and worked on previous projects may readily come to mind. Other very valuable resources for membership on such a committee are the former leaders of your professional association. Generally these individuals are deeply committed to the profession and, because of their previous leadership experience, have considerable knowledge about group structures and decision-making processes. A general invitation to the full membership of your professional organization to identify affiliate members interested in serving in this capacity is still another very beneficial strategy, and while most organizations will, for practical reasons, choose to keep official committees small, the sociopolitical concerns committee will want to set up an advocacy network among the membership so that key individuals can easily be called upon as the organization commits to specific projects and as related tasks need to be addressed. Thus, an open call to all members interested in serving on the association's advocacy committee might well serve a dual function: that of identifying members for the formal advocacy committee and that of identifying key players in the association-wide advocacy network.

Developing an advocacy network

Once your affiliate's sociopolitical concerns committee is in place, a very important task for that committee is to develop such an advocacy network throughout the organization. Basically this is a bi-directional process, i.e. making sure that the full membership has access to information about issues of relevance and the wide variety of ways that they can participate in working on an issue, and eliciting input from members of the organization who are willing and interested in being immediately and actively involved at all levels. Providing information about issues to the members of your association involves gathering information, researching issues, and identifying individuals with the expertise to write articles for your newsletter or to make presentations at organizational conferences. Sometimes it means keeping regular contact with a legislator's office and periodically putting out a brief mailing, an "issue update" for the membership of your organization. It may also involve letting the members of your association know what other organizations have done and what has or hasn't worked for them. Project models from other professional or community organizations can serve as effective sources of information for your association and can catalyze members to initiate creative activities relevant to their front-burner issues.

Providing information to your membership also means providing information about how various decisions are made as well as offering suggestions about activities that can affect the decision that is ultimately reached. For example, when ESOL professionals in New York State decided that underemployment might be reduced if institutions who did not meet a certain ratio of full- to part-time teaching positions were denied accreditation, they needed to find out how the process for amending the existing processes for accreditation and reaccredidation worked so that they would know where and how they might participate in the discussions pertinent to that process. When ESOL professionals in California wanted to share their concerns about Proposition 187—proposed legislation which among other thing would have obligated teachers (including ESOL teachers) to report to "the authorities" any suspicion that one of their students might be the child of immigrants who had entered the U.S. illegally—they too, needed to know where and how to give their input into that legislative process. In order to participate effectively in such decision making processes, it is essential that the members of your professional organization become knowledgeable about those processes. The socio-political leadership of your organization needs to ensure that information is made available to the full membership. There is no reason for ESOL pro-fessionals to feel alienated or intimidated by such processes. Through newsletter articles, conference presentations, discussions, and work-shops, the rhetoric pertinent to decision-making will become common and, in so doing, knowledge will translate into power.

A well-informed membership needs to understand not only the issues facing them and how decisions pertinent to those issues are made, they also need to understand how they can most effectively participate in related decision-making processes. Thus, another very important respon-sibility of the sociopolitical leadership of your organization is to help members discover the endless variety of meaningful ways that they can work on an issue and to help them build the skills that they need. Not everybody is a keynote speaker, nor need they be. When there's serious issue-related work to be done, there are usually as many (or more!) important "behind-the-scenes" tasks as there are needs for people to serve "in the limelight." If you are in a sociopolitical leadership position, it is critical that you realize that every member of your association has something to offer. Some individuals will NEVER be comfortable speak-ing directly with a legislator, but those same people may be invaluable in researching information relevant to the issue. They may be willing to call a legislative aide for regular updates or, gather current information from the library. They may be willing to check key web sites for the associa-tion's advocacy team. Other members may be willing to participate in panel discussions or may agree to meet with a decision-maker. Still oth-ers may choose to organize letter-writing parties, while others may offer to use their desk-top publishing skills to put together eye-catching fliers and issue updates. Never forget that the individual working steadfastly in the shadows is as important as the person meeting with a public offi-cial. Our singular voices are varied: deep, soft, high, strong, graveled; together they blend into a rich and powerful chorus. Like our voices, the members of your organization represent a colorful tapestry of insights and talents. Recognize them. Welcome them. Put them to good use!

While your organization develops its own internal advocacy network, it is essential to extend that network to other ESOL affiliates, and to other professional and community organizations. Many of these organizations are "old pros" at advocacy, and many of them are concerned about the same issues that concern you. They can be invaluable resources to your affiliate, sources of information, of strategies (e.g. what works and what doesn't), and of expertise. They may permit you to reprint and distribute articles that they have written on an issue. They may share their ideas and models of successful advocacy projects. They may provide you with very helpful information about a particular legislator's stance or about how to secure an audience with a key decision-maker, and at times they may publicly "join forces" with you and your colleagues, thus strengthening the impact of your message.

Prioritizing concerns

For a professional association, an important dimension of becoming sociopolitically active beyond identifying issues of concern is prioritizing them. Some issues, by their very nature, will be of more importance than others. Some will move into positions of urgency because of the imminence of the date when the vote is to be taken and the final decision made. Establish clear priorities and know when votes are to be taken so the organization will be more realistic in setting goals related to those issues and more effective in addressing them.

As issues are identified and prioritized and as members of the organization become well informed, the leadership may want to develop position statements that articulate the organization's stance on an issue and the rationale for it. Such position statements serve as useful tools for affiliate members who choose to communicate with a decision-maker or who inadvertently find themselves participating in an impromptu discussion about the issue. They serve as an educational resource for affiliate members who may not be knowledgeable about the issue and who would like information about the organization's official position. Finally, they readily enable members of the organization to distinguish their personal viewpoints on an issue from that of the organization. It is absolutely essential that ESOL professionals who are speaking out on an issue be clear about whether they are speaking for themselves or whether they are officially representing their affiliate.

To summarize, for the professional organization, the first phase of becoming sociopolitically active is organizational, i.e. establishing a sociopolitical concerns committee as an official part of the affiliate structure, developing an internal advocacy network throughout the affiliate, and extending that network outward to other professional and community organizations. The second and equally important task for the organization is that of building advocacy skills, i.e. becoming well informed about issues of concern and the related decision-making processes and learning both from others and from personal experience how to effectively give input to those making the decisions. Finally, if an organization's sociopolitical voice is to become effective, it is necessary that advocacy skills and information be transferred throughout the affiliate membership. Unless affiliate leaders, including the members of the sociopolitical concerns committee, work to assure a well-informed membership and to promote the ongoing development of advocacy skills among that membership, the advocacy structure of the organization will falter; those at the hub bearing the weight of too many tasks and spread too thin without the support of a strong network of colleagues will eventually tire and be unable to continue. It is therefore essential that a fundamental goal of the affiliate's sociopolitical concerns committee be the transfer of information and advocacy skills to the full membership, and at times to other professional colleagues and to the wider community. Before people can advocate, they need to be informed about issues and related decision-making processes. They need to understand reasons for advocacy and they need to know what they can do that might make a difference. Finally, wherever possible, they need to have opportunities to develop advocacy skills, e.g. to learn how to write a brief but effective letter to a legislator, how to disagree without creating hostility, how to motivate others to get involved in a project.

Transferring information and skills can be done in many ways. Newsletter articles, email lists, action alerts, issue updates, conference presentations, round table and panel discussions, and workshops are all useful vehicles for exchanging information and ideas. Whatever the format, it is very important that a professional organization promote an environment where questions are welcome, where affiliate and advocacy leaders realize that there is no such thing as a stupid question, and where members are never embarrassed to ask about something that they are still grappling with. If issues were clear and simple, there would be very little disagreement; decisions could be made quickly and with ease. However, most concerns are not simple. There are financial, pedagogical, political, and emotional ramifications. Professional colleagues, affiliate members, and community neighbors need to know that they are welcome to raise questions and concerns and that inherent in sharing information is the process of exploring the complexities of an issue.

While articles, fliers, presentations, and discussions are effective ways of transmitting information, workshops, manuals, and advocacy "how-to" packets are particularly useful tools for the transfer of skills. Workshops enable participants to practice certain skills and to benefit from immediate feedback. Participants can role-play a meeting with a "busy legislator," with an "unconvinced neighbor," or with an "irate opponent." Through the vehicle of the workshop, participants can watch models of both productive and counterproductive interactions. They can discuss the strengths of one and the shortcomings of the other. They can then tackle their own role-play "assignments" with self-assessment and group feedback as follow-up. Such experiences not only strengthen individual communication skills, but spotlight important arguments and concerns related to an issue and reinforce the importance of keeping oneself well informed. Skill-building workshops can be designed around the development of certain "target" skills or can focus on a particular issue and the array of skills related to that issue. Both skill-based and issue-based workshops are important in the development of the advocacy skills of the membership of your affiliate, and both should become regular components of the organization's conference offerings.

Manuals, like that produced by the members of NYSTESOL to address the problem of underemployment among ESOL teachers, can also be very useful skill-building tools. In this case, the manual is issue specific, offering historical background information about the issue, providing arguments for or against particular positions, reporting on actions that have already been taken and their outcomes, and proposing possible strategies for addressing the issue in other settings.

Finally, as professional organizations learn from their individual experiences and from each other, they can develop "how-to" packets to be shared with their own members and with colleagues in other organizations. Such packets contain position statements and resolutions, skill-building tips (do's and don'ts), and samples of letters to legislators as well as letters to the editor.

Advocacy is a very big job. People don't easily realize that they can make a difference. They don't seem to believe that their input is of significance. That's why education is an ongoing and critical part of advocacy. We need to learn that we can make a difference, that our voices matter. We need to teach others what advocacy is; we need to help them discover the multiplicity of forms that it can take. Becoming sociopolitically active is a lot of hard work, but the more we do it, the better we get at it. Advocacy is real on-the-job training. If we sit back and let others make decisions for us, then we get what we deserve. Participating in the process doesn't always mean that we get what we want; it doesn't mean that there are no disappointments. But, when we take part in decision-making, we often find that we have succeeded in keeping or changing a situation for the better. As we participate in professional advocacy we strengthen our awareness of the connections between the quality of our work and the quality of our lives, we strengthen our organizational and communication skills, and we discover the vibrant network of individuals and organizations that share our goals.

Discussion Questions and Activities

1. Is there a local association of ESOL professionals where you are now studying/working?

    A. If so, how can you go about getting involved in the organization?

    B. What strengths do you have to offer?

    C. Does it have a sociopolitical concerns committee?

    D. What are its front-burner issues?

    E. How has the organization been addressing these concerns? What has worked? What hasn't?

    F. How can you best serve the organization? What can it offer you?

2. Some ESOL professionals are concerned that organizational leadership is too often dominated by native speakers of English (especially Americans!), including those working outside of their native country. Is there a relationship between one's nationality and the appropriateness of holding positions of professional leadership? Should there be some sort of "balance" in the proportion of organizational leadership positions held by ESOL professionals who are citizens of a country and those who are not? Explain your point of view.

3. Are there any ESOL programs in the community where you are now living? What are the working conditions in these programs? Do instructors have job security? Benefits? Are their salaries commensurate with their level of education and the local cost of living? What is a typical workload?

4. Page 197 contains a list of concerns raised by members of the international organization TESOL. In small groups, review the list and add any additional concerns that you may have. Together prioritize the concerns according to the needs of your teaching contexts. Be ready to explain your decisions. Together choose one concern and develop a plan for addressing it.

5. Interview five TESOL teachers in your area about their views on their roles as ESOL teachers and in particular on the role that advocacy plays in their professional lives. What are their concerns? How do they address them? What "tips" can they offer newcomers to the field?

Additional Questions and Activities

1. Describe any experiences you have had with course and/or program materials design and evaluation. Who were the primary participants? What did you find easy about the process? Difficult about the process? In your opinion, in any kind of ESL program for adults, who should be responsible for choosing materials? Why? How important is it for everyone who is teaching the same course to use the same materials and the same syllabus?

2. If a particular dialect is not selected as a standard for English language instruction, how will instructors choose which "accent," vocabulary, etc., to teach and how can testing and certification be meaningful across borders?

3. Write down the three most significant learning experiences you have had, in or out of the formal classroom context. What made them significant? What role did language play? What role did the teacher play? How did they transform your beliefs about teaching and learning? What implications can you draw for the English language teaching situations in which you expect to be involved in the future?

4. Tutor a person for whom English is not a native language for a minimum of 20 hours. If you do not have easy access to someone, contact your local public library or community social services. They can help you locate someone. Create a portfolio of your involvement as a tutor. Include a description of the person, of yourself, the site of your tutoring sessions, a needs assessment, materials you developed for the student, examples of his or her work, and your reflections on how successful your involvement was for both you and the student.

5. In a small group, consider some of the more serious obstacles beginning teachers face on the job. How might these differ for language dominant and language minority teachers? Create a list of suggestions for improving the professional lives of beginning teachers and share them with your classmates.

6. Gather yourselves into small working groups. Find out what services and organizations exist in your community for helping recently arriving immigrants. Begin by contacting your local churches, public library, chambers of commerce, adult education programs, and public schools. Make a list of the services and organizations and divide it among the working groups. Each group is responsible for finding out as much as they can about the services and organizations to which they are assigned. Once the research has been completed, as a large group, compile the information and create a pamphlet that describes these services and organizations for public distribution.

7. Find out as much as you can about local, state, and national professional organizations devoted to teachers of English as an additional language. If possible, attend a meeting of the organization, or ask a member to come to speak to your class about the role of the organization in helping teachers of English and membership possibilities.

8. There are many listservs that provide discussion opportunities for English teachers from around the world on topics such as, for example, bilingual education, language policies and practices, teaching language minority students, second language learning, and the study of language use. Find one that appeals to you and become a member. Document the discussions over a six week period. At the end of this time, prepare a report in which you summarize your findings and reflect on the personal and professional value of having joined the list.

9. Write an essay in which you articulate your philosophy of teaching. Use the following questions to help guide your writing: What are the goals of education? How are they best achieved? What kind of classroom community will you build? What language policies will be created in your classroom? What role(s) will you play as teacher? What role(s) will the students play? What are some important rules/principles underlying successful classrooms? What are some effective practices? What will you strive NOT to do in the classroom?

Additional Reading and Resources

Arnold, B., Burke, B., James, C., Martin, D. and Thomas, B. (1991) *Educating for a Change*. Toronto: Between the Lines and the Doris Marshall Institute for Education and Action.

Auerbach, E. (with B. Barahona, J. Midy, F. Vaquerano, A. Zambrano and J. Arnaud) (1996) *From the Community to the Community: A Guidebook for Participatory Literacy Training*. Mahwah, NJ: Lawrence Erlbaum Associates.

Bardovi-Harlig, K. and Hartford, B. (eds) (1997) *Beyond Methods: Components of Second Language Teacher Education*. New York: McGraw-Hill.

Bereiter, C. and Scardamalia, M. (1993) *Surpassing Ourselves: An Inquiry into the Nature and Implications of Expertise*. Chicago: Open Court Press.

Bull, B.L., Fruehling, R.T., and Chattergy, V. (1992) *The Ethics of Multicultural and Bilingual Education*. New York: Teachers College Press.

Carroll, D.W. (1994) *Psychology of Language*. Pacific Grove, CA: Brooks/Cole.

Chevalier, M. (1994) (Spring) Developing a trusting community: Dilemmas in ESL adult instruction. *Adult Basic Education* 4 (1), 3–18.

Crookes, G. (1997) What influences what and how second and foreign language teachers teach. *Modern Language Journal* 81 (1), 67–79.

Csikszentmihalyi, M. (1990) *Flow: The Psychology of Optimal Experience*. New York: Harper & Row.

Csikszentmihalyi, M. (1997) *Finding Flow: The Psychology of Engagement with Everyday Life*. New York: HarperCollins.

Cummins, J. (1995) Empowering minority students: A framework for intervention. In O. Garcia and C. Baker (eds) *Policy and Practice in Bilingual Education* (pp. 103–117). Clevedon: Multilingual Matters.

Freeman, D. and Richards, J.C. (eds) (1996) *Teacher Learning in Language Teaching.* New York: Cambridge University Press.

Genesee, F. and Upshur, J. (1996) *Classroom Based Evaluation in Second Language Education.* New York: Cambridge University Press.

Kornblum, H. with Garshick, E. (1995) *Directory of Professional Preparation Programs in TESOL in the United States and Canada: 1995–1997.* Alexandria, VA: TESOL.

Lessow-Hurley, J. (1996) *The Foundations of Dual Language Instruction.* New York: Longman.

McCarthy, M. and Carter, R. (1994) *Language as Discourse.* New York: Longman.

McKay, S.L. and Hornberger, N.H. (1996) *Sociolinguistics and Language Teaching.* New York: Cambridge University Press.

Nonesuch, K. (1996) *Making Connections: Literacy and EAL Curriculum from a Feminist Perspective.* Toronto: Canadian Congress for Learning Opportunities for Women.

Numrich, C. (1996) On becoming a language teacher: Insights from diary studies. *TESOL Quarterly* 30 (1), 131–153.

Odlin, T. (ed.) (1994) *Perspectives on Pedagogical Grammar.* New York: Cambridge University Press.

Palmer, P. (1998) *The Courage to Teach: Exploring the Inner Landscape of a Teacher's Life.* San Fransisco: Jossey-Bass.

Posner, G. (1996) *Field Experience: Methods of Reflective Teaching* (4th edn). New York: Longman.

Postman, N. (1995) *The End of Education: Redefining the Value of School.* New York: Knopf.

Richards, J.C. (1998) *Beyond Training.* New York: Cambridge University Press.

Schiffrin, D. (1994) *Approaches to Discourse.* New York: Blackwell.

Shor, I., and Pari, C. (1999) *Critical Literacy in Action: Writing Words, Changing Worlds: A Tribute to the Teachings of Paulo Freire.* Portsmouth, NH: Heinemann.

Skehan, P. (1998) *A Cognitive Approach to Language Learning.* New York: Oxford University Press.

Smoke, T. (ed.) (1998) *Adult ESL: Politics, Pedagogy, and Participation in Classroom and Community Programs.* Mahwah, NJ: Lawrence Erlbaum Associates.

Stoller, F.L. (1997) The catalyst for change and innovation. In M.A. Christison and F.L. Stoller (eds) *A Handbook for Language Program Administrators* (pp. 33–48). Burlingame, CA: Alta Book Center.

van Lier, L. (1996) *Interaction in the Language Curriculum: Awareness, Autonomy and Authenticity.* New York: Longman.

Vella, J. (1994) *Learning to Listen, Learning to Teach: The Power of Dialogue in Educating Adults.* San Francisco: jossey-Bass.

Wallace, M.J. (1998) *Action Research for Language Teachers.* New York: Cambridge University Press.

Wallterstein, N. (1983). *Language and Culture in Conflict: Problem-posing in the ESL Classroom.* Reading, MA: Addison-Wesley.

Wright, T. and Bolitho, R. (1993) Language awareness: A missing link in language teacher education? *ELT Journal* 47 (4), 292–304.

Epilogue

L. Smith

"You Gotta Serve Somebody" was written with the hope that it might stimulate thought and be of modest entertainment value. It was inspired by the Bob Dylan song entitled "Gotta Serve Somebody" and by the debate over language policy in the United States. The connection of a Dylan song and the debate about the role of English and non-majority languages in American education and government might be difficult to grasp at first, but it came to me in a rare moment of satori. With the "din" of Pennycook, Phillipson, Skutnabb-Kangas, Thomas, and other authors, as well as the voices of the official English proponents dancing in my head, I pushed a cassette into my car stereo and found myself enveloped in Dylan's gospel call to service: "It may be the Devil, or it may be the Lord, but you're going to have to serve somebody." Regardless of one's religious convictions, the song is a powerful call to arms. Neutrality is unacceptable. You must take a stand! So it is in this debate over language policy, official English, and the role of English as an International Language. As teachers, administrators, researchers, and graduate students, we need to stay informed and aware of the relevant discussions. We are in a position to be advocates on behalf of those who may be marginalized or even deprived of their rights. This song represents an attempt to synthesize some of the more important issues related to the debate over language policy in the U.S. and the official English Movement.

You Gotta Serve Somebody

(A pedagogical call to arms)

by Lavon Smith (based on a song by Bob Dylan)

1

You may be an English teacher
Teaching overseas
You may have got a Master's
Maybe you've got a Ph.D.
You may have studied theory
Maybe you studied methodology
You may think that you're objective
Maybe you think you can "just teach"

CHORUS:

BUT YOU'RE GOING TO HAVE TO SERVE SOMEBODY
YES, YOU ARE. YOU'RE GOING TO HAVE TO SERVE SOME-
    BODY
IT MAY BE THE MONOLINGUISTS
IT MAY BE THE POLYGLOTS
BUT YOU'RE GOING TO HAVE TO SERVE SOMEBODY

2

You may speak Korean
You may speak Chinese
You may be trilingual
In English, German, and Japanese
Your Spanish may be impeccable
Your French is never snubbed
But, friend, if you want to teach English
Let me tell you, here's the rub
(chorus)

3

You may be an author
"Writing back" and taking 'em on
Maybe you're a critical pedagogue
Using words like "panopticon"
You may know about the discourse of EIL

Language and Culture are interrelated
You may think English "Worldliness"
Is overestimated
(chorus)

4

You may be a policy wonk
Maybe you boned up on Ebonics
Students failing, students dropping out
You can see the problem's chronic
You may blame the individual
Maybe you see society's role
You may accuse the liberals
Maybe you blame the status quo
(chorus)

5

You may be a columnist
Afraid of Balkanization
Maybe you're a media mogul
With the power of communication
You may be an advocate
For Ronald McDonaldization
You may own tall buildings
You're the Donald (or his agent)
(chorus)

6

Maybe you process poultry
Hiring illegals again and again
Maybe you're just a good ol' boy
Trying to protect your skin
You may be a patriot
Maybe you're just confused
You may raise up English only
Like you raise up the Red, White, and Blue
(chorus)

7

You may be a linguist
Talking language equality
Interacting with Vygotsky

In the ZPD
Maybe you raise your affective filter
When Krashen comes to dinner
You can "generate" Chomsky on demand
But you "behave" like B. F. Skinner
(chorus)

8

You may be a grad student
And though some of your friends may scoff
You're probably busting your butt
Wondering if it's going to pay off
And you're working part time at the carpet plant
You've got a couple of rug rats, too
You may think that politics
Has nothing to do with you
 (chorus)

9 (extra verse)

You may be a legislator
In Washington D.C.
Thinking about the next election
Thinking about your constituencies
You may be a Democrat
You may be a Republican
U.S. ENGLISH makes a contribution
So do the Freedom Forum fans
(chorus)

References

Ahai, N. and Faraclas, N. (1993) Rights and expectations in an age of "debt crisis": Literacy and integral human development in Papua New Guinea. In P. Freebody and A.R. Welch (eds) *Knowledge, Culture and Power: International Perspectives on Literacy as Policy and Practice.* London: Falmer.

Algeo, J. (1988) British and American grammatical differences. *International Journal of Lexicography* 1 (1), 131.

American Council on Education: Committee on Foreign Students and Institutional Policy. (1982) *Foreign Students and Institutional Policy: Towards an Agenda for Action.* Washington, D.C.: American Council on Education.

Associated Press. (March 9, 1994) Use of Parody test costs teacher his job.

Auerbach, E. (1992) *Making Meaning, Making Change: Participatory Curriculum Development for Adult ESL/Literacy.* Washington, D.C.: Center for Applied Linguistics/Delta.

Auerbach, E. (1995) The politics of the ESL classroom: Issues of power in pedagogical choices. In J. Tollefson (ed.) *Power and Inequality in Language Education* (pp. 9–33). New York: Cambridge University Press.

Auerbach, E. (in press) "Yes, but": Problematizing participatory ESL pedagogy. In B. Burnaby and P. Campbell (eds) *Participatory Approaches in Adult Education.*

August, D. and Hakuta, K. (eds) (1997) *Improving Schooling for Language-Minority Children: Research Agenda.* Washington, D.C.: National Academy Press.

Baldauf, R.B., Jr. and Rainbow, P.G. (1996) Gender bias and differential motivation in LOTE learning and retention rates: A case study of problems and materials development. Canberra: Australian Government Publishing Services. [Department of Employment, Education and Training; Australian Second Language Learning Program 1991 National Project.]

Ball, A. (1991) *Organizational Patterns in the Oral and Written Expository Language of African American Adolescents.* Stanford: Unpublished Ph.D. Dissertation.

Ball, A. (1992) Cultural preference and the expository writing of African-American adolescents. *Written Communication* 9 (4), 501–532.

Ball, A. (1995) Investigating language, learning, and linguistic competence of African-American children: Torrey revisited. *Linguistics and Education* 7, 23–46.

Bamgbose, A. (1992) Standard Nigerian English: Issues of identification. In B. Kachru (ed.) *The Other Tongue: English across Cultures* (2nd edn) (pp. 148–161). Urbana: University of Illinois Press.

Banks, J.A. (1991) Teaching multicultural literacy to teachers. *Teaching Education* 4, 135–144.

Banks, J. (1993) The canon debate: Knowledge construction, and multicultural education. *Educational Researcher* 22 (5), 4–14.

Banks, J. (1994) *Multiethnic Education: Theory and Practice.* Boston: Allyn and Bacon.

Barber, B.R. (1997) Public schooling: Education for democracy. In J.I. Goodlad and T.J. McMannon (eds) *The Public Purpose of Education and Schooling* (pp. 21–32). San Francisco: Jossey-Bass Publishers.

Bardovi-Harlig, K. and Hartford, B. (eds) (1997) *Beyond Methods: Components of Second Language Teacher Education.* New York: McGraw-Hill.

Barndt, D. (1991) *English at Work: A Tool Kit for Teachers.* Syracuse, NY: New Readers Press.

Bartolome, L. (1994) Beyond the methods fetish: Toward a humanizing pedagogy. *Harvard Educational Review* 64 (2), 173–194.

Baugh, J. (1983) *Black Street Speech: Its History, Structure, and Survival.* Austin: University of Texas Press.

Baugh, J. (1988) Language and race: Some implications for linguistic science. In F. Newmeyer (ed.) *Linguistics: The Cambridge Survey* 4 (pp. 64–74). Cambridge: Cambridge University Press.

Baugh, J. (1994). *Learning Partners: Helping Children and Parents Learn Together.* Thousand Oaks, CA: Learning Partners Inc.

Baugh, J. (1998) Linguistics, education, and the law: Educational reform for African-American language minority students. In S. Mufwene *et al.* (eds) *African American English: Structure, History, and Usage* (pp. 282–301). London: Routledge.

Baugh, J. (1999) *Out of the Mouths of Slaves: African American Language and Educational Malpractice.* Austin: University of Texas Press.

Bennett, L. (1993) *Before the Mayflower: A History of Black America* (6th rev. edn). New York: Viking.

Benson, P. (1997) The philosophy and politics of learner autonomy. In P. Benson and P. Voller (eds) *Autonomy and Independence in Language Learning* (pp. 18–34). London: Longman.

Bereiter, C. and Scardamalia, M. (1993) *Surpassing Ourselves: An Inquiry into the Nature and Implications of Expertise.* Chicago: Open Court Press.

Berman, R. and Slobin, D. (1994) *Relating Events in Narrative: A Crosslinguistic Developmental Study.* Hillsdale, NJ: L. Erlbaum.

Boas, F. (1911) *Handbook of American Indian Languages.* Washington, D.C.: Bureau of American Ethnology, Smithsonian Institution.

Boggs, G.L. (1998) *Living for Change.* Minneapolis: University of Minnesota.

Bokamba, E.G. (1992) The Africanization of English. In B. Kachru (ed.) *The Other Tongue: English across Cultures* (2nd edn) (pp. 125–147). Urbana: University of Illinois Press.

Boudin, K. (1993) Participatory literacy education behind bars: AIDS opens the door. *Harvard Educational Review* 63 (2), 207–232.

Bourdieu, P. (1986) The forms of capital. In J.G. Richardson (ed.) *Handbook of Theory and Research for the Sociology of Education.* New York: Greenwood Press.

Bourdieu, P. and Passeron, J.C. (1977) *Reproduction in Education, Society and Culture.* Los Angeles: Sage.

Bowles, S. and Gintis, H. (1976) *Schooling in Capitalist America.* New York: Basic Books.

Brecht, R.D. and Ingold, C.W. (1998) Tapping a national resource: Heritage languages in the United States. *ERIC Digest.* [webmaster@cal.org; eric@cal.org; http://www.cal.org/ericll].

Breen, M. (1984) Process syllabuses for the language classroom. In C.J. Brumfit (ed.) *General English Syllabus Design.* Oxford: Pergamon Press. [ELT Documents 118]

Bronner, E. (1998, June 4) Defeat of bilingual education is challenged in federal court. *New York Times*, A25.

Bruner, J. (1985) Vygotsky: A historical and conceptual perspective. In J.V. Wertsch (ed.) *Culture, Communication, and Cognition: Vygotskian Perspectives*. New York: Cambridge University Press.

Buber, M. (1965) *Between Man and Man*. New York: Collier Books.

Bull, B.L., Fruehling, R.T., and Chattergy, V. (1992) *The Ethics of Multicultural and Bilingual Education*. New York: Teachers College Press.

Bullough, R. and Gitlin, A. (1995) *Becoming a Student of Teaching: Methodologies for Exploring Self and School Context*. New York: Garland Publishers.

Canagarajah, A.S. (1993) Critical ethnography of a Sri Lankan classroom: Ambiguities in student opposition to reproduction through ESOL. *TESOL Quarterly* 27 (4), 601–626.

Carrasquillo, A.L., and Rodriquez, V. (1995) *Language Minority Students in the Mainstream Classroom*. Clevedon: Multilingual Matters Ltd.

Carroll, D.W. (1994) *Psychology of Language*. Pacific Grove, CA: Brooks/Cole.

Casanova, U. (1995) Bilingual education: Politics or pedagogy? In O. García and C. Baker (eds) *Policy and Practice in Bilingual Education: Extending the Foundations* (pp. 15–24). Clevedon, England: Multilingual Matters Ltd.

Castro, M. (1992) On the curious question of language in Miami. In J. Crawford (ed.) *Language Loyalties: A Source Book on the Official English Controversy* (pp. 178–186). Chicago: University of Chicago Press.

Cazden, C. (1988) *Classroom Discourse*. Portsmouth, NH: Heinemann.

Chapa, J. (1990) Population estimates of school age language minorities and limited English proficiency children of the United States, 1979–1988. [On-line] Availability: http://www.ncbe.gwu.edu/iasconferences/index.htm

Chavez, L. (1991, March) Why bilingual education fails Hispanic children. *McCall's* 118, 59–60.

Chen, L. (1993) *Primary Six New PSLE Examination: English Practice Papers*. Singapore: Success Publications.

Chisanga, T. (1989) "Non-problematic Zambianisms" and their implications for the teaching of English in Zambia. In J. Schmied (ed.), *English in East and Central Africa*, 99 (pp. 63–83). Bayreuth University. [African Studies Series 15].

Christison, M.A. and Stoller, F.L. (1997) *A Handbook for Language Program Administrators*. Burlingame, CA: Alta Book Center.

Clary, M. (1997a, March 23) Black, Cuban racial chasm splits Miami. *Los Angeles Times*, A1, A20, A21.

Clary, M. (1997b, Aug. 28) Finding a "muy friquiado" way to speak. *Los Angeles Times*, A5.

Collier, V. (1989) How long: A synthesis of research on academic achievement in a second language. *TESOL Quarterly*, 23, 509–531.

Commission on Teacher Credentialing, State of California. (1992) Standards of program quality and effectiveness for professional teacher preparation programs for multiple and single subject teaching credentials with a (bilingual) crosscultural, language and academic development (CLAD/BCLAD) emphasis. Sacramento, CA: Author.

Counts, G. (1932) *Dare the School Build a New Social Order?* Yonkers, NY: World Book.

Crawford, J. (1992) *Hold Your Tongue: Bilingualism and the Politics of "English Only."* Reading: Addison-Wesley Publishing Company.

Crawford, J. (1995) *Bilingual Education: History, Politics, Theory, and Practice*. Los Angeles: Bilingual Education Services Inc.

Crookes, G. (1997) What influences what and how second and foreign language teachers teach. *Modern Language Journal* 81 (1), 67–79.

Crystal, D. (1997) *English as a Global Language*. Cambridge: University Press.

Csikszentmihalyi, M. (1990) *Flow: The Psychology of Optimal Experience*. New York: Harper & Row.

Csikszentmihalyi, M. (1997) *Finding Flow: The Psychology of Engagement with Everyday Life*. New York: HarperCollins.

Cummins, J. (1986) Empowering minority students: A framework for intervention. *Harvard Educational Review* 56 (1), 13–36.

Cummins, J. (1995) Power and pedagogy in the education of culturally diverse students. In J. Frederickson (ed.) *Reclaiming Our Voices: Bilingual Education, Critical Pedagogy, and Praxis* (pp. 139–162). Ontario: California Association for Bilingual Education.

Cummins, J. (1998, Feb. 9) *Beyond Adversarial Discourse: Searching for Common Ground in the Education of Bilingual Students*. Presentation to the California State Board of Education.

Cutri, R.M. and Ferrin, S. (1999) The moral dimensions of bilingual education: Identifying the power and limitations of political and spiritual moralities. *Bilingual Research Journal* (submitted).

Darder, A. (1991) *Culture and Power in the Classroom: A Critical Foundation for Bilingual Education*. Westport, CT: Bergin & Garvey.

Darling-Hammond, L. (1997) *The Right to Learn: A Blueprint for Creating Schools that Work*. San Francisco: Jossey-Bass Publishers.

DeGroot, A. and Kroll, J. (eds) (1997) *Tutorials in Bilingualism: Psycholinguistic Perspectives*. Mahwah, NJ: L. Erlbaum.

Delgado-Gaitan, C. (1990) *Literacy for Empowerment: The Role of Parents in Children's Education*. New York: Falmer Press.

Dewey, J. (1938) *Experience and Education*. New York: Macmillan Publishing Company.

Díaz-Rico, L.T. and Weed, K.Z. (1995) *The Crosscultural, Language, and Academic Development Handbook: A Complete K-12 Reference Guide*. Boston: Allyn and Bacon.

Durkheim, E. (1961a) *The Elementary Forms of the Religious Life*. New York: Collier Books.

Edelsky, C. (1991) *With Literacy and Justice for All: Rethinking the Social in Language and Education*. London: Falmer Press.

Educational Testing Service. (1980) *Test of English for International Communication*. Princeton: ETS. [retired version provided by Educational Testing Service]

Educational Testing Service. (1990) *Bulletin of Information, Test of English for International Communication*. Princeton: ETS.

Educational Testing Service. (1991) *The Reporter*, Number 7.

Educational Testing Service. (1993) *Test of English for International Communication*. Princeton: ETS. [retired version provided by Educational Testing Service]

Educational Testing Service. (1996a) *TOEFL Test and Score Data Summary, 1996–97 Edition*. Princeton: ETS.

Educational Testing Service. (1996b) *Test of Written English guide* (4th edn). Princeton: ETS.

Educational Testing Service. (1998) *TOEIC Examinee Handbook*. Princeton: ETS.

Ericsson, K. (ed.) (1996) *The Road to Excellence: The Acquisition of Expert Performance in the Arts and Sciences, Sports, and Games.* Mahwah, NJ: Lawrence Erlbaum.

Fairclough, N. (1989) *Language and Power.* London: Longman.

Farr, M. (1994) En los dos idomas: Literacy practices among Chicano Mexicans. In B. Moss (ed.) *Literacy across Communities* (pp. 9–48). Cresskill, NJ: Hampton Press.

Fenstermacher, G.D. (1990) Some moral considerations on teaching as a profession. In J.I. Goodlad, R. Soder, and K.A. Sirotnik (eds) *The Moral Dimensions of Teaching* (pp. 130–151). San Francisco: Jossey-Bass.

Ferguson, C.A. (1992) Forward. In B. Kachru (ed.) *The Other Tongue: English across Cultures* (2nd edn) (pp. xiii–xvii). Urbana: University of Illinois Press.

Fiji's fledgling English television network as an English as a second language curriculum. Paper presented at AILA/IRAAL International Conference, Dublin, June 1994.

Fix, M. and Passel, J.S. (1994) *Immigration and Immigrants: Setting the Record Straight.* Washington, D.C.: The Urban Institute.

Flaster, D.J. (1983) *Malpractice.* New York: Scribner.

Fleischman, H.L. and Hopstock, P.J. (1993) *Descriptive Study of Services to Limited English Proficient Students, Volume 1. Summary of Findings and Conclusions.* Arlington, V.A: Development Associates.

Foster, M. (1997) Ebonics and all that jazz: Cutting through the politics of linguistics, education, and race. *Quarterly of the National Writing Project* 19 (1), 7–12.

Freeman, D. and Richards, J.C. (1993) Conceptions of teaching and the education of second language teachers. *TESOL Quarterly* 27 (2), 193–216.

Freeman, D. and Richards, J.C. (eds) (1996) *Teacher Learning in Language Teaching.* New York: Cambridge University Press.

Freire, P. (1970) *Pedagogy of the Oppressed.* New York: Herder and Herder.

Freire, P. (1996) *Letters to Cristina: Reflections on My Life and Work.* New York and London: Routledge.

Garcia, E. (1994) *Understanding and Meeting the Challenge of Student Cultural Diversity.* Boston: Houghton Mifflin.

García, O. (1985) Bilingualism in the U.S.: Present attitudes in the light of past policies. In S. Greenbaum (ed.) *The English Language Today* (pp. 147–158). Oxford: Pergamon Institute of English.

García, O. (1995) Spanish language loss as a determinant of income among Latinos in the United States: Implications for language policy in schools. In J. Tollefson (ed.) *Power and Inequality in Language Education* (pp. 142–160). Cambridge: Cambridge University Press.

Gebhard, J., Gaitan, S. and Oprandy, R. (1990) Beyond prescription: The student teacher as investigator in J. Richards and D. Nunan (eds) *Second Language Teacher Education* (pp. 16–25). Cambridge: Cambridge University Press.

Gee, J.P. (1994) Orality and literacy: From the savage mind to ways with words. In J. Maybin (ed.) *Language and Literacy in Social Practice.* Clevedon: Multilingual Matters.

Genesee, F. and Upshur, J. (1996) *Classroom Based Evaluation in Second Language Education.* New York: Cambridge University Press.

Giroux, H. (1983) *Theory and Resistance in Education: A Pedagogy for the Opposition.* South Hadley, MA: Bergin and Garvey.

Giroux, H. (1988) *Schooling and the Struggle for Public Life: Critical Pedagogy in the Modern Age.* Minneapolis: University of Minnesota Press.

Giroux, H. (1992) *Border Crossings: Cultural Workers and the Politics of Education.* New York: Routledge.

Glazer, N. and Moynihan, D.P. (1963) *Beyond the Melting Pot: The Negroes, Puerto Ricans, Jews, Italians, and Irish of New York City.* Cambridge, MA: MIT Press.

Gonzalez, A. (1983) When does an error become a feature of Philippine English? In R. Noss (ed.) *Varieties of English in Southeast Asia* (pp. 150–172). Singapore: Regional Language Centre. [Anthology Series 11]

Goodlad, J.I. (1990) The occupation of teaching in schools. In J.I. Goodlad, R. Soder, and K.A. Sirotnik (eds) *The Moral Dimensions of Teaching* (pp. 3–34). San Francisco: Jossey-Bass Publishers.

Goodlad, J.I. and Keating, P. (1994) *Access to Knowledge: The Continuing Agenda for Our Nation's Schools.* New York: College Entrance Examination Board.

Goodlad, J.I., Soder, R. and Sirotnik, K.A. (eds) (1990) *The Moral Dimensions of Teaching.* San Francisco: Jossey-Bass Publishers.

Goodman, S. and Graddol, D. (1996) *Redesigning English: New Texts, New Identities.* London: Routledge.

Grant, R. (1995) Meeting the needs of young second language learners. In E. Garcia and B. McLaughlin (eds) *Meeting the Challenge of Linguistic and Cultural Diversity in Early Childhood Education* (pp. 1–17) New York: Teachers College Press.

Green, L. (1995). Study of Verb Classes in African American English. *Linguistics and Education* 7, 65–82.

Greene, M. (1988) *The Dialectic of Freedom.* New York: Teachers College Press.

Grin, F. (1990) The economic approach to minority languages. *Journal of Multilingual and Multicultural Development.* 11, 153–171.

Gumperz, J.J. and Levinson, S. (eds) (1996) *Reexamining the Whorfian Hypothesis.* New York: Cambridge University Press.

Haberman, M. (1995) *STAR Teachers of Children of Poverty.* West Lafayett, IN: Kappa Delta Pi, an International Honor Society in Education.

Heath, S.B. (1983) *Ways with Words: Language, Life and Work in Communities and Classrooms.* London: Cambridge University Press.

Hispanic Link Weekly Report (1995, Oct. 2) 99.94% of documents are printed in English, 1.

hooks, b. (1994) Eros, eroticism, and the pedagogical process. In H.A. Giroux and P. McLaren (eds) *Between Borders: Pedagogy and the Politics of Cultural Studies* (pp. 113–118). New York: Routledge.

Hornbeck, D. Speech before the National Council of Churches of Christ in the U.S.A. Chicago, IL, November 11, 1998.

Howe, D.H. (1974) *New Guided English, Book 1.* Kuala Lumpur: Oxford University Press. [Reprinted by Penerbit FaJar Bakti Sdn. Bhd., Kuala Lumpur, 1986.]

Howe, M. (1990, January 6) Immigrants swell language classes. *New York Times,* 26L.

Hymes, D. (1972) On communicative competence. In J.B. Pride and J. Holmes (eds) *Sociolinguistics* (pp. 269–293). Harmondsworth, Middlesex: Penguin Books.

Imhoff, G. (1990) The position of U.S. English on bilingual education. *The Annals of the American Academy of Political and Social Science* 508, 48–61.

Ingram, C. (1986, November 24) Prop. 63 backers aim at bilingual education. *Los Angeles Times,* 3, 16.

Jenkins, R. (1992) *Pierre Bourdieu.* London: Routledge.

Johnson, K.E. (1992) Learning to teach: Instructional actions and decisions of pre-service ESL teachers. *TESOL Quarterly* 26 (3), 507–535.

Johnson, K.E. (1996) The role of theory in L2 teacher education. *TESOL Quarterly* 30 (4), 765–771.

Jordan, G. and Weedon, C. (1995) *Cultural Politics: Class, Gender, Race and the Modern World.* Oxford: Blackwell.

Kachru, B.B. (1983) *The Other Tongue: English across Cultures.* Urbana: University of Illinois Press.

Kachru, B.B. (1986) *The Alchemy of English.* Oxford: Pergamon Press. [Reprinted by University of Illinois Press, Urbana, 1990]

Kachru, B.B. (1992a) Introduction: The other side of English and the 1990s. In B. Kachru (ed.) *The Other Tongue: English across Cultures* (2nd edn) (pp. 1–15). Urbana: University of Illinois Press.

Kachru, B.B. (1992b) Models for non-native Englishes. In B. Kachru (ed.) *The Other Tongue: English across Cultures* (2nd edn) (pp. 48–75). Urbana: University of Illinois Press.

Kachru, B.B. (1992c) Meaning in deviation: Toward understanding non-native English texts. In B. Kachru (ed.) *The Other Tongue: English across Cultures* (2nd edn) (pp. 301–326). Urbana: University of Illinois Press.

Kachru, B.B. (ed.) (1992d) *The Other Tongue: English across Cultures* (2nd edn). Urbana: University of Illinois Press.

Kachru, B.B. (1998) Past imperfect: The other side of English in Asia. In L.E. Smith and M.L. Forman (eds) *World Englishes 2000* (pp. 68–89). Honolulu: University of Hawaii Press.

Kachru, Y. (1988) Interpreting Indian English expository prose. *IDEAL* 3, 39–50. [Published by Division of English as an International Language, University of Illinois, Urbana.]

Kang, K.C. (1997, June 29) Chinese in the Southland: A changing picture. *Los Angeles Times*, A1, A32.

Kaplan, R.B. and Baldauf, Jr., R.B. (1997) *Language Planning from Practice to Theory.* Clevedon, UK: Multilingual Matters.

Kempf, S. (1997) *Finding Solutions to Hunger: A Sourcebook for Middle and Upper School Teachers.* New York: World Hunger Year. http://www.iglou.com/why.

Kolln, M. (1997) *Understanding Grammar* (5th edn). New York: Macmillan.

Kornblum, H. with Garshick, E. (1995) *Directory of Professional Preparation Programs in TESOL in the United States and Canada: 1995–1997.* Alexandria, VA: TESOL.

Korthagen, F.A.J. and Kessels, J.P.A.M. (1999, May) Linking theory and practice: Changing the pedagogy of teacher education. *Educational Researcher.*

Kozol J. (1991) *Savage Inequalities.* New York: Crown.

Krashen, S., Tse, L. and McQuillan, J. (1998) *Heritage Language Development.* Language Education Associates.

Krauss, M. (1992) The world's languages in crisis. *Language* 68 (1), 4–10.

Kretzschmar, W.A. (ed.) (1993) *Handbook of the Linguistic Atlas of the Middle and South Atlantic States.* Chicago: University of Chicago Press.

Kubota, R. (1999) Japanese culture constructed by discourses: Implications for applied linguistic research and ELT. *TESOL Quarterly* 33 (1), 9–35.

Labov, W. (1972) *Language in the Inner-City: Studies in the Black English Vernacular.* Philadelphia: University of Pennsylvania Press.

Labov, W. (1982) Objectivity and commitment in linguistic science: The case of the Black English trial in Ann Arbor. *Language in Society* 11, 165–201.

Ladson-Billings, G. (1994) *The Dreamkeepers.* San Francisco: Jossey-Bass.

Lantolf, J. and Appel, G. (1994) *Vygotskian Approaches to Second Language Research.* Norwood, NJ: Ablex Publishers.

Lau v. Nichols. (1974) 414 U.S. 563.

Leap. W. (1993) *American Indian English.* Salt Lake City: University of Utah Press.

Lee, C. (1995) A culturally based cognitive apprenticeship: Teaching African-American high school students skills in literary interpretation. *Reading Research Quarterly* 30, 608–630.

Lima, E.S. and Lima, M.G. (1998) Identity, cultural diversity and education: Notes towards a pedagogy of the excluded. In E.T. Trueba and Y.L. Zou (eds) *Ethnic Identity and Power: Cultural Contexts of Political Action in School and Society.* Albany: State University of New York Press.

Lippi-Green, R. (1997) *English with an Accent: Language, Ideology and Discrimination in the United States.* London: Routledge.

Lo Bianco, J. (in press). Language policies: State texts for silencing and giving voice. In P. Freebody and S. Muspratt (eds) *Difference, Silence and Cultural Practice.* Creskill. NJ: Hampton Press.

Lotherington-Wolozyn, H. (1994) Unintended pedagogy: Fiji's fledgling English television network as an English as a second language curriculum. Paper presented at AILA/IRAAL International Conference, Dublin, June 1994.

Lowenberg, P. (1986) Non-native varieties of English: Nativization, norms, and implications. *Studies in Second Language Acquisition* 8 (1), 1–18.

Lowenberg, P. (1990) Nativization and interlanguage in Standard English: Another look. In J.E. Alatis (ed.) *Linguistics, Language Teaching and Language Acquisition: The Interdependence of Theory, Practice and Research* (pp. 157–168). Washington, D.C.: Georgetown University Press. [Georgetown University Round Table on Languages and Linguistics 1990]

Lucas, T., Henze, R. and Donato, R. (1990) Promoting the success of Latino language-minority students: An exploratory study of six high schools. *Harvard Educational Review* 60, 315–340.

Luke, A. (1995) Text and discourse in education: An introduction to critical discourse analysis. In M. Apple (ed.) *Review of Research in Education* 21. Washington, D.C.: AERA.

Luke, C. and Gore, J. (1992) *Feminisms and Critical Pedagogy.* London: Routledge.

Macias, R. (1999) Survey of the states' LEP students and available educational programs and services, 1996–97. *Part II: Survey Data, Tables and Figures.* [On-line]. Availability: http://www.ncbe.gwu.edu/iasconferences/index.htm

Mayes, C. (1998) A transpersonal model for teacher reflectivity. Unpublished manuscript, Brigham Young University.

McArthur, E.K. (1993) *Language Characteristics and Schooling in the U.S., A Changing Picture: 1979 and 1989.* National Center for Education Statistics, Office of Educational Research and Improvement. Document number NCES 93–699. Washington, D.C.: U.S. Government Printing Office.

McCallen, B. (1989) *English: A World Commodity.* London: The Economist Intelligence Unit.

McCarthy, M. and Carter, R. (1994) *Language as Discourse.* New York: Longman.

McCormick, M. (1994) *Creating the Nonsexist Classroom.* New York: Teachers College Press.

McDermott, R. (1987) Achieving school failure: An anthropological approach to literacy and social stratification. In G. Spindler (ed.) *Education and Cultural Process: Anthropological Approaches* (pp. 173–209). New York: Holt, Rinehart and Winston.

McGroarty, M. (1998) *Partnerships with Linguistic Minority Communities.* TESOL Professional Papers #4. Alexandria, VA: Teachers of English to Speakers of Other Languages.

McKay, S.L. and Hornberger, N.H. (1996) *Sociolinguistics and Language Teaching.* New York: Cambridge University Press.

McLaughlin, B. (1992) *Myths and Misconceptions about Second Language Learning: What Every Teacher Needs to Unlearn.* Santa Cruz, CA: National Center for Research on Cultural Diversity and Second Language Learning.

McLaughlin, D. (1994) Toward a dialogical understanding of literacy: The case of Navajo print. In B. Moss (ed.) *Literacy across Communities* (pp. 9–48). Cresskill, NJ: Hampton Press.

Mehan, H. (1991) *Sociological Foundations Supporting the Study of Cultural Diversity.* Santa Cruz, CA: National Center for Research on Cultural Diversity and Second Language Learning.

Michaels, S. (1981) Sharing time: Children's narrative styles and differential access to literacy. *Language in Society* 10, 423–440.

Microsoft Corporation (1998) MicrosoftWord '98 [Computer software].

Moll, L. (1990) *Vygotsky and Education: Instructional Implications and Applications of Sociohistorical Psychology.* Cambridge: Cambridge University Press.

Morgan, B. (1997) Identity and intonation: Linking dynamic processes in an ESL classroom. *TESOL Quarterly* 31 (3), 431–450.

Moss, M. and Puma, M. (1995) Prospects: The Congressionally Mandated Study of Educational Growth and Opportunity. First-Year Report on Language Minority and Limited English Proficient Students. Prepared for Office of the Under Secretary. U.S. Department of Education by Abt Associates, Cambridge, MA.

Mujica, M. (1994, November 9) U.S. English membership letter.

Mujica, M. (1995, July 28) U.S. English membership letter.

Murray, D. (1992) *Diversity as Resource: Redefining Cultural Literacies.* Alexandria, VA: Teachers of English to Speakers of Other Languages.

Nakanishi, D.T. and Hirano-Nakanishi, M. (eds) (1983) *The Education of Asian and Pacific Americans: Historical Perspectives and Prescriptions for the Future.* Phoenix: AZ: Oxford Press.

Nakanishi, D.T. and Nishida T.Y. (eds) (1995) *The Asian American Educational Experience: A Sourcebook for Teachers and Students.* New York: Routledge.

Nandy, M. (1995) *Effective Business Letters: A Guide to All Forms of Business Correspondence.* Selangor, Malaysia: Pelanduk Publications.

Nash, A., Carson, A., Rhum, M., McGrail, L. and Gomez-Sanford, R. (1992) *Talking Shop: A Curriculum Sourcebook for Participatory Adult ESL.* Washington, D.C. and McHenry, IL: Center for Applied Linguistics and Delta Systems.

Nieto, S. (1992) *Affirming Diversity: The Sociopolitical Context of Multicultural Education.* White Plains, NY: Longman.

Norton Peirce, B. (1995) Social identity, investment, and language learning. *TESOL Quarterly* 29, 9–31.

Norton, B. (1997) Language, identity and the ownership of English. *TESOL Quarterly* 31 (3), 409–429.

Numrich, C. (1996) On becoming a language teacher: Insights from diary studies. *TESOL Quarterly* 30 (1), 131–153.

Odlin, T. (ed.) (1994) *Perspectives on Pedagogical Grammar.* New York: Cambridge University Press.

Palmer, P. (1993) *To Know as We Are Known: Education as a Spiritual Journey.* New York: Harper.

Palmer, P. (1998) *The Courage to Teach: Exploring the Inner Landscape of a Teacher's Life.* San Francisco: Jossey-Bass Publishers.

Pattanayak, D.P. (1986) Language, politics, region formation, regional planning. In E. Annamalai, B. Jernudd, and J. Rubin (eds) *Language Planning: Proceedings of an Institute* (pp. 18–42). Mysore: Central Institute of Indian Languages.

Pease-Alvarez, L., Garcia, E.E., and Espinosa, P. (1991) Effective instruction for language-minority students: An early childhood case study. *Early Childhood Research Quarterly* 6, 347–361.

Peirce, B.N. (1989) Toward a pedagogy of possibility in the teaching of English internationally. *TESOL Quarterly* 23, 401–420.

Peirce, B.N. (1995) Social identity, investment, and language learning. *TESOL Quarterly* 29, 9–31.

Pennington, M.C. (1996) *Phonology in English Language Teaching: An International Approach.* London: Longman.

Pennycook, A. (1994a) Critical pedagogical approaches to research. *TESOL Quarterly* 28 (4).

Pennycook, A. (1994b) *The Cultural Politics of English as an International Language.* London: Longman.

Pennycook, A. (1997) Vulgar pragmatism, critical pragmatism, and EAP. *ESP Journal* 16 (4), 253–269.

Pennycook, A. (1998) *English and the Discourses of Colonialism.* London: Routledge.

Phillipson, R. (1992) *Linguistic Imperialism.* Oxford: Oxford University Press.

Phillipson, R. and Skutnabb-Kangas, T. (1996) English Only worldwide, or language ecology. In T. Ricento and N. Hornberger (eds) *TESOL Quarterly, Special-Topic Issue: Language Planning and Policy*, 429–452.

Platt, J., Weber, H. and Ho, M.L. (1984) *The New Englishes.* London: Routledge & Kegan Paul.

Pollock, K. and Berni, M. (1996) Vocalic and postvocalic /r/ in African American Memphians. Paper presented to the 25th annual New Ways of Analyzing Variation in English conference, University of Nevada at Las Vegas.

Porter, D. and Roberts, J. (1987) Authentic listening activities. In M.H. Long and J.C. Richards (eds) *Methodology in TESOL* (pp. 177–87). New York: Newbury House.

Purple, D.E. and Shapiro, H.S. (1998) Beyond liberation and excellence: A discourse for education as transformation. In H.S. Shapiro and D.E. Purple (eds) *Critical Social Issues in American Education: Transformation in a Post-modern World* (pp. 373–409). Mahwah, NJ: Lawrence Erlbaum Associates, Publishers.

Quirk, R., Greenbaum, S., Leech, G. and Svartvik, J. (1985) *A Comprehensive Grammar of the English Language.* London: Longman.

Ramirez, D.J., Yuen, S.D., and Ramey, D.R. (1991) *Longitudinal Study of Structured Immersion Strategy, Early-Exit and Late-Exit Transitional Bilingual Education Programs for Language-Minority Children.* San Mateo: Aguirre International.

Reveron, D. (Reporter) (1999, January 25) *Marketplace.* Los Angeles: Public Radio International.

Richards, J.C. (1998) *Beyond Training.* New York: Cambridge University Press.

Richardson, V. (ed.). (1997) *Constructivist Teacher Education: Building New Understanding.* Washington, D.C.: Falmer Press.

Rickford, J. (1986) Social contact and linguistic diffusion: Hiberno-English and New World Black English. *Language* 62, 245–89.

Rickford, J. and Rickford, A. (1995) Dialect readers revisited. *Linguistics in Education* 7, 107–128.

Riley, R.W. (1998, April 27) *Statement by U.S. Secretary of Education Richard W. Riley on California Proposition 227*. Press release.

Rogers, E.M. (1995) *Diffusion of Innovations* (4th edn). New York: Free Press.

Rogoff, B. (1990) *Apprenticeship in Thinking Cognitive Development in Social Context*. New York: Oxford University Press.

Ross, L.Q. (1937) *The Education of Hyman Kaplan*. New York: Harcourt, Brace & Company.

Sahgal, A. (1991) Patterns of language use in a bilingual setting in India. In J. Cheshire (ed.) *English around the World: Sociolinguistic Perspectives* (pp. 299–307). Cambridge University Press.

Said, E.W. (1994) *Representations of the Intellectual*. London: Vintage.

Schenke, A. (1996) Not just a "social issue": Teaching feminism in ESL. *TESOL Quarterly* 30 (1), 155–159.

Schiffrin, D. (1994) *Approaches to Discourse*. New York: Blackwell.

Schlesinger, Jr., A.M., (1992) *The Disuniting of America: Reflections on a Multicultural Society*. New York: W.W. Norton.

Schmidt, R. (1998) The politics of language in Canada and the United States: Explaining the differences. In T. Ricento and B. Burnaby (eds) *Language and Politics in the United States and Canada: Myths and Realities* (pp. 37–70). Mahway, NJ: Lawrence Erlbaum Associates.

Scollon, R. and Wong Scollon, S. (1995) *Intercultural Communication*. Oxford, UK: Blackwell.

Sharma, M.K. (1987) *Cannon 'N' Level Guide: English Language Test Papers and Additional Exercises*. Singapore: Cannon International.

Shaw, W. (1981) Asian student attitudes toward English. In L.E. Smith (ed.) *English for Cross-cultural Communication* (pp. 108–122). New York: St. Martin's Press.

Short, D.J. (1994) Expanding middle school horizons: Integrating language, culture and social studies. *TESOL Quarterly* 28 (3), 581–608.

Siao, G.W.T. (1988, September 16) 1,000 Chinese books given to Monterey Park Library. *Asian Week*.

Simon, R. (1992) *Teaching against the Grain: Texts for a Pedagogy of Possibility*. Toronto: OISE Press.

Sirotnik, K.A., and Oakes, J. (1990) Evaluation as critical inquiry: School improvement as a case in point. In *New Directions for Program Evaluation* 45 (Spring, 1990).

Skehan, P. (1998) *A Cognitive Approach to Language Learning*. New York: Oxford University Press.

Skutnabb-Kangas, T. (ed.) (1995) *Multilingualism for All*. Lisse, The Netherlands: Swets and Zeitlinger.

Smith, J.W.A. and Elley, W.B. (1997) *How Children Learn to Read: Insights from the New Zealand Experience*. Katonah, NY: Richard C. Owen Publishers.

Smitherman, G. (1977) *Talkin' and Testifyin': The Language of Black America*. Boston: Houghton Mifflin Co.

Smitherman, G. (ed.) (1981) *Black English and the Education of Black Children and Youth*. Detroit: Wayne State University Press.

Smitherman-Donaldson G. and van Dijk., T. (1988) *Discourse and Discrimination*. Detroit: Wayne State Press.

Spolsky, B. (1998) *Sociolinguistics*. New York: Oxford University Press.

Stanley, W. (1992) *Curriculum Utopia*. Albany: SUNY Press.

Steele, C., Spencer, S., and Lynch, M. (1993) Self-image resilience: The role of affirmational resources. *Journal of Personality and Social Psychology* 64, 885–896.

Stephens, L. (1995) *The Complete Guide to Learning through Community Service.* (K–9) Needham Heights, MA: Allyn and Bacon.

Stockman, I. and Vaughn-Cooke, F. (1992) Lexical elaboration in children's locative action constructions. *Child Development* 63, 1104–1125.

Stoller, F.L. (1997) The catalyst for change and innovation. In M.A. Christison and F.L. Stoller (eds) *A Handbook for Language Program Administrators* (pp. 33–48). Burlingame, CA: Alta Book Center.

Strevens, P. (1992) English as an international language: Directions in the 1990s. In B. Kachru (ed.) *The Other Tongue: English across Cultures* (2nd edn) (pp. 24–47). Urbana: University of Illinois Press.

Stupak, S.A. (ed.) *The TOEIC and the TOEFL Programs: Their Purpose, Design, Language, Scoring, Score Interpretation and Administration.* Princeton: ETS.

Subrahmanian, K. (1977) Penchant for the florid. *English Teaching Forum* 15, 23–24.

Suerez-Orozco, M. M. (1998) State terrors: Immigrants and refugees in the post-national space. In Y. Zhou and E.T. Trueba (eds) *Ethnic Identity and Power: Cultural Contexts of Political Action in School and Society.* Albany: State University of New York Press.

Takaki, R. (1990) *Strangers from a Different Shore: A History of Asian Americans.* New York: Penguin.

Takaki, R. (1995) *A Different Mirror: A History of Multicultural America.* Boston: Little, Brown and Company.

Tannen, D. (1984) *Conversational Style: Analyzing Talk among Friends.* Norwood, NJ: Ablex.

Tarone, E. and Yule, G. (1989) *Focus on the Language Learner: Approaches to Identifying and Meeting the Needs of Second Language Learners.* New York: Oxford University Press.

Tay, M.W.J. and Gupta, A.F. (1983) Towards a description of Standard Singapore English. In Noss (ed.) (pp. 173–189). Singapore: SEAMEO Regional Language Centre. [Anthology Series 11]

Teemant, A., Cutri, R.M., Gibbs, G. and Squires, D. (1999, April) Developing inclusive pedagogy for special populations: Meeting the challenge of preparing pre-service teachers. Paper presented at the annual meeting of the American Educational Research Association, Montreal, Canada.

TESOL 1984. *Statement of Core Standards for Language and Professional Preparation Programs.* Washington, DC: Teachers of English to Speakers of Other Languages.

TESOL 1986. *The TESOL Core Standards for Language and Professional Preparation Programs.* Washington, DC: Teachers of English to Speakers of Other Languages.

Thomas, W.P. and Collier, V.P. (1997) *School Effectiveness for Language Minority Students.* Washington, D.C.: National Clearinghouse for Biligual Education.

Tickoo, M.L. (1991) Introduction. In M.L. Tickoo (ed.) *Languages and Standards: Issues, Attitudes, and Case Studies* (pp. iv–x). Singapore: SEAMEO Regional Language Centre. [Anthology Series 26]

Tickoo, M. (1993) When is language worth teaching? Native languages and English in India. *Language, Culture and Curriculum* 6, 225–239.

Tollefson, J.W. (1991) *Planning Language, Planning Inequality: Language Policy in the Community.* London: Longman.

Tollefson, J.W. (in press) Language policy and ideology. In T. Ricento (ed.) *Ideology, Politics, and Language Policies*. Amsterdam, The Netherlands: John Benjamins.

Tongue, R.K. (1979) *The English of Singapore and Malaysia* (2nd edn). Singapore: Eastern Universities Press.

Toohey, K. (1998) Breaking them up, taking them away: ESL students in Grade 1. *TESOL Quarterly* 32 (1), 61–84.

Torres-Queral, M. (1998) Living on the hyphen: An exploration of the phenomenon of being Cuban-American. Unpublished Ph.D. dissertation. The University of Maryland, College Park.

Trudgill, P. (1983) *Sociolinguistics: An Introduction to Language and Society* (rev. ed.). Harmondsworth, Middlesex: Penguin.

Tsuda, Y. (1994) The diffusion of English: Its impact on culture and communication. *Keio Communication Review* 16, 49–61.

U.S. English Update XI (1) (1994) U.S. Senate joins in effort to stop INS, 1, 4.

U.S. English (1998, March/April) Advertisement. *American Language Review*, 25.

van Lier, L. (1996) *Interaction in the Language Curriculum: Awareness, Autonomy & Authenticity*. New York: Longman.

Vygotsky, L. (1978) *Mind in Society*. Cambridge, MA: Harvard University Press.

Wallace, M.J. (1998) *Action Research for Language Teachers*. New York: Cambridge University Press.

Washington, J. and Craig, H. (1994) Dialectal forms during discourse of poor, urban, African American preschoolers. *Journal of Speech and Hearing Research* 37, 816–823.

Watson-Gegeo, K.A., and Gegeo, D.W. (1995) Understanding language and power in the Solomon Islands: Methodological lessons for educational intervention. In J. Tollefson (ed.) *Power and Inequality in Language Education* (pp. 59–72). Cambridge: Cambridge University Press.

West, C. (1990) The limits of neopragmatism. *Southern California Law Review* 63, 1747–1751.

Wexler, P. (1996) *Holy Sparks: Social Theory, Education, and Religion*. New York: St. Martin's Press.

Wildavsky, A. (1992) Finding universalistic solutions to particularistic problems: Bilingualism resolved through a second language requirement for elementary public schools. *Journal of Policy Analysis and Management* 11 (2), 310–314.

Wiley, T. (1996) *Literacy and Language Diversity in the United States*. McHenry, IL: Center for Applied Linguistics/Delta Books.

Williams, R. (1975) *Ebonics: The True Language of Black Folks*. St. Louis: Robert L. Williams and Associates.

Wink, J. and Almanzo, M. (1995) Critical pedagogy: A lens through which we see. In J. Frederickson (ed.) *Reclaiming Our Voices: Bilingual Education, Critical Pedagogy, and Praxis* (pp. 210–223). Ontario: California Association for Bilingual Education.

Wolfram, W. (1969) *A Sociolinguistic Description of Detroit Negro Speech*. Washington, D.C.: Center for Applied Linguistics.

Wolfram, W. (1991) *Dialects and American English*. Englewood Cliffs, NJ: Prentice-Hall.

Wolfson, N. (1989) *Perspectives: Sociolinguistics and TESOL*. New York: Newbury House.

Wong, S. (1993) Cultural context: Exploring the nexus between medicine and ministry. In T. Boswell, R. Hoffman and P. Tung (eds) *English for Professional Communication* (pp. 115–126). Hong Kong: City Polytechnic.

Wong, S. and Grant, R. (1995) Addressing poverty in the Baltimore-Washington metropolitan area: What can teachers do? *Literacy Issues and Practices* 12, 3–12.

Wong, S., and Teuben-Rowe, S. (1996) Critical perspectives on the language of family literacy research: Use of native language with involved parents from diverse linguistic backgrounds. *Journal of Educational Issues of Language Minority Students* 16, 235–261.

Wong Fillmore, L. (1992) Against our best interest: The attempt to sabotage bilingual education. In J. Crawford (ed.) *Language Loyalties: A Source Book on the Official English Controversy* (pp. 367–376). Chicago: University of Chicago Press.

Wright, T. and Bolitho, R. (1993) Language awareness: A missing link in language teacher education? *ELT Journal* 47 (4), 292–304.

Wyatt, T. (1995) Language development in African American English child speech. *Linguistics and Education* 7, 7–22.

Yule, G. (1996a) *The Study of Language* (2nd edn). New York: Cambridge University Press.

Yule, G. (1996b) *Pragmatics*. New York: Oxford University Press.

Zeichner, K.M. (1993, February) *Educating Teachers for Cultural Diversity* (National Center for Research on Teacher Learning Special Report). East Lansing, MI: National Center for Research on Teacher Learning.

Author Biographies (June 2, 1999)

Elsa R. Auerbach is Associate Professor of English and Bilingual/ESL Studies at the University of Massachusetts/Boston. Her work focuses primarily on adult ESL and literacy, participatory curriculum development, and family literacy. She is the author of numerous articles and books including *Making Meaning, Making Change: Participatory Curriculum Development for Adult ESL/Literacy* (Center for Applied Linguistics & Delta Systems) and *From the Community to the Community: A Guidebook for Participatory Literacy Training* (Lawrence Erlbaum Publishers).

John Baugh is Professor of Education and Linguistics at Stanford University. He is a past President of the American Dialect Society and formerly served as Vice Chairman of the Board at the Center for Applied Linguistics. His research explores the social stratification of linguistic diversity in the United States and elsewhere, with particular attention to matters of public policy in the fields of education, medicine, and law.

Ramona M. Cutri is an assistant professor at Brigham Young University in the Department of Teacher Education. Her work focuses on the socio-political and spiritual dimensions of multicultural and bilingual/ESL education and teacher education.

Susan J. Dicker is Associate Professor of English at Hostos Community College, CUNY. She is the author of *Personal Expressions: Writing your Way into English* (1992, Heinle & Heinle) and *Languages in America: A Pluralist View* (1996, Multilingual Matters). Her articles appear in *The Bilingual Review/La Revista Bilingüe, The Educational Forum, The Journal of Policy Analysis and Management, College ESL, Education and Society,* and *The Journal of Multilingual and Multicultural Development.* She was a member of TESOL's Sociopolitical Concerns Committee and was chair of the sociopolitical concerns committee of New York State TESOL. She has given papers and advocacy workshops on the official English movement nationally and internationally, and has appeared on U.S. television in discussion of the issue.

William G. Eggington is Professor of English Language and Linguistics and Associate Chair of the English Department at Brigham Young University, Provo, Utah. Originally from Australia, He has researched and written extensively on language policy and planning in Australia, South Pacific, and general and educational contexts. He has been the chair of TESOL's Sociopolitical Concerns Committee and the Applied Linguistics Interest Section.

Linn E. Forhan is the Coordinator for Academic Listening and Speaking in the Ohio Program of Intensive English at Ohio University, where she is a senior member of the continuing faculty. In addition to extensive work in curriculum development, intercultural communication, and teacher education, she has long been involved in professionally related socio-political activism. She was a member of TESOL's Sociopolitical Concerns Committee for six years, serving as Committee Chair from 1993–1995. She has also served as the sociopolitical representative for Ohio TESOL, as the President of Ohio TESOL, and as the Chair of Ohio University's Human Relations Standing Committee.

William Grabe is Professor of English in the English Department at Northern Arizona University. His research interests include the development of reading and writing abilities in both first and second languages. More generally, he is also interested in literacy, written discourse analysis, cognitive processing, and curricular efforts to move from theory to instruction in literacy. He has published a number of articles and chapters on reading and writing issues, and his most recent book, co-authored with R. B. Kaplan, is *The Theory and Practice of Writing* (Longman, 1996). He is also editor of the *Annual Review of Applied Linguistics* (Cambridge University Press).

Joan Kelly Hall is Associate Professor of Language Education at the University of Georgia. Her research interests include classroom-based language development, language use and identity, and intercultural communication. Her work appears in such journals as *Applied Linguistics, Foreign Language Annals, The Journal of Linguistic Anthropology, Linguistics and Education, Modern Language Journal,* and *Research on Language and Social Interaction.* Together with Lorrie Verplaetse, she is currently completing an edited volume entitled *Second and Foreign Language Learning through Classroom Discourse* (Lawrence Erlbaum Associates).

Robert B. Kaplan is Professor Emeritus of Applied Linguistics and past Director of the American Language Institute at the University of Southern California, where he was a member of the faculty since 1960. Kaplan is the past Editor-in-Chief and currently a member of the Editorial Board of the *Annual Review of Applied Linguistics,* which he founded in 1980; he is a member of the Editorial Board of the *Oxford University Press International Encyclopedia of Linguistics,* and he serves on the editorial boards of several scholarly journals. He has authored or edited 28 books, more than 125 articles in scholarly journals and chapters in books, more than 80 book reviews and other ephemeral pieces in various newsletters, as well as 8 special reports to government both in the U.S. and elsewhere. He has held three separate Senior Fulbright Fellowship Awards (Australia, 1978; Hong Kong, 1986; New Zealand, 1992), two Vice Chancellors' Awards (one in Britain and one in New Zealand), and a special research award from the New Zealand Council on Educational Research (1979). He has received the first Distinguished Faculty Service Award from the Academic Senate, University of Southern California, and the first Distinguished Service Award from the Black Administrators' Alliance, County of Los Angeles. He has previously served as President of

(1) the American Association for Applied Linguistics,
(2) the Association of Teachers of English as a Second Language,
(3) the California Association of Teachers of English to Speakers of Other Languages,
(4) the National Association for Foreign Student Affairs,
(5) the international organization Teachers of English to Speakers of Other Languages, and
(6) the University of Southern California Faculty Senate.

Peter H. Lowenberg, Associate Professor of Linguistics and Language Development at San Jose State University, has served on the Committee of Examiners for the Test of English as a Foreign Language (TOEFL) and on the Technical Research Panel of the Test of English as a world language and on language testing for the United States Information Agency in Mexico, Brazil, the Philippines, Belgium, and Uzbekistan, and for two years he has directed the language teaching programs at the United States Binational Center in Surabaya, Indonesia. He has published on the spread of English as a world language, language policy and planning, and second language acquisition and testing, and has been Review Editor and Associate Editor of the journal *World Englishes.*

Alastair Pennycook is Professor of Language in Education at the University of Technology, Sydney. He was previously at the University of

Melbourne, and has also worked in Japan, China, Hong Kong, and Canada. His interests include ethics, culture, and difference in language and teacher development projects; plagiarism and intertextuality; colonialism and language policy; and implications of the global spread of English. He is the author of *The Cultural Politics of English as an International Language* (Longman) and *English and the Discourses of Colonialism* (Routledge). He was guest editor of a special edition of *TESOL Quarterly* for 1999 on *Critical Approaches to TESOL*.

Mona Scheraga, M.A., is consultant, author, editor, teacher, and teacher trainer. She is past chair of the Materials Writers Interest Section and Secondary Schools Interest Section for International TESOL, where she has also served on the Sociopolitical Concerns Committee. She has supervised programs for former Soviet émigrés and worked with corporations training staff in ESP (English for specific purposes). She has taught ESL at the high school and adult levels and has done teacher training at various colleges and universities. She has also trained teachers in Puerto Rico for the Department of Defense and in the Baltics, Poland, and Belarus for the United States Information Agency, USIA. She is a recipient of the Princeton University Award for Distinguished Secondary School Teaching and of a National Education Association Hilda Maehling Fellowship for developing vocational education materials for non-native English speakers. She has served as Vice Chairperson of the New Jersey State Bilingual Advisory Board and as a member of the New Jersey State Test Selection Committee for Limited English Proficient Students. She is the author of *Consumer Sense* (Contemporary Publishers, Chicago, IL); *Practical English Writing Skills* (National Textbook Co., Lincolnwood, IL); *Content Connection Activity Book* (Santillana Publishers, Compton, CA); and co-author of *The Complete ESL/EFL Resource Book: Strategies, Activities and Units for the Classroom*, and *Hello, English* (both for National Textbook Co.).

Tove Skutnabb-Kangas, has a B.A., M.A. and Ph.D.-equivalent (fil.lic), University of Helsinki, Finland; dr.phil. (advanced doctorate), Roskilde University, Denmark. Reader (docent) in Minority Education and Linguistic Human Rights, Åbo Akademi University, Vasa, Finland. She taught and/or researched in Lund, Harvard, and Helsinki (lecturer, assistant professor) before coming to Roskilde University as a guest researcher. Her main research interests are linguistic human rights; minority education and educational models for high levels of multilingualism; ethnicity, identity, and integration; language and gender; the role of language in power relations; linguistic imperialism; the relationship between biodiversity and linguistic and cultural diversity. She has published and/or (co)edited over 20 books and over 300 scientific and many popular articles in books and journals, in Danish, English, Estonian, Finnish, French, German, Hungarian, Kannada, Kurdish, Latvian, Norwegian, Portuguese, Serbocroatian, Slovak, Spanish, Swedish, and Turkish. Her books in English include *Bilingualism or Not— The Education of Minorities* (1984), *Minority Education—From Shame to Struggle* (1988, ed. with Jim Cummins), *Linguistic Human Rights* (1994, ed. with Robert Phillipson), *Multilingualism for All* (ed., 1995), *Language Rights* (1998, ed. with Phil Benson & Peter Grundy). She is currently working on a book on linguistic genocide in education and editing another book on linguistic human rights. She lives with her husband (Robert Phillipson) on a small ecologically run farm in Denmark.

Fredricka L. Stoller is Associate Professor of English at Northern Arizona University, Flagstaff, Arizona, where she teaches in the Teaching English as a Second Language (TESL) and Applied Linguistics graduate programs. Her professional interests include content-based instruction, language teaching methodology, curriculum design, materials development, and program administration. She has published in *Applied Linguistics, TESOL Journal, English Teaching Forum*, and *Applied Language Learning*. She co-edited a volume entitled *A Handbook for Language Program Administrators* (with Alta Book Center) and co-authored a reading text for developing readers entitled *Javier Arrives in the US* (Prentice Hall Regents). She has trained EFL teachers and language program administrators in many parts of the world including Bolivia, Croatia, the Czech Republic, Italy, Malaysia, Mexico, Morocco, Panama, Poland, Slokavia, and Tunisia. She is an active member of international TESOL.

Christine Tardy is an Instructor of English in the Faculty of Business Administration at Bilkent University, Ankara, Turkey, where she is also the Writing Center Director. Her research interests include EAP/ESP, genre theory and pedagogy, and L2 writing issues. She has published and presented on ESP course and materials development, needs analysis, and written discourse in business settings. A graduate of Northern Arizona University's MA-TESL program, she has also taught in the Czech Republic, the United States, and Japan.

James W. Tollefson holds a Ph.D. in Linguistics from Stanford University and is currently Professor of English at the University of Washington. His research focuses on language and politics, especially the role of language policy in second language acquisition and the links between language and other areas of social policy. His books include

Power and Inequality in Language Education (Cambridge); *Planning Language, Planning Inequality* (Longman); *Alien Winds: The Reeducation of America's Indochinese Refugees* (Praeger); and *The Language Situation and Language Policy in Slovenia* (University Press of America).

Shelley Wong has taught English to Speakers of Other Languages (ESOL) and Bilingual Education (BE) in Hong Kong, Los Angeles, New York, the Washington, D.C., area, and Columbus, Ohio. She has taught middle school, secondary, adult, and community college and university ESOL/BE. She is interested in dialogic approaches to teaching and research, sociocultural perspectives on literacy and multicultural curriculum transformation. Her current research involves collaborating with ESOL elementary teachers to strengthen home-school communication. She received a B.A. in Sociology from the University of California at Santa Cruz (UCSC); a TESL certificate, secondary and adult credentials in Social Studies and E.S.L. and an M.A. in Teaching English as a Second Language from UCLA; and a Doctor of Education degree in Applied Linguistics from Columbia Teachers College. She is an Assistant Professor in Foreign/Second Language Education in Language, Literacy and Culture at the Ohio State University in Columbus, Ohio.

Index

Academics, and language 70
Action research 187
Active, being sociopolitically 196
Activities, structured 156
Adjuncts 203
Advocacy
    effective 198, 210
    and professional organizations
        212
    and understanding 197–198
    and the workplace 201
    and you 208
Alphabetic language 181
American, average 45
American dream 117
Anthropology 185
Articles of Confederation 46
Assessment, language 75
Assumptions, about students 98
Autonomy 96
    classroom 90
    learner 91
Awareness, lack of 41

Background
    cultural 38
    influence of 121
    linguistic 38
    need for diverse 128
    and teachers 151
Beliefs 170
    articulating and identifying 171
    implications of 172
    questioning 172
Bilingual education 52, 54, 58
    anti- 64

battle to end 62
case for 60
and commitment 169
and ESL professionals 64
lack of funding 133
legally distinguished 111
and morals 166
Bilingual Education Act (1968) 47
    Official English attacks on 60
Bilingual professionals, need for
    127–128
Bilingualism 52
    anti- 57
    as a right 32
    squandered 126–127
Black English trial 109
Braceros 120
Business writing 79

Civil Rights movement 47
Classrooms
    autonomy in 90
    based on social research 101
    critical ethnographies of 100
    and dialogical processes 148
    as microcosm 93, 102
    and outside factors 149
    as part of larger social world 94
    relation to outside world 97
    as site of cultural struggle 98
    as social and cultural spaces 89,
        90–92
    as social domain 94
    teacher-centered 144
    and tone 152–154
Communicative competence 70, 186

Communities
  and teachers 151
  learning 143
  vs. individualism 145
Community development 130, 132
Competence
  analytical 38
  functional 38
  multilingual 39
Concerns
  European 205
  prioritizing 215
  sociopolitical 196–197
Conditional, use of 73–74
Confidentiality, medical vs. educational 112
Content, and social context 148, 150
Contextual factors 149
Contradictions 162
Convention on Prevention and Punishment of the Crime of Genocide 26
Court Interpreter's Act (1965) 48
Cross-cultural communication 186
Cultural capital 95, 122
Cultural politics 97
Cultural preferences 98
Cultural reproduction 95
Culture
  as an asset 127
  reproduces inequality 96
Curriculum
  design 187
  ESOL 130–132
  legislation of 33

Dialect 182
Dialogic pedagogy 129
  and classrooms 148
Diffusion of English, paradigm of 40–41
Discourse analysis 183
Discrimination, and TESOL 203
Divergence
  morphological and syntactic 71–73
  in style 73–73

Diversity
  as a resource 127
  as a response 41
Early-exit programs 61–62
Ebonics 105, 108
Ecology of languages, paradigm of 41
Economic disparities 204
Education
  as a discipline 186
  minimum standards of 109
  public vs. private 106–107
Educational language rights 26
Educational malpractice 104
  definition of 106
Educators, see also Teachers
  dilemma in politics 133
  and leadership 133
Elementary and Secondary Education Act (1965) 64
Embellishment, in non-native English 74, 79
Engagement focus 101
English
  changes in 69
  changing demographics of 125
  differences in 71, 73
  as dominant language 68
  economic value of 11
  hegemony of 16, 18
  as an international language 8–9
  language of colonists 46
  learning advantages of 10
  non-native varieties of 68
  non-Western use of 69
  proficiency in 75–76
  promoters of 49
  resistance to 18
  spread of 12, 67, 97
  status of 9, 55, 68
English for the Children Act 64
"English Only" in ESL 160
Equal Educational Opportunity Act (1994) 111

Equality, 17 _see also_ Inequality
  and attention 56
Equality (cont.)
  and education 117
  and public education 121
  in society 93
Equitable education, and politics 168
Equity, and morality 175–176
ESL professionals, _see also_ Educators
  support for bilingual education 64
ESL teachers, incompetence of 37
ESOL, international support 205
ESOL organizations 208
Ethical questions 166
Euphemisms, use of 32
Experience
  first-hand 38
  shaped by individual 146
  sharing of 154. 175
  and social analysis 148
Expertise 151

Federal Voting Rights Act (1975) 48
Filipino English 7, 14
Foreign language learning
  capacities needed 38–39
  five tenets of 36–37
  and national defense 47
Framework Convention 28
Fullbright-Hays Act (1961) 47
Funding
  and curriculum 151
  restrictions on 199

Grammar 180

Hague Recommendations, The 32, 37
Hawaiian pidgin 108
Head Start 122
Hispanic enrollment 59
Holistic scoring 78
Human rights, _see_ Linguistic human
  rights

Identities, complexity of 147
Identity
  American 51–52

  and classrooms 99
  and issues 101
  national 51–52
  social 101
  social and cultural 87
  students' 61
  Theodore Roosevelt on 51–52
Ideologies 99
  in the classroom 97
  of language 16
  linked to social relations 93
Immersion, 34 _see also_ Submersion
  programs of 61
  structured 63
Immigrants 54–55
  African-American 118
  Asian-American 119
  Chinese 119
  coddling of 117
  history of 118
  inferiority of 48
  Latino 120
  Mexican-American 119
  and proficiency 109
Immigration
  Chinese 56
  Cuban 57
  and language policy 46
  in Miami, FL 57
  in Monterey Park, CA 56
Inclusivity 100
India, English use in 68
Individuals, as effective advocates
  210
_Individuals with Disabilities Educational
  Act_ 105
Inequalities, challenging 146
Inequality 121
  global 13
  in scholastic achievement 95
  social 13, 95
Information
  and advocacy 198
  providing to members 213–214
  transferring 216
Innovation, _see_ Linguistic innovation
Inquiry 161

Interdependency 175
International English 77, 78
International language, need for 8–9
Issues
    and context 150
    embracing 91
    ethical 166
    identifying 155
    including in curriculum 100
    moral 64
    understanding 210–211
    use of 19

Kashmiri 18

Labeling 122, 123
Language
    defined as 23
    and government 170
    standard 16
    structure of 180
Language communities 29
Language competencies 94
Language policy, policies
    assimilation 15
    creating 169
    external 173
    monolingual 14, 19
    and national unity 50
    promotion-oriented 46
    purpose of 14
    restrictive 46,47
    in spreading of English 13
    tolerance-oriented 46
    and understanding language 91
Languages
    as an asset 127
    distribution of 23
    endangered 9, 24
    extinction of 24, 43
    murder of 25, 31
Late-exit programs 61–62
Lau v. Nichols 111
Learner-centeredness, as a false construct 145
Learners, empowering 145
Learning, and environment 149

Learning theory 185
Legislation
    American 46–48, 50
    local 57
Limited English Proficient 122
Lingua franca 29
Linguicism 40, 65
Linguistic diversity 22
Linguistic genocide 25, 31, 64
Linguistic human rights 22, 25, 29, 30
Linguistic innovation 72
Linguistic norms, *see also* Norms
    in Standard English 70
Linguistic stereotypes, *see*
    Stereotypes
Linguistics 179
    applied 178
Listening 156
Literacy, as measure of achievement
    123

Majority-minority 126
Malpractice, *see* Educational malpractice
Marginalized people, changing their
    lives 145
Mayes' 4 levels of teaching 168
Methodology courses, value of
    189–191
Meyer v. Nebraska 47
Minorities 31,32
Minority language, and curriculum
    33
Minority language learning 54
Minority students 165
Misconceptions, *see* Myths
Monolingual stupidity
    and Americans 39
    a dangerous illness 42
    ideology of 24
    and T-shirts 41
Moral courage 176
Moral dimensions, definition of 166
Morality
    political 167
    secular 166–167
    spiritual 168, 174

Morals 64
Motivation 184–185
    spiritual 176
Multilingualism, advantages of 39
Myths, list of 209

National Defense Act (1958) 47
Native-language instruction 3
    for children 53
    as a crime 53 *see also* Languages,
        murder of
    effectiveness of 62
    principles of 60–61
Native speaker, discrimination of
    203–204
Needs 155
NELLE 205
Network, developing 213
Non-native varieties
    Black English 109, 113
    embellishment in 74, 79
Norms
    assumptions about 81
    and Black English 109–110
    linguistic 67
Nouns, countability 71

Official English
    and anti-immigration 60
    founder of 48
    movement 48
    promises of 50
    proposed legislation 54–55

Papua New Guinea 18
Participatory action research 101
Participatory classrooms 3
    factors of 161
Participatory education, and curricu-
    lum 147
Participatory pedagogy, defined 144
Participatory vs. participation 145
Part-time, problems with 202
Philippines 14
Phonology 181
Pluralism 45
    linguistic 51

Policies, and professional goals 198
Political morality 167
Position statements 215
Poverty, increase in 126
Power, use of 145
Power sharing 92
Prepositions, differences between
    varieties 72, 76, 78
Problems, addressing 154
Process, and content 146
Professional ESOL goals 201
Professional ESOL issues 201
Professional organizations, and advo-
    cacy 212
Professionals, and unions 125
Proposition 187, 214
Proposition 227, 34, 63, 111
Psycholinguistics 183–184
Psychology 184

Racism 40
    and affirmative action 104–105
Ramirez Report 61
Reductionism 24, 42
Refugees, education of 94
Resistance, student 161
Resources
    allocation of 112, 129
    human 127
Restrictionism 48, 55

Salaries, international disparities 204
Second Language Acquisition, and
    individual learners 145
Secular morality 166–167
    bases of 168
Segregation, economic 35
Social context, and content 148
Social stratification 121
    begins at first grade 123
Sociolinguistics 182
Solomon Islands 18
Spanish, as a threat 59
Spanish-speaking communities 58
Spiritual morality 168, 174
Squandered bilingualism, *see*
    Bilingualism

Standard English 69 *see also* English, differences in 71, 73
States, duties of 33
Status, *see also* English, status of
   economic 121
   of a population 61
   securing higher 68
Stereotypes
   linguistic 123
   negative 200
   and textbooks 207
Students
   and advocacy 200
   and decisions 160
Submersion, model of 34
Supreme court
   Arizona 50
   rulings of 47, 111
Syntax 180

Teachers *see also* Educators
   as activists 152
   and authority 146
   and background 151
   beliefs 170
   and communities 151
   as a community 162
   differing expectations of 123
   influence of 171–172
   and L1 use 160
   personally engaged 175
   as problem-posers 148, 160
   role in schools 134
   and sensitivity 153
   training 33
Teaching
   impact of courses on 190–192
   Mayes' 4 levels of 168
Teaching-in-training 188
Testing 124
Tests
   results from 104
   standardized 75
Textbooks, stereotypes in 207
Tolerance, Zero 42
"Toolkit" techniques 158–159
Traditional vs. non-traditional 152–153

Transpersonal 168

UN Declaration on the Rights of Persons 27
UN Human Rights Committee 31
UN International Covenant on Civil and Political Rights 31
Underemployment, reducing 214
United Nations 25–26
Universal Declaration of Linguistic Rights 28–29
U.S. English 48, 59

Verbs, differences between varieties 72, 78
Vocational ESL programs 131–132

Workshop tours 206